Europe and America

'In this pathbreaking book, Peterson employs the empirical record of US–European relations since 1989 to assess four major theories of international relations, thus linking detailed historical understanding, general social scientific theory, and prudent policy prescription. This comprehensive *tour d'horizon* is a splendid point of departure for understanding this critical yet puzzling transition in modern international relations.'

Andrew Moravcsik, *Harvard University*

'John Peterson's book contains a well-informed, original and eloquent analysis of EU–US relations. *Europe and America* is a "must" for those readers who want to look ahead and go beyond the traditional presentation of transatlantic relations.'

Youri Devuyst, *Free University*, Brussels

The conflict in Bosnia, disputes within the new World Trade Organization and debates about NATO enlargement all illustrate a single point: no relationship is more important in determining the state of international relations than the alliance between Europe and America. Contrary to accepted wisdom, John Peterson argues that the end of the Cold War actually enhances the prospects for partnership between the United States and the European Union. Based on original research and presented here in its second edition, this book offers a clear and penetrating analysis of the problems and opportunities facing the transatlantic alliance.

John Peterson is Jean Monnet Senior Lecturer at the University of Glasgow, UK, and Visiting Research Fellow at the Centre for European Policy Studies, Brussels, Belgium. He has taught previously at the universities of Oxford, Essex and York in the UK, at the Institut d'Etudes Politiques in Grenoble, France, and at the University of California, Santa Barbara, USA.

Europe and America

The prospects for partnership

Second edition

John Peterson

London and New York

The first edition of this book,
under the title *Europe and America in the 1990s*
was published by Edward Elgar in May 1993

This edition first published 1996
by Routledge
11 New Fetter Lane, London EC4P 4EE

Simultaneously published in the USA and Canada
by Routledge
29 West 35th Street, New York, NY 10001

Routledge is a Thomson International Publishing Company I T P

© 1996 John Peterson
John Peterson asserts his moral right to be identified as the author of this work

Phototypeset by Intype London Ltd
Printed and bound in Great Britain by Mackays of Chatham PLC,
Chatham, Kent

British Library Cataloguing in Publication Data
A catalogue record for this book is available from the British Library

Library of Congress Cataloging in Publication data
A catalogue record for this book has been requested

ISBN 0–415–14653–4 (hbk)
ISBN 0–415–13864–7 (pbk)

To Miles
for being such a good-timer

Contents

Tables

Preface

What follows is very much an 'interview-driven' study. All interviews were contributed on a non-attributable basis to encourage frank and open responses and are cited as such in the text. A warm expression of thanks is due to those on both sides of the Atlantic who offered interviews when the first edition of this book was being researched between 1989 and 1992. Revisions for the present edition were informed by conversations with more than sixty interviewees who were consulted in connection with a report prepared for the European Commission on US foreign and security policies in 1995. I owe a special debt to Fraser Cameron for playing facilitator on this project and to his colleagues in the Commission for their comments during a 'brain-storming' session on transatlantic relations in May 1995. Of course, any views expressed in this book are mine alone and do not represent the views of the Commission.

For the sake of simplicity, the term 'European Union' and the abbreviation 'EU' are often used to refer to the pre-Maastricht European Community. The same applies to the Organization (formerly Conference) for Security and Cooperation in Europe (OSCE). The term 'Atlantic Alliance' is used throughout the book to refer to the membership of NATO while the 'Transatlantic Alliance' denotes bilateral relations between the US and EU. 'Eastern Europe' is employed as shorthand for the former Warsaw Pact states in Eastern and Central Europe. Monetary amounts are expressed in US dollars throughout the book and ECU values are calculated at a rate of $1.25 per ECU. Italics in cited passages indicates that the emphasis appears in the original.

Research leading to the book's first edition was supported by a grant from the staff research fund of the Department of Politics at the University of York. Work on the second edition was facilitated by the European Commission, the Bertelsmann Foundation and the Centre for European Policy Studies in Brussels. Paul Najsarek, Clare McManus, Ricardo Gomez and, especially, Christine Matthews contributed an enormous amount to the study as my research assistants. The staffs at the documents library of the US Embassy in London and the European Commission office in Edinburgh provided crucial assistance in tracking down key documents.

Any errors or omissions are my own and not the fault of numerous colleagues in the US and Europe who contributed valuable insights and suggestions. Thanks are due to Phil Cerny of the University of Leeds, Youri Devuyst of the Vrije Universiteit Brussel, Patrick Dunleavy of the London School of Economics, Roy Ginsberg of Skidmore College, Wolfram Hanrieder of the University of California at Santa Barbara, Erik Jones of Central European University, Adrian Leftwich of the University of York, Hideki Mimura of Mitsui, Andrew Moravcsik of Harvard University, Thomas Risse-Kappen of the University of Konstanz, Rod Rhodes of the University of Newcastle, Neil Robinson and Hugh Ward of the University of Essex, Michael Smith of Loughborough University and Nicholas Ziegler of the Massachusetts Institute of Technology. Steve Breyman of Rensselaer Polytechnic Institute and Mary M. McKenzie of the University of San Diego reminded me that there are no friends like the old friends. Elizabeth Bomberg of the University of Stirling read every word of the text and proved to be an indispensable editor. I am very glad that I married her.

Abbreviations

ACP	African, Caribbean and Pacific
APEC	Asia Pacific Economic Cooperation forum
AT&T	American Telephone and Telegraph
CAP	Common Agricultural Policy (EC)
CEN/	European Committee for Standardization/
CENELEC	European Committee for Electrotechnical Standardization
CFE	Conventional Forces in Europe
CFSP	Common Foreign and Security Policy
CIA	Central Intelligence Agency
CIS	Commonwealth of Independent States
CJTF	Common Joint Task Forces
CMEA	Conference for Mutual Economic Assistance
CNN	Cable News Network
CO_2	carbon dioxide
DG	Directorate-General
EBRD	European Bank for Reconstruction and Development
EC	European Community
ECJ	European Court of Justice
ECSC	European Coal and Steel Community
ECU	European Currency Unit
EDC	European Defence Community
EEC	European Economic Community
EFTA	European Free Trade Association
EMS	European Monetary System
EMU	Economic and Monetary Union
EP	European Parliament
EPC	European Political Cooperation
ESDI	European Security and Defence Identity
EU	European Union
Euratom	European Atomic Energy Community
FAO	Food and Agriculture Organization (UN)
FDI	foreign direct investment

FTAA	Free Trade Area of the Americas
G-7	Group of Seven industrialized nations
G-24	Group of Twenty-Four industrialized nations
GATT	General Agreement on Tariffs and Trade
GDP	gross domestic product
GNP	gross national product
HDTV	high-definition television
IGC	intergovernmental conference
IMF	International Monetary Fund
INF	intermediate nuclear forces
JCG	Joint Consultative Group (on Science and Technology)
JESSI	Joint European Silicon Structures
LDC	less developed country
MBFR	Mutual and Balanced Force Reductions
MFN	most favoured nation
MITI	Ministry of International Trade and Industry (Japan)
MNCs	multinational corporations
MTCR	Missile Technology Control Regime
NACC	North Atlantic Cooperation Council
NAFTA	North American Free Trade Area
NATO	North Atlantic Treaty Organization
NPT	Nuclear Non-Proliferation Treaty
NTBs	non-tariff barriers
OECD	Organization for Economic Cooperation and Development
OEEC	Organization for European Economic Cooperation
OSCE	Organization for Security and Cooperation in Europe
PHARE	Poland and Hungary: Aid for the Reconstruction of Economies
QMV	qualified majority voting
R&D	research and development
RRF	Rapid Reaction Force
SDI	Strategic Defense Initiative (US)
SEA	Single European Act
UK	United Kingdom
UN	United Nations
US	United States
USSR	Union of Soviet Socialist Republics
USTR	United States Trade Representative
WEU	West European Union
WTO	World Trade Organization

Introduction

This book seeks to make an original contribution to the literature on relations between the United States (US) and the European Union (EU). It is intended primarily for advanced undergraduate and postgraduate students of international relations or Western foreign policies. Since the publication of its first edition in 1993, the literature on US–EU relations has expanded considerably. Yet this literature still lacks a concise, accessible and theory-based study which examines how the transatlantic relationship has evolved against a backdrop of sweeping changes in the global system. In its second edition, as in its first, this book aims to fill that gap.

The pace of change in both international and transatlantic relations has been breathtaking since research for this book was begun. During this time, I have sympathized with the more diligent of my students – on both sides of the Atlantic – who have imbibed the available literature only to find a minefield of mistaken premises about how much and how fast the international system, the EU or US politics could change.

A similar sympathy must be held for political scientists whose good works were overtaken by events that no one expected. The editor of a collection of essays by prominent Americans and Europeans published in 1990 asserted that German unification was 'not on the agenda' (Treverton 1990: 13). Two years before the collapse of communism, the authors of a competent text on comparative politics argued that 'the durability of liberal democracy is open to question; more so, indeed, than communist party states, none of which have so far changed to a different regime type' (Hague and Harrop 1987: 310). With the wisdom of hindsight, we can chuckle at the opening line of an international relations textbook: 'much has changed in the international arena since the first edition . . . was published in 1984' (Papp 1991: v). Who could fault the author for failing to predict that far *more* would change before his revised manuscript could make it into print?

I do not wish to mock these authors, but cite them to illustrate the enormous difficulties faced by students of international relations in the period since the collapse of the Soviet bloc in 1989. In this book's first edition, I aired my intuition that many international relations scholars were hoping that 'the tumult of 1989–92 will pass and yield a more stable, predictable period in international affairs', thus facilitating more 'definitive analysis' of a post-Cold War world (Peterson 1993a: 2). Arguably, the dust is no more settled now than when I began working on this project in 1989.

Nonetheless, I remain convinced of the validity of the essential argument set out in the first edition and now further developed in this one: that the bilateral relationship between the US and the EU is the most important relationship between any two major international actors, that both sides are nearly always more powerful acting together than separately, and that a transatlantic partnership is well within the grasp of the US and EU. It remains possible to imagine a more stable, peaceful and even just global system which is shaped and led by an alliance between an ex-hegemon and a confederation of autonomous and often fiercely independent states (Peterson and Ward 1995). No historical precedent exists for this kind of leadership.

This study primarily seeks to explain why the US and EU have sought stronger bilateral ties since the Cold War ended, how their relations are conducted, and what international relations theory can tell us about the prospects for a US–EU partnership in the twenty-first century. It tries to identify the essential *prerequisites* of such a partnership. The analysis is organized into three parts. Part I introduces the study's major themes and places US–EU relations in historical perspective. Part II links broad changes in the international system with changes in the internal political landscapes of Europe and America. Part III examines changing notions of security and their implications for the transatlantic relationship.

The first chapter surveys recent theoretical debates in the international relations literature, and outlines the main assumptions of four leading theories of international relations. Each subsequent chapter ends by reviewing the competing perspectives offered by advocates of each of these theories on issues raised in the chapter. The intent of this exercise is threefold. First, the actual application of theory helps to clarify debates which are interesting and important, but often hermetic and jargon-ridden, between proponents of different schools. I cannot believe that my undergraduate students are alone in finding much of the theoretical literature on international relations to be either impenetrable or dull as ditchwater. Second, each of the four theories offers distinct insights and helps order empirical evidence in novel ways. Third, the exercise demonstrates that any interpretation of US–EU relations crucially depends on the analyst's assumptions about international relations more generally.

The idea is not to see which theory 'wins' by the end of the book; it is to highlight debates between them and to illustrate that 'truth [is] not an attribute of any one tradition but of the dialogue between them'

(Smith 1995: 13). Advocates of any of the four theories may quibble with my characterizations of their main assumptions and analytical claims. Others may complain that the book does not treat the theories in sufficient detail.

Given the book's empirical focus and relatively modest length, I have chosen to distil only the very essential characteristics of each theory. To do so, of course, is to simplify dramatically. The alternative was to ignore theory altogether, to write a purely empirical study, and thus to perpetuate a curious crevice between theory and history which characterizes much of the existing literature. As Halliday (1994: ix) argues, 'International Relations, like all branches of knowledge, faces two dangers – that of factual accounts devoid of theoretical reflection, explanatory or ethical, and that of theorizing unanchored in, or tested by, the analysis of history itself.'

Many theorists resist my rather neat categorizations, thus posing the danger that 'a false sense of unity is created, and nuances and subtleties are lost' (Smith 1995: 12). Because an author is referenced in a section on one of the theories does not necessarily imply that they should be 'pigeonholed' as a neorealist or reformist or whatever. It simply means that the author has included a point of argument associated with that particular theoretical school in the work which is referenced. The reader who is stimulated by the sections of the book which examine the competing theories is urged to consult the original sources. Without illusions about the possibility of value-free analysis, I have done my damnedest to give fair treatment to all of the theoretical perspectives.

The book is not intended to be an exercise in theory-building. Nor is it designed to test, clarify or criticize the theories in any systematic way. Substantial literatures already exist which perform these tasks. Besides, although international relations tends to move slowly as a discipline, it has yielded several new and truly innovative works of theory which offer interesting explanations for the recent tumult in the international system (Baldwin 1993; Buzan *et al.* 1993; Halliday 1994; Booth and Smith 1995).

What this book *does* aim to do is to show that theories of international relations are valuable heuristic tools which often yield powerful explanations for real-world outcomes. I do not wish to encourage the reader to accept the assumptions of any single theory as it is presented here. I do hope to encourage them to examine their own assumptions in order to understand how their own views of US–EU relations are shaped by them.

In the book's second edition, I have altered the labels used to refer to two of the four leading theories of international relations. *Institutionalism* has become a more widely accepted category of theory in the literature than was the case several years ago. It replaces the label 'interdependence theories', which seems a 1970s-era categorization, although both terms essentially refer to the same broad and varied literature. It took some cajoling, but I finally have become convinced by colleagues that a distinct *liberal* school of international relations has begun to emerge, which offers actual theory, as opposed to mere ideology. I thus have junked the category 'liberal trade theory' which was employed in the first edition of the book.

The book's structure is the same as before, although most chapters are expanded and all are updated. The introduction to the final section of Chapter 1, which introduces the four theories, has been considerably revised to take account of recent developments in the theoretical literature. In bringing the empirical analysis up to date, I have drawn heavily on two works (Peterson 1994a; Peterson and Ward 1995) which were published between this book's first and second editions. It is my hope that readers of the first edition may find this second one a rather different and perhaps even better book.

Part I

US–EU relations in perspective

Chapter 1

The New Transatlanticism

The end of the twentieth century is an extraordinarily exciting time to study international politics. It has become routine to talk of a 'post-Cold War world' which is no longer constricted by the grim imperatives of East–West conflict and nuclear stand-off. Yet the idea of a 'New World Order' – a peaceful and enlightened new epoch in international relations – now seems the product of a conspiracy of optimism in the early 1990s. Since the term was coined, American and West European governments have appeared weak and unimaginative, particularly when faced with tragic civil wars in Somalia, Rwanda and the former Yugoslavia. Nevertheless, whatever type of global system emerges in a post-Cold War world, the US and the EU will be crucial in determining how it will differ from the system it is replacing.

The central arguments of this study are that the US and EU are the most powerful actors in the international system, and that usually they are much more powerful acting together than separately. The scope for *choice* in the conduct of bilateral relations, or the design of Western foreign policies more generally, is far wider for both sides now than ever before in the post-war period. Paradoxically, however, Western foreign policies are subject to more *constraints* in a post-Cold War world because a more diverse and intense set of domestic pressures shape foreign policy-making processes on both sides of the Atlantic.

The demise of the Soviet Union means that bipolarity along an East–West axis is no longer the defining feature of the international system. The EU has become a new centre of power in a more multipolar world. A US–EU coalition of rough equals on political, economic, environmental and other issues is no longer precluded by their asymmetrical military relationship, as during the Cold War. A 'New Transatlanticism' emerged soon after the end of the Cold War as political links between the US and EU were deepened and institutionalized. It became possible to envisage a true transatlantic partnership which could define and pursue an integrated policy agenda on a range of issues far wider than military security.

At the same time, the potential sources of conflict in US–EU relations are now more numerous due to the emergence of three distinct features of international relations after the Cold War. First, a monolithic Soviet threat no longer exists as a force for unity in Western foreign policies. Before 1989, the security threat to the West was clear. It made collective Western action absolutely essential. Pressures rooted in their dependence on US security guarantees often pushed EU states towards compromise and conciliation in transatlantic disputes. These pressures are now much weaker.

Second, domestic politics no longer 'stops at the water's edge'. Potential electoral costs have declined for members of Congress or parliaments who choose to oppose their executives on matters of foreign policy. Meanwhile, foreign policy agendas have expanded: trade, foreign direct investment (FDI) and environmental protection have become 'core' issues. Foreign policies have become subject to a wider range of domestic pressures. They are now more politicized and less insulated from domestic political competition than during the Cold War.

By the mid-1990s, ostensibly 'domestic' debates were under way on both sides of the Atlantic which promised to have profound effects on the future of transatlantic relations. European integration seemed stalled as the EU faced vexing new problems connected with its enlargement. It became difficult to be optimistic about the EU's future ability to interact with the US as a unified and equal partner. Meanwhile, the United States was consumed with a debate about the acceptable costs of internationalism in the face of new limits to US fiscal resources and crushing economic and social problems.

Third, the US and EU are challenged by their declining collective power to dictate the terms of global trade and investment. New economic challengers have emerged, particularly in Asia. With Japan and, especially, China enjoying higher economic growth rates than Western states in the 1990s, the combined US and European share of total global production and consumption has declined. Both the US and EU now have more alternative partners with whom they can form alliances on specific economic issues. Their declining economic power may actually *strengthen* incentives for collective US–EU action (Kahler 1995). However, bilateral relations could also become subject to new strains as alternative alliances drive a wedge between the transatlantic allies.

In any event, the economic dimension has become a more important determinant of US–EU relations. Levels of trade and investment which flow between the US and EU have increased exponentially since the early 1970s. On one hand, most of this economic exchange is relatively untouched by political changes on either side of the Atlantic (Featherstone and Ginsberg 1993). On the other, more domestic interests on both sides now have a higher stake in their government's trade and investment policies. The heightened importance of trade and investment for Western foreign policies enhances the potential for conflict on these issues.

In the defence and security arena, the end of bipolarity has encouraged the EU to seek a European Security and Defence Identity (ESDI). Debates about how an ESDI will mesh with existing Western security structures are acrimonious and often theological. They reflect widely divergent views between EU member states about the future role of the United States in European affairs, and starkly different outlooks within the US political class about the desirability of an ESDI.

More broadly, the very meanings of national and international security have changed. A military balance of power does nothing to check accelerating environmental degradation, rising ethnic and regional tensions or widening disparities between rich Northern and poorer Southern states. National security can no longer be equated with military strength. International security can be assured only if a far larger number of states become satisfied with the status quo.

The end of East–West conflict means that mutual vulnerability and fear no longer need to be the primary guarantors of global peace. It is plausible, if perhaps unfashionable, to argue that a more 'stable peace' (Boulding 1987) is possible if the US and EU can provide leadership, particularly within strengthened international institutions. The crucial point is that they are far more likely to inspire others to follow, and thus lead effectively, by acting together than by acting alone.

This chapter proceeds in four sections. Section 1 explains why one response to the end of the Cold War was enhanced US–EU cooperation. Section 2 considers alternative scenarios for a post-Cold War world and the possible role of the transatlantic alliance in each. Section 3 examines the diametric trends towards integration and fragmentation in the international system and the challenges they present to US–EU relations. The four leading theories of international relations which guide the book's analysis are introduced in section 4.

1 FORCES FOR CHANGE IN TRANSATLANTIC RELATIONS

The 1992 project and 'Fortress Europe'

A considerable transformation in US–EU relations occurred before the end of the Cold War seemed remotely possible. A political relaunch of the EU culminated in 1987 with the adoption of the Single European Act (SEA) and acceptance of a programme to create a 'single European market' by the end of 1992. The so-called 1992 project provided the US with clear incentives to upgrade its ties to the EU, as distinct from its constituent parts. In particular, the US needed to ensure that the EU did not erect new barriers to American access to the single market as it tore down barriers to internal trade between its member states.

Two key factors propelled the 1992 project. First, the recessions of the 1970s and early 1980s concentrated the minds of European decision-makers on the fact that the 'Common Market' simply did not exist. Western Europe enjoyed unprecedented levels of economic growth, spurred by increased, tariff-free internal trade after the European Economic Community was created in 1957. But trade between its member states remained restricted by complicated border controls and a range of non-tariff barriers (NTBs). Incompatible national standards acted to keep domestic markets for goods such as electronics and pharmaceuticals protected and segmented. Governments usually awarded public contracts to monopolistic 'national champion' producers, and markets worth up to 15 per cent of EU gross domestic product (GDP) thus remained insulated from meaningful competition. Trade in most services remained heavily restricted. The integration of the rest of the global economy, as measured by the volume of trade across national borders, actually proceeded further and faster than it did *within* the EU in the ten years after 1975 (Neven and Röller 1991: 1296–300). The 1992 project aimed to 'kick-start' European economies by freeing trade between them.

A second factor in the EU's relaunch was the declining capacity of European states to control their domestic economies. After 1980, EU governments found themselves confronted by a US administration under President Ronald Reagan which paid little heed to the impacts of its macroeconomic policies on European economies. Renewed European interest in the idea of moving towards full economic and monetary union (EMU) and a single European currency was reflected in the SEA. Its section on EMU hinted at an emerging consensus on the need to increase the EU's autonomy and power to defend the collective interests of its member states in international economic diplomacy.

The 1992 project was as much a political as an economic project. Its architects – particularly the European Commission – viewed the creation of the internal market as a means to justify more integrated political structures and stronger EU institutions to regulate it (see Appendix). A politically unified EU would be a more powerful international actor because the 'politics of scale' would provide it with more clout than could be wielded by its member states acting alone (Ginsberg 1989). The 1992 project was designed to enhance the EU's 'supranational' power, or its power to define and pursue collective interests which transcend national boundaries, authorities or interests.

The SEA amended the Community's founding document, the Treaty of Rome, for the first time in its history. It strengthened the EU's central institutions and streamlined decision-making related to the creation of the internal market. The SEA also increased the EU's powers over environmental, research and development (R&D), regional development and other policies. However, it was silent on the question of how the creation of the single market might affect the EU's external trade policy. The Commission clearly calculated that the implications of the 1992 project for the EU's external relations were so potentially explosive as to be a threat to the project itself (Holmes 1990: 20). Supporters of the internal market sought to draw a veil over concerns that large Japanese and US multinational corporations (MNCs) would be the principal benefactors from the creation of a large, barrier-free market. EU member states thus committed themselves to opening their domestic markets to more competition from other EU states, but gave no parallel commitment to open their markets to foreign states or, in the Union's jargon, 'third countries'.

Fears arose in Washington of a hidden agenda to create new barriers for non-European competitors as barriers to internal EU trade were swept away. Three distinct factors fuelled American anxieties. First, the US trade deficit meant that any threat to US access to foreign markets was viewed with alarm. US apprehension about the development of a 'Fortress Europe' was fuelled by Commission statements which asserted that 'where international obligations do not exist . . . we see no reason why the benefits of our internal liberalization should be extended unilaterally to third countries' (De Clercq 1988).

Second, the British government's anti-EU rhetoric shaped US perceptions. The strong personal and ideological affinity between Reagan and the British Prime Minister, Margaret Thatcher, made the Anglo-American 'special relationship' perhaps more palpable in the 1980s than ever before in the post-war period. Thatcher's initial opposition to the SEA and her reluctance to expand the EU's supranational authority struck deep chords in Washington.

Third, 'Fortress Europe' was in part a product of a historical lack of understanding of the EU in the United States. As the 1992 project took shape, one US 'expert' argued that while the Community had been created to promote free trade, 'under the leadership of [the Commission President] Jacques Delors and his socialist allies, who have an overall majority in the European Parliament in Brussels, this admirable goal of the European Community is being shoved aside' (Roberts 1990). More careful observers would have noted that the European Parliament (EP) met as a whole in Strasbourg (not Brussels), its powers were in no way fused with those of the Commission, and neither it nor the Commission could force its own agenda on EU member states. Delors's solidly pro-US credentials often went unnoticed by American pundits because he was a 'socialist'.

American trepidation about the possible effects of the 1992 project peaked as Reagan neared the end of his Presidency (Devuyst 1990: 7–8).

A senior official in the Commission's External Affairs Directorate-General (DG I) admitted, 'At that point in 1988 it became clear that the Commission actually hadn't considered what the impact of the single market would be on third countries and it didn't have a policy.'[1]

The EU thus moved to convene a special task force on the external policy implications of the 1992 project. Its members warned that increased EU protectionism against outsiders would erode many of the single market's expected benefits, such as increased employment and economic growth. A subsequent study found that the 1992 project might benefit foreign firms as much or more than EU producers, but also warned

> that is not to say, however, that keeping NTBs in place is going to make European industry more competitive in the future. On the contrary, competition from non-EU imports can be expected to lead European firms to restructure in order to stay competitive.
>
> (Neven and Röller 1991: 1302).

A declaration issued by the Commission (1988b) finally gave the 1992 project the external relations element it had lacked. Politically, it amounted to at least a tentative commitment to avoid erecting new external barriers while knocking down barriers to intra-EU trade. The declaration was a necessary, if far from sufficient, condition for closer US–EU relations.

The GATT and the Japanese challenge

The broad outlines of the 1992 project emerged at the same as the Uruguay Round of the General Agreement on Tariffs and Trade (GATT) was launched in 1986. This confluence of events posed considerable political difficulties for the EU. By unilaterally committing itself to liberalization of the internal market, the EU was effectively reducing its own bargaining power in multilateral negotiations on global liberalization within the GATT (see Calingaert 1988; Sek 1989).

The GATT's central instrument was the most favoured nation (MFN) principle. It required that trade concessions given to one country had to be extended without conditions to all GATT members. The EU's commitment to ensuring that the 1992 project did not discriminate against foreign competitors carried an implicit guarantee to treat all foreign competitors equally. Measures which allowed American firms access to the internal market also had to be extended to Asian competitors. A primary effect of the EU's pledge not to construct a 'Fortress Europe' was to focus attention on the Union's chronic trade deficit with Japan.

The subsequent debate within the EU mirrored one which had arisen in the US during the Reagan years. Western trade policies became subject to fierce protectionist pressures from domestic producers threatened by powerful competition from Japan, as well as the newly-industrialized Asian countries. In some respects, moves to strengthen US–EU cooperation after 1988 were propelled by shared perceptions about the threat posed to Western producers by the competitive challenge from Japan.

The US bilateral trading relationship with Japan contrasted sharply with US–EU trade relations. By the early 1990s, the Union accounted for nearly a quarter of US exports, while Japan took less than 12 per cent. The EU remained a critical market for American goods in high-growth, expanding industries. Nearly 45 per cent of American exports to the EU were high-technology goods, compared with less than 30 per cent of US sales to Japan (Hufbauer 1990: 21). The two main priorities for US trade policy became maintaining access to the EU's market and pressuring the Japanese to increase their imports of US goods.

However, the central US goal in the Uruguay Round was to agree sweeping, multilateral reforms of agricultural regimes. Agriculture had always been the main source of transatlantic trade disputes after the creation of the EU's Common Agricultural Policy (CAP) in 1962. More than 80 per cent of GATT legal actions taken by the US against the EU resulted from agricultural or fishery disputes (Hudec 1988). Sales of American farm goods accounted for 16 per cent of the EU's agricultural imports in 1960 but only 6 per cent by the late 1980s (Hufbauer 1990: 28).

In the early stages of the Uruguay Round, the US under George Bush, Reagan's successor, insisted that all countries should work towards the elimination of all agricultural subsidies by the year 2000. This goal was never taken seriously by the EU or many other US trading partners. But US negotiators proved resourceful and creative in isolating the EU on the agricultural issue. Eventually, EU member states were faced with a choice between radically reducing subsidies to their farmers or accepting blame for the total collapse of the Uruguay Round.

Agriculture remained one of America's 'last indisputable world-class industries' (Runge 1988: 143). Along with the Japanese challenge, reform of the CAP emerged as the most important focus of US trade diplomacy. Substantial cuts in EU farm subsidies became a prerequisite for a successful outcome of the Uruguay Round and US–EU partnership more generally.

Geopolitical change and the New Transatlanticism

The primary catalyst for the New Transatlanticism after 1988 was rapid geopolitical change in Eastern Europe. The fall of communist governments in the former Eastern bloc altered the balance of power within the transatlantic alliance. The EU's ethnic, historical and economic ties to Eastern Europe gave it unmatched influence and leverage in the region. Nearly all of the first governments to be elected democratically in post-war Eastern Europe cited EU membership as their country's number one foreign policy priority. The Bush administration thus sought stronger links to the Union and encouraged it to take the lead in developing Western policies which could help to promote and consolidate democratic reforms in the East.

Geopolitical change made a genuine transatlantic partnership imaginable, of a sort that had been quite unimaginable when the combination of the Soviet threat and the military superiority of the US made the alliance one of clearly unequal partners. US–EU relations were often marked by bitter clashes of interest and outlook during the Cold War. Still, East–West conflict reduced international politics to a 'zero-sum game that everyone could understand' (Maynes 1990: 5). In many respects, rapid geopolitical change between 1989 and 1992 yielded a more unpredictable and unstable system of international relations. The perceived need for common Western strategies to manage or at least influence events in a radically altered international environment inspired the New Transatlanticism. But there remained no guarantee that the dangers of further geopolitical instability could provide a new 'glue' to hold the West together and override new disputes in a post-Cold War world.

2 COMPETING VISIONS OF A POST-COLD WAR WORLD

The Cold War ended quite suddenly. Despite the expenditure of vast resources on intelligence and surveillance, Western political classes were caught nearly as unaware as those of the Soviet bloc when popular revolutions erupted in Eastern Europe in late 1989. Most of the assumptions which flowed from the bipolar balance of power of the Cold War were useless as guides for Western policy by the middle of 1990. By this time, agreement had been reached within the Community on the need to convene two new intergovernmental conferences (IGCs) to overhaul further the EU's institutions and treaties to accommodate EMU and strengthen political unity. Events in Eastern Europe gave EU member states new incentives to develop mechanisms which could facilitate common actions on foreign and security issues as they moved for the second time in five years to revise the Treaty of Rome.

Meanwhile, the US pushed the Union to acknowledge that it faced new and pressing external responsibilities in Eastern Europe. In a landmark speech in Berlin in December 1989, Bush's Secretary of State, James Baker, called for a 'new European architecture' to be built on the existing institutions of the post-war alliance and for a more politically unified EU. Throughout 1990 Bush repeatedly urged that US–EU relations needed to be upgraded. By November 1990, agreement had been reached on the Transatlantic Declaration, which committed both sides to more intensive and institutionalized consultations. Crucially, the declaration mandated that a new series of bilateral exchanges would take place outside the North Atlantic Treaty Organization (NATO), which traditionally had acted as the primary channel for exchanges of views between the US and Western Europe.

American insistence on strengthened ties to the Community flowed from the Bush administration's assumption that the EU's power would increase as the 1992 project neared completion. A Commission official observed:

> By the middle of 1989, that problem of the perception of the single market as a fortress essentially had been dealt with. But that process had a curious side-effect. Those who'd been looking at it were given a heightened awareness of the importance of the single market programme and thus of the economic and legislative role of the Community. That led the administration in the US to take the Community far more seriously than it had before.[2]

The Bush administration was also motivated by fears that accelerated European integration would yield a more assertive and unified EU caucus within NATO or even an EU defence community which might supersede NATO. Baker's Berlin speech urged that NATO be transformed from a purely military alliance into a broader forum for promoting Western political unity. Such urgings reflected apprehension within the Bush administration about a perceived decline in the salience of the institution which had done the most to guarantee a powerful US role in European affairs during the Cold War.

As the EU became preoccupied with transforming its own institutions in 1990, it was left to the Americans to develop a broad vision of what a post-Cold War world might look like. Bush's own vision was unveiled in a speech to a joint session of the US Congress in September 1990. Notably, Bush had convened the session to seek Congressional approval for the use of American military force to liberate Kuwait from occupying Iraqi forces. He urged that a 'New World Order' was within reach: a 'historic period of cooperation . . . freer from the threat of terror, stronger in the pursuit of justice, and more secure in a quest for peace' (US State Department 1990: 2). But, according to Bush, all of this was possible *only* if the US took immediate and decisive action in the Persian Gulf.

Bush stressed that his decision to send American troops to the Gulf was supported by a wide cross-section of the international community. At that point, the United Nations (UN) Security Council had endorsed US policy in five separate declarations. Bush's message was clear and politically shrewd, if extremely ironic. Congress would show itself to be out of step with seismic changes leading towards a more stable, humane and peaceful era in international relations unless it granted him a free hand to overwhelm the Iraqis with the full brunt of US military power.

The Gulf War featured neither US–EU partnership nor much European unity. It confirmed that only the US possessed the political will, international influence and military might to form and lead an international coalition which could repel an aggressor anywhere in the world. The war also demonstrated that the EU's loose arrangements for the coordination of national foreign policies remained poorly suited to unified action in a crisis. Subsequent discussions on the creation of new EU mechanisms to develop a Common Foreign and Security Policy (CFSP) were marked by sharp disagreements about how much EU unity was either desirable or practical. These divisions were not reconciled conclusively when the new CFSP arrangements were revealed at the Maastricht summit of December 1991. After they had been in place for several years, a notable lack of increased European unity led many observers – especially non-European ones – to belittle the CFSP as a device for legitimating EU inaction (Pfaff 1994; Shearman 1995). A more effective CFSP remained a critical and elusive prerequisite of a true US–EU partnership.

During the first half of the 1990s, Bush's vision of a 'New World Order' characterized by united, purposeful Western leadership became progressively less conceivable as a model for international relations in the twenty-first century. The Gulf War was in many respects a triumph of US unilateralism, despite the impression that the country's actions were backed by a broad-based international coalition. Domestic support for the war effort and US internationalism more generally waned quickly after the war ended. A vocal group of opinion leaders began to argue that the end of the Cold War would lead US allies such as the EU 'increasingly [to] assert control over their own destinies no matter what America wants or does, cultivating their own strengths, pursuing their own goals, and placing their interests above everyone else's' (Tonelson 1991: 46).

Bush's preoccupation with foreign policy cost him dear at the polls in 1992. Bill Clinton was elected, albeit with only 43 per cent of the popular vote, largely on the strength of his pledge to focus 'like a laser beam' on the US economy and other domestic problems. Clinton's 1992 campaign generally avoided foreign policy. One of his only substantive comments on the EU was 'it is too early to say whether the integration of Western Europe will be a plus or minus for America. If they keep opening trade, well, that's good.'[3] Clinton also offered vague promises to adopt new policies towards China, Haiti and Bosnia which would be more firmly guided by moral considerations.

Like Jimmy Carter, the last Democrat to hold the White House before him, Clinton found that a foreign policy based on moral principles was often impractical. Without a clear vision to guide national policy, the

Clinton administration often flip-flopped on its international commitments and thus enraged its allies. The Clinton Presidency became bogged down in policy rows over Somalia, North Korea and Bosnia which combined to damage the administration's credibility and hamper progress on its domestic agenda (Drew 1994).

The 1994 mid-term election found US voters in an ugly mood. The Democrats were thrashed at both the state and Congressional levels. A new breed of extremely ideological Republicans took power in Congress. In the midst of disputes over Bosnia and US foreign aid, the Clinton administration condemned the Republican Congressional majorities as 'new isolationists'.

The 'neo-isolationist' vision of a post-Cold War world is based on a narrow definition of national interests. It is shared by 'nativists', such as the maverick Republican, Pat Buchanan, as well as some Congressional Republicans, such as David Funderburke, formerly Reagan's ambassador to Romania. US neo-isolationists urge a retreat from international commitments and a slashing of budgets for foreign aid and the main foreign policy agencies. Needless to say, there is no room in this worldview for US–EU partnership.

By the mid-1990s, few outright neo-isolationists occupied positions of power in US politics. A more accurate label for most right-wing, 'America-first' politicians was 'aggressive unilateralist'. Their vision was rooted in history and informed by the Gulf War experience. Aggressive unilateralists tended to define US interests more broadly than neo-isolationists, but also to insist that 'American lives should not be risked – and lost – in places like Somalia, Haiti, and Rwanda with marginal or no American interests at stake' (Dole 1995: 41).

Most Americans of this ilk insisted that the US should remain a global military power which was capable of policing and disciplining the Third World as it did in Lebanon, Grenada, Central America, Libya, Panama and Haiti in the 1980s and early 1990s. Many assumed that even if the Soviet threat had receded, Russia remained politically unstable and a potential threat. Thus, the US had to maintain its traditional military presence in Europe, as well as Asia, in order to maintain a balance of power in both regions. Aggressive unilateralists found allies in the US Pentagon, which continued to insist that the US had to be prepared to fight two regional wars simultaneously.

Aggressive unilateralism may seem the product of a US mindset which is trained to find enemies where none exist, and which cannot accept the paradigm shift to a post-Cold War world. Yet, this mindset lurked behind the Bush administration's cautious approach to the reform of NATO and reductions in US military spending. It was not dispelled under the Clinton administration, whose control over the Pentagon was, to put it charitably, tenuous.

Aggressive unilateralists remained deeply sceptical about the idea that the US and EU could develop an integrated foreign and security policy agenda. In the words of the Senate majority leader and leading Republican Presidential candidate, Robert Dole (1995: 33–9): 'The United States, as the only global power, must lead. Europe – as individual states or a collective – cannot.'

An aggressively unilateralist vision of international relations was by no means confined to the US: a vocal 'Euro-sceptic' minority nearly tore apart the ruling British Conservative Party in the mid-1990s by insisting that it embrace fervent nationalism and opposition to closer European integration. After his election in 1995, the French President, Jacques Chirac, defied global opinion by resuming French nuclear testing in the South Pacific. More generally, the rise of nationalism in Europe threatened to lead to a stagnation or reversal of the movement towards closer European unity.

In the East, the splintering of the Soviet Union and Yugoslavia yielded a plethora of new 'micro-states' such as Estonia and Slovenia as well as acute tensions between 'reborn' states such as Russia and Ukraine or Croatia and Serbia. The long-term trend towards smaller and less stable political units in Europe seemed likely to complicate the inevitable expansion of the EU's membership and bog down its decision-making structures. In the shorter term, the rise of nationalism on the European continent threatened to make the Union a less unified political entity and preclude much meaningful cooperation between it and the US.

Another plausible scenario in a post-Cold War world would see the increased salience of trade, foreign investment and economic security provoke a break-up of the global trading system into three regional economic blocs in Europe, Asia and North America. Logically, the demise of the Soviet threat increases the possibility that the world's three capitalist centres of power – the US, EU and Japan – will drift apart and into conflict. Each could erect new barriers to trade with the others and develop its own rules and institutions for purely regional economic cooperation (see Bergsten 1990; Stoeckel et al. 1990; Thurow 1992).

There are clear grounds for extreme pessimism about the prospects for a 'New World Order' based on lofty ideals such as the consolidation of democracy, the defence of human rights and protection of the environment. Still, the end of the Cold War has at least created new opportunities for enhanced cooperation between states, fortified international institutions and stronger international law. The scenario which actually emerges depends crucially on choices taken by the US and EU about their relationship to one another and to the rest of the world.

3 INTEGRATION AND FRAGMENTATION IN THE GLOBAL SYSTEM

The key features of the international system of the early twenty-first century remain impossible to foresee with any precision. Clearly, however, they will be shaped dramatically by the interplay between two broad trends which have been accelerated and reinforced by the end of the Cold War (see Gaddis 1990; Rosenau 1990; Shaw 1994; Weiss *et al.* 1994). One is the movement towards the *integration* of the international system. Traditionally, the term has been used most often by international relations scholars to describe the process by which regional groups of states, such as the EU, increasingly develop common policies or decision-making arrangements across a progressively wider array of issues (see Keohane and Nye 1975).

In the latter part of the twentieth century, integration has become perceptible on a global scale, thus prompting a growing literature on 'globalization' (see Luard 1990; Held and McGrew 1993; Humbert 1993). Regions, states and peoples have become more closely associated due to modern global communications, which provide the infrastructure for the further integration of politics, economics, culture and technology (see Reich 1991: 220–1). Globalization has provoked new interest among international relations scholars in notions such as 'global society' or 'world community' (Shaw 1994; Brown 1995). The validity of such ideas is debatable and work on them is often shrouded in dense jargon. But the simple point is that a trend towards the integration of ideas or values which are variously termed Western, liberal or cosmopolitan has become perceptible. One rather optimistic assessment suggests that 'the old nineteenth-century liberal vision of a peaceful, integrated, interdependent and capitalist world may at last be coming true' (Gaddis 1990: 105)

Buttressed by the spread of democratic and, above all, capitalist ideas, the global economy is where integration has proceeded the furthest. Increases in global trade volumes are more a consequence than a cause of global economic integration. The structural bases for an integrated global economy are emerging in the form of accelerated technology transfers across borders, increased FDI, the embrace of capitalism throughout the developing world, and the creation of global markets for finance, currency and stocks. National and regional economies are increasingly bound together through complex interdependence as 'events occurring in any given part . . . of a world system affect (either physically or perceptually) events taking place in each of the other parts' (Young 1969: 726).

The integration of the global economy has been bolstered by the diminished utility of military-strategic power and the increased primacy of economic strength as determinants of international power. These trends were first visible in the 1970s when the Soviet Union achieved rough strategic parity with the US. The restraints imposed by the nuclear balance limited the degree to which any state could enhance its international power by increasing its military strength (Hanrieder 1978). Ho Chi Minh, the Afghans, Saddam Hussein and others in the Third World defied this logic. But the primary forum for competition between major states became the international economy. States had to trade and compete in order to satisfy domestic welfare demands. The integration of the global economy was reinforced in the process.

The power which states derive from the possession of nuclear weapons has not withered away and is unlikely to do so in the twenty-first century. Yet military conflict between any of the major nuclear powers has become almost unimaginable. Regional rivalries between superpowers playing a zero-sum game for international influence are no longer a primary feature of international politics. State security is now more than ever rooted in the ability of states to provide a basic system of welfare, a functioning economic infrastructure and links to the rest of the world. These are the keys to peaceful domestic political competition and a decent national standard of living.

Of course, the security equation is not that simple. Many nation-states have borders which are artificial creations imposed by past imperialist powers. Only half of all existing nation-states have one ethnic group which accounts for as much as 75 per cent of its population (Nye 1992: 91). Many face growing or latent ethnic or regional rivalries. These rivalries are historically entrenched features of the political landscape across Europe from Belfast to Belgrade and from the Basque country to the Baltic republics. Such tensions have been reawakened in many East European countries now that the repressive interior security regimes of the communist era no longer exist to keep them in check.

Heightened tension between ethnic groups is one manifestation of a wider trend towards national and regional *fragmentation* in the international system. The post-1945 'imaginary war' between East and West led societies to identify themselves in terms of ideas – capitalism or socialism – instead of race or ethnicity (Kaldor 1990). The effect was to mute nationalist impulses and integrate the economic, security and foreign policy agendas of most states into one bloc or the other. The resurgence of nationalist impulses, particularly in Europe, is evidenced by the fact that nearly twenty different nation-states now appear on the map where only two – Yugoslavia and the Soviet Union – appeared in 1990. The security threats posed by aggressive nationalism are more salient than any prospect of conflict along the traditional East–West axis of the Cold War.

It is easy to assume that integration is a positive force and fragmentation a negative one. However, the political integration of Germany after 1990 exposed latent xenophobia which was unleashed in ugly attacks on asylum-seekers. The integration of the global market for arms made the proliferation of nuclear and chemical weapons more difficult to police and prevent. The political uproar surrounding the ratification of the Maastricht Treaty on European Union in 1992 pointed to deep-seated doubts in several EU countries about the desirability of further political integration in Western Europe. In short, integration can yield conflict and instability as much as peace and mutual understanding between different cultures.

On the other hand, the political fragmentation of the Warsaw Pact can only be considered a positive development in human affairs. The unfreezing of the East–West divide at least creates the potential for Western policies towards less-developed countries (LDCs) which shed their post-war obsession with checking the spread of Soviet influence and focus instead on promoting economic development, environmental protection or respect for human rights. While the splintering of centralized political power in Yugoslavia has led to much bloodshed and human tragedy, its former republics could have been held together only by repression of the sort used to quell ethnic rivalries in Eastern Europe during the Cold War.

Joffe (1992–3: 43) summarizes the conflict as one between 'the logic of economics and interdependence that spells community, and the logic of ethnicity and nationality that demands separation'. Put another way, a dialectic has emerged between economic integration and political fragmentation. Balancing the two poses profound new challenges for Western foreign policies. The EU countries must design mechanisms which can legislate between the different interests of member states yet still secure the mutual benefits which can be gained through cooperation. Unless the EU can reconcile conflicting national interests more effectively on issues related to the internal market project – immigration, taxation, the environment, social legislation and so on – it is difficult to foresee truly 'common' European foreign or security policies.

The EU must also widen its membership to include the new democracies in Eastern Europe. The inevitable enlargement of the EU will complicate the Union's efforts to present itself to the rest of the world as a single actor in international relations. It also threatens to exacerbate political fissures which already exist within the present membership. EU institutions which were originally designed for a Community of six member states appear ill-suited to a Union of as many as twenty-five or even thirty.

After the EU dramatically relaunched itself in the 1980s with the single market project, it underwent a profound crisis of legitimacy in the early 1990s. Referendums called to ratify the Maastricht Treaty in 1992 saw the Danish voters reject it and the French approve it only narrowly. The

European Monetary System (EMS), which many viewed as a transitional arrangement on the road to full EMU, nearly collapsed amid bitter exchanges between Germany and the UK over who was to blame. The political climate sparked anti-EU revolts within the governing British Conservative Party and reinforced profound hesitations in Germany about EMU. Even after Maastricht was finally ratified, closer European political unity seemed far from inevitable and often unlikely.

At the same time, it must be acknowledged that the EU is, and is likely to remain, one of the most successful experiments in the history of international cooperation. The unprecedented political experiment upon which the EU is embarked is mostly about balancing the forces of integration and fragmentation. How well it manages this balancing act will go far towards determining its relationship with the US in the twenty-first century.

United States foreign policy also has reached a crossroads. In some respects the end of the Cold War accentuated American power. Initially, at least, the collapse of communism and victory in the Gulf War appeared to debunk Kennedy's (1989) thesis that US power was in decline due to 'imperial overstretch'. Fukuyama's (1992) celebration of the 'end of history' and the clear victory of US-style liberal democracy over Soviet communism in the battle for ideological ascendancy led many students of international relations to be bullish about the prospects for a 'new American hegemony'.

Ironically, one effect of the apparent triumph of US foreign policy was to focus the nation's attention on its own domestic problems. Huntington's (1989–90: 96) claim that US pre-eminence would remain unchallenged turned on his argument that the 'self-renewing genius of American politics' could solve its most pressing problems at home. On the contrary, the response of the Bush administration to a deteriorating education system, the drug epidemic, inner city decay and the federal debt was usually to play down their severity. Reich (1991) – who became a key player in the Clinton administration – insisted that these problems were the root causes of declining US economic competitiveness. Yet the Clinton years saw only very limited public investments due to overwhelming political concern about cutting the federal budget deficit.

By the mid-1990s, the growing US federal budget deficit created a budget-cutting fervour among Republicans who wanted to 'reduce government'. Clinton's initiative to 'reinvent' government struck relatively few chords with voters. Debates about the proper role of government in American life had effects on foreign as well as domestic policy, as fierce and ill-tempered competition for strictly limited federal resources began to permeate the US foreign policy agenda.

Accordingly, domestic and foreign policy agendas began to merge in the minds of many voters. As never before, American workers showed themselves to be aware that their livelihoods often depended on economic forces beyond their country's borders. Meanwhile, a growing chorus of domestic voices began to insist that it was time to 'bring America home' and concentrate limited federal resources on domestic problems while toughening its trade policy. The domestic political consensus which supported US internationalism throughout the post-war period began to splinter. The forces of integration and fragmentation thus became visible in new debates about the future of US foreign policy.

These forces are also at play within the myriad international and bilateral institutions in which the US and EU interact. Nearly all these institutions have had to expand to take in new states created after the end of the Cold War. At the same time, most have been the subject of new efforts to reform, consolidate and strengthen their powers and central bodies. The transformation of NATO, the creation of the World Trade Organization (WTO), the reform of the UN, the institutionalization (and widening and renaming) of the Organization for Security and Cooperation in Europe (OSCE), and above all the evolution of the EU itself will all fundamentally alter the way in which the US and EU interact with one another.

The international system as a whole is where the forces of integration and fragmentation are visible in boldest relief. Rapid and sweeping geopolitical changes have unleashed centrifugal and centripetal forces: 'nationalism and transnationalism' (Nye 1992), 'anarchy and interdependence' (Buzan 1991: 43) or 'fusion and fission' (Halliday 1995: 44). This study is primarily concerned with assessing the prospects for an integrated transatlantic partnership against a backdrop of fragmented global power.

4 EXPLAINING US–EU RELATIONS IN THEORY

Using theory to guide the study of empirical political events means being selective. Competing theories are always on offer and they inevitably provide competing explanations for the same events or outcomes. The most important criterion to guide the selection process is the validity of the *assumptions* which underpin different theories. Theorists who study international relations often invoke entirely contradictory explanations for the same events or outcomes because they start from different assumptions.

The four theories employed throughout this book clearly illustrate the maxim that different theoretical assumptions can lead to radically different interpretations of the same evidence. Each of them makes different assumptions about the nature of power, cooperation and competition in the international system. Accordingly, they provide competing explanations for vital aspects of US–EU relations.

None of these four theories offer convincing explanations for all events and outcomes. All are 'abbreviations of reality' (Hanrieder 1989: x). The end of the Cold War and the heightened unpredictability of international relations have chastened all but the most dogmatic theorists. Witness Keohane's (1993b: 297) remarkable confession: 'when we use our weak theories to offer predictions about the future, we must be humble, since during the last several years we have failed to anticipate major changes in world politics'.

Whatever its shortcomings, the literature on international relations theory remains one of the richest and most provocative offered by political science as a discipline. Even a leading critic of mainstream approaches insists that 'theoretical diversity is a strength, not a weakness of International Relations' (Halliday 1994: 1). The four theories chosen to guide this book's analysis all have rich historical traditions and offer clear sets of assumptions.

This section provides a brief overview of each theory. The focus is on the *assumptions* made by advocates of each about three critical determinants of international politics: the nature of competition between states, the relative importance of international cooperation, and the impact of domestic politics on the behaviour of states as international actors.

Neorealism

Against the odds, neorealism remains the leading theory of international relations: it 'has established a secure place despite continuing dissatisfactions with it, and a fair measure of outright hostility' (Buzan *et al.* 1993: 14–15; see also Ashley 1984; Kratochwil 1993). Neorealism seeks to update the principles of classical realism.

Works by Thucydides (1954) and Kissinger (1964) may be viewed as the theoretical start and end points for classical realism. Bull's *The Anarchical Society* (1977) represents one of its most eloquent expressions, and Morgenthau's *Politics Among Nations* (1985) its clearest and most convincing portrayal. For realists, international relations was a Hobbesian 'struggle for power, "a war of all against all" ' (Kegley and Wittkopf 1993: 23). States behaved as 'unitary-rational' actors. They sought to maximize their power, primarily by military means, and remained 'essentially warmaking machines' (Gilpin 1981: 131) whose 'every act . . . in its power aspects, is directed to war' (Carr 1940: 139). The international system thus bred competition and insecurity.

The era of superpower détente in the mid-1970s appeared to make classical realism obsolete. Subsequently, the Soviet invasion of Afghanistan, the bellicosity of the Reagan administration and the 'Second Cold War' of the early 1980s made realist assumptions respectable again. Neorealism emerged to refine and systemize realism while retaining most of its major assumptions. Where realism had stressed hierarchy between states, neorealism concerned itself more with polarity, or the number of centres of power in the international system and its effects on the behaviour of states. The notion of a 'balance of power' between states was a critical focus of realism, but realists were vague on how such a balance might change over time. Neorealism explained change in international politics as a product of the impact of the international system's structure on the behaviour of its individual units (see Gilpin 1984; Keohane 1986).

The seminal neorealist work remains Kenneth Waltz's *Theory of International Politics*(1979). Waltz argued that alliances changed quite naturally as states adjusted to shifts in the distribution of power in the international system. He held out hope – although of a somewhat sceptical kind – that the competitive pressures of the international system could lead the balance of power to dissolve and reform continuously without dire consequences. International cooperation on specific issues might be possible between actors such as the US and EU as long as they approached cooperation with no illusions about the relative distribution of power between them. But Waltz and other neorealists doubted that sustained cooperation was possible between sovereign states within international organizations such as the EU.

Neorealism has four core premises. First, it accepts the classical realist assumption that the international system is 'anarchic': it possesses no overarching authority to force states to behave in a certain way. Thus interstate conflict is inevitable. Nation-states are the only actors that really matter in international politics and there is little 'interdependence' between them (Waltz 1979: 143–6). Coalitions between states are fleeting. The ability of transnational actors, such as the EU, to impose some semblance of order in the midst of anarchy is mostly denied. Waltz (1979: 95) berates analysts who view transnational actors as powerful actors in their own right for having 'developed no distinct theory of their subject matter or of international politics in general'.

Second, the primary level of analysis for neorealists is the international system as a whole. Thus the internal characteristics of states or their domestic politics 'drop out', and are theoretically irrelevant in explaining their behaviour as international actors. For Waltz (1979: 97), 'national politics consists of differentiated units performing specified functions. International politics consists of like units duplicating one another's activities'. The point is that it matters little whether states are democracies or dictatorships or something in between. Because they operate in the same anarchic environment all states are alike in the functions they perform and in the goals they pursue. They differ only in their relative capabilities. This point is more explicit in neorealism than realism.

Third, neorealism assumes that power in international relations is 'fungible': a state's power in one arena can compensate for weakness in another. Thus American military power can be used to pursue US interests in the economic arena. Waltz argues that the classical realist distinction between 'high' and 'low' politics, or between issues of war and peace as against those of economy and welfare, is 'misplaced. States use economic means for military and political ends; and military and political means for the achievement of economic interests' (Waltz 1979: 94). Neorealists do not share classical realist assumptions about the absolute primacy of military power.

The fourth and most important neorealist assumption is that the *structure* of the international system is a more important determinant of international politics than are the discretionary choices taken by individual nation-states:

> States have no choice about their concern for security and, indeed, survival. The system may not determine their behavior, but it does condition it. And from the anarchical nature of the state system everything else flows: the need for states to pay attention to their power, to maintain an equilibrium, and to be aware of the ever-present dangers of conflict and war.
>
> (Spanier 1987: 681)

Neorealism offered powerful explanations for international politics in the 1980s. However, neorealists found it more difficult to explain the dramatic changes of the post-1989 period by reference to shifting patterns of relative power in the international system. As Kratochwil (1993: 63) points out, Soviet military power was virtually the same the year before and the year after the Berlin Wall fell.

Nonetheless, the early 1990s brought several (previously rare) attempts to develop neorealism further. Moran (1993) urged an 'economics agenda' upon neorealists which acknowledged that the decline of US international power had domestic roots: it resulted primarily from Americans consuming far more than they saved. Powell (1994) insisted that neorealism had to specify more clearly the conditions under which international institutions did *not* constrain states or shape their actions.

Perhaps above all, Buzan *et al.*'s (1993) theory of 'structural realism' tried to take account of the internal characteristics of states and to conceptualize power in a more sophisticated way than Waltz. The result was a theory which went beyond the almost exclusive neorealist concern with structure and units. In emphasizing the *systemic* quality of relations between states, Buzan *et al.* held that relations between certain groups of states, such as those of the EU, might become systemized. A group might contain states which were internally different (i.e. Luxembourg and Germany), with these differences actually preserved by a balance of power between that group and other, relatively autonomous groups of states. Buzan *et al.* (1993: 245) concede that they raise as many questions as they answer, but their provocative book illustrates a wider point:

neorealism, however altered, has proved to be a remarkably resilient model for understanding international politics despite new challenges to its central assumptions.

Institutionalism

Theorists who view complex interdependence between nation-states as an important determinant of international politics are precisely those whom Waltz accuses of having developed no distinct theory. One of Waltz's theoretical soulmates observes that: 'Realists and institutionalists particularly disagree about whether institutions markedly affect the prospects for international stability. Realists say no; institutionalists say yes' (Mearsheimer 1994/5: 7).

Institutionalists insist that the nature of international politics has changed as nation-states have become progressively more interlinked in a complex web of institutions which help them manage their political, security and (especially) economic relationships. Institutionalists argue that:

> Interdependence means that even great powers cannot act effectively on their own. To regain some influence over events, governments and firms have to collaborate with one another; they have to sacrifice their unilateral freedom of action for some degree of mastery over transnational flows of goods, capital, technology, ideas, and people.
>
> (Keohane 1993a: 48)

Institutionalists share several common assumptions. One is that nation-states can cooperate with one another even if they are motivated by self-interest. Many institutionalists draw inspiration from Hugo Grotius (1913), a seventeenth century Dutchman who was the first great proponent of international law as a force for cooperation in international relations.

Another institutionalist assumption is that international organizations and other transnational actors (such as MNCs) can develop their own resources and agendas independently of nation-states. International agencies such as the European Commission and UN Secretariat assume key roles in communications networks between states and other actors. They act as 'brokers and negotiators without having significant tangible sources of power' (Keohane and Nye 1975: 399).

Finally, institutionalists challenge the realist assumption that national security and military concerns must always be paramount in foreign policy-making. Complex interdependence forces more issues of an eclectic nature onto governments' foreign policy agendas. One consequence is that the distinction between international and domestic issues is eroded

(Keohane 1984). 'Intermestic' issues such as the price of oil thus become central concerns for both international and domestic policies.

Institutionalism is a broad church. It includes theorists who might be called 'liberal neorealists' because they borrow from balance of power analysis, but argue from a Lockean rather than a Hobbesian position (see Keohane and Nye 1975, 1977, 1987; Krasner 1983; Keohane 1986, 1989). They allow that states may be happy to pursue self-preservation, as opposed to power-maximization. Meanwhile, international institutions can mitigate the anarchy of the international system.

Institutionalism 'grew up' out of a body of work concerned with foreign policy analysis: the study of what determines foreign policy decisions and outcomes. Advocates of foreign policy analysis tried to show that the approach, incorporating domestic factors, could provide a more persuasive account of the making of foreign policy, and of its irrationalities, than could realism. Clearly, 'societies were interacting in ways that were "transnational" rather than inter-state and these "linkages" were in turn having an impact on foreign policy' (Halliday 1994: 13).

Institutionalism gradually lost it focus on the domestic–international connection as attention shifted to international 'regimes' (see Young 1980; Krasner 1983; Haggard and Simmons 1987; Smith 1987; Rittberger 1993). Regimes were defined broadly as 'sets of implicit or explicit principles, norms, and decision-making procedures around which actors' expectations converge in a given area of international relations' (Krasner 1982b: 186). Theorizing about regimes tended to be clouded in jargon. One prominent analyst even dismissed it as a 'fad' (Strange 1982). Subsequent work, often grouped together under the rubric of 'liberal institutionalism', offered more clarity by focusing more narrowly on formal institutions such as the EU and less on informal norms, principles or procedures (see Keohane 1984, 1989; Lipson 1984; Young 1986; Grieco 1990).

Many regime theorists – along with some neorealists – saw the post-war period as proving that a stable system of regimes requires a single hegemonic power to enforce rules and norms (Keohane 1980; Gilpin 1981; Avery and Rapkin 1982; Snidal 1985). 'Hegemonic stability theory' maintained that the unprecedented peace, stability and economic growth of the post-war period was possible only because the US founded and then supported regimes such as NATO, the GATT and the Bretton Woods arrangements on exchange rates. Its advocates argued that a hegemon might use coercion to enforce a global order which served not only its own national interest but those of many or even most other states in the international system. The 'afterglow' of hegemonic stability, in the form of international institutions, might last far longer than the distribution of power which prompted it in the first place: 'institutions are the shadows of the past that shape visions and choices about the future' (Nye and Keohane 1993: 125).

The increasingly technical nature of international policy-making led some institutionalists to focus on 'epistemic communities' or 'network[s] of professionals with recognized expertise and competence in a particular domain' (Haas 1992a: 3). These theorists argued that closely linked communities of scientists, activists and other experts often shared specialized knowledge and causal understandings. Epistemic communities could define problems, identify compromises between different interests and devise international solutions for governments. Thus, when governments selected policies, they were supplied with 'readymade' expert arguments which could be used to justify their choices and build domestic political consensuses to support them (see Goldstein 1989; Haas 1990, 1992b; Haas *et al.* 1993). Work on epistemic communities sought to link 'institutions to the dynamic interaction between domestic and international political games' (Adler and Haas 1992: 369). It often built on theories which tried to identify links between domestic politics and the behaviour of states in international relations (see Putnam 1988, 1993).

Institutionalism, with its stress on cooperation, eventually became a competitor with neorealism, with its emphasis on conflict. A logical, and rather banal, next step was to argue that the two approaches needed to be integrated or reconciled (Buzan *et al.* 1993: 4; Niou and Ordeshook 1994). Yet the assumptions of the two schools remain incompatible in key respects. Leading advocates of one approach frequently offer no quarter to the other (see Kratochowil 1993; Mearsheimer 1994/5).

During the post-war period, theorists who stressed the importance of complex interdependence and cooperation in international relations often had to apologize for the failure of their theories to explain state behaviour on security issues. The end of the Cold War then altered definitions of security. The expansion of foreign policy agendas to include issues such as trade, environmental protection and drug trafficking enhanced the explanatory power of institutionalism. Certainly, the increased importance of the EU as an institution and the New Transatlanticism after 1989 may be viewed as responses to increasing interdependence, thus validating institutionalist assumptions.

Liberalism

Concepts developed in classic works of economics by Adam Smith (1937) and David Ricardo (1911) form the building blocks for a third theory of international relations. Liberalism starts with the most powerful single idea in the history of economic theory: the law of comparative advantage. It teaches that the more that states trade with one another, the more they may specialize and the more all benefit. Liberals view international relations as a positive-sum game: if states would eliminate all barriers to economic exchange between them, all states would benefit from the economic growth engendered by free trade.

Strictly speaking, liberalism is an ideology, not a theory. Liberals believe that people are almost 'programmed' to trade. Ridley (1996) argues that trade is one of the oldest human traits, that it is inherent to people and a hallmark to their species in the same way as language. With its relatively narrow focus on trade, liberalism may be criticized as offering an incomplete picture of international relations. Liberals are often accused of being agnostic about how power is distributed in the international system, especially by Marxists who argue that free trade provides disproportionate benefits to rich states.

Many neorealists and even more institutionalists would consider themselves to be both liberals and free traders. However, a distinct liberal view of international relations has begun to emerge in recent years (see Doyle 1986; Rosecrance 1986; Burley 1993; Moravcsik 1992, 1993, 1995). Its proponents argue that degrees of cooperation or competition between states are determined neither by the distribution of international power, as neorealists claim, nor by the type of institutions available to facilitate bargaining, as institutionalism teaches. For liberals, cooperation is determined by the extent to which national preferences converge on particular issues, which in turn is determined by the demands of powerful domestic interest groups. The functional benefits of cooperation tend to create their own supply. Thus, stable international institutions reflect stability in underlying national interests or strategic problems that states must solve. By contrast with institutionalists, liberals argue that 'international institutions are not *causes* of cooperation but mechanisms through which cooperation occurs' (Haggard and Moravcsik 1993: 285).

Liberalism offers plausible explanations for the behaviour of states on matters related to human rights (Moravcsik 1995) and international law (Burley 1993). But its most germane theoretical insights concern the political economy of international trade. Liberals take satisfaction in a growing body of empirical evidence which suggests that increased competition promotes innovation and sustained economic growth far more than does protection (see Geroski and Jacquemin 1985; Porter 1990; Bayard and Elliott 1994). This trend has profound implications for international relations between states. A distinct theoretical model is needed to explain state behaviour on international trade and 'economic security' issues as they become 'core' issues for Western foreign policies.

Liberalism offers a powerful heuristic guide to understanding the emergence of the 1992 project and the evolution of US–EU relations. The former attracted political support largely because the predicted results of increased trade within a liberalized internal market were an increase of more than 5 per cent in European GDP and the creation of five million new jobs (see Cecchini *et al.* 1988; Padoa-Schioppa 1987). Liberals argue that the very existence of the EU has shifted the preferences of its member states towards embracing free trade more enthusiastically because it has empowered pro-free trade forces in domestic politics. As for transatlantic relations, the root cause of most bilateral conflicts has been deviation from the liberal prescription that each side eliminate barriers to economic exchange with the other.

Liberalism's explanatory power is not limited to economic relations between states. Historically, free trade has consistently been pursued only by states which have embraced more general liberal values. Thus, 'liberalism asserted a close relation of democracy and peace, not just as the first determining the second, but as an interactive process' (Halliday 1994: 32). Doyle's (1986) empirical treatment of wars throughout modern history supports Kant's (1932) contention that liberal states do not make war upon each other. Historical exceptions may be cited (Ray 1994), but liberal states generally create a 'separate peace' between themselves as they become imbued with the goal of promoting unfettered commerce.

Liberalism's prescriptions may be criticized as naive because they assume that governments can resist the domestic political pressures which prevent unencumbered free trade from becoming a reality. This point is crucial for advocates of the 'managed' or 'fair trade' school of theoretical economics, which emerged in the 1980s as a formidable challenger to liberalism (see Dixit 1986; Prestowitz 1988; Nivola 1990). The fair trade school, which shares many neorealist assumptions, rejects the strategy of unilaterally eliminating barriers which protect home markets in the hope that others will reciprocate and embrace free trade. Its advocates insist that trade patterns will always be politically influenced. Individual states must bargain with their competitors to seek concessions which satisfy domestic interests. Trade is 'not about utopian notions of the evolution of the world's industrialized nations towards a "post-protectionist" or "post-industrial" economy. Free trade is about competing. It is about defending existing comparative advantages while developing new ones' (de la Mothe and Ducharne 1990: 4). The fair trade school is anathema to liberals, but it has inspired unilateralism in EU and (especially) US trade policies.

The best-known liberal statement on contemporary international relations is Fukuyama's *The End of History and the Last Man* (1992). Only half in jest, Fukuyama (1989) has said that he takes great pride in having achieved 'a uniquely universal consensus, not on the current status of liberalism . . . but on the fact that I was wrong'. Despite the persistence of attacks on Fukuyama and liberalism more generally, the power of the essential liberal argument – as summarized by Gaddis (1990: 104) – cannot be denied: 'if only one could maximize the flow of ideas, commodities, capital and people across international borders, then the causes of war would drop away'.

Reformism

A final set of perspectives on international relations must be included because 1989 and its immediate aftermath marked 'one of those rare moments in history when everything seems to change' (Maynes 1990: 3). Many theorists argue that international politics is no longer simply about what is necessary given practical realities. It is now about what may be possible if new ideas and assumptions replace existing ones.

Reformism is used throughout this study to refer to a set of views which is shared by an eclectic group of theorists and thinkers. Its roots and assumptions may be traced back to Rousseau (1975), who believed that individuals could put their needs aside for the common good, and forward to the political idealism of the interwar period (see Kegley and Wittkopf 1993: 20–2). Idealists argued that nation-states were capable of mutual assistance and cooperation and denied that war was an inevitable feature of international politics. For them, war was a product of inadequate international institutions or avoidable structural conditions.

Reformists build on idealist assumptions. First, reformists insist on 'holism' as an approach to international relations. They stress interconnections between issues which are usually viewed as distinct and separate by governments. Reformists argue that the most important modern threats to international security – inequalities between rich and poor countries, environmental degradation and nuclear proliferation – are part of a single crisis in international affairs which threatens all states. Links between emigration pressures and rapid population growth in LDCs, Western arms sales to Iraq and the Gulf War, and the Chernobyl disaster and the contamination of British farmland are cited as evidence.

Second, reformists claim that states are the problem in international relations, not the solution (Walker 1995). The reformist critique of the state is primarily what distinguishes it from other theories. Reformists argue that 'the emergence of the state is a historical not a natural occurrence' (Walker and Mendlovitz 1987: 4). Most wish to accelerate the decline of nation-states by linking new social movements devoted to ecological, feminist or pacifist causes in global networks. The ultimate goal is to pressure governments to develop transnational solutions to modern problems (Hurrell 1995).

Third, while reformists often condemn international organizations as slaves to state interests, international cooperation is viewed as desirable in principle. Thus, reformists tend to be split about whether the EU is a tool at the service of petty national interests or a potential vehicle for overcoming them. Shaw (1994: 166) sums up the reformist critique of existing international organizations:

> The major Western states have resisted endowing international institutions with real substance, have refused to give real priority to means of anticipating international difficulties, still cling too much to the idea of national 'sovereignty', and above all react to crises too little, too unimaginatively, and too late.

Fourth, reformists argue that the moral content of foreign policies must supersede abstract and increasingly meaningless notions of national interest. Reformists chide governments for tolerating human misery beyond their national borders, and often within them. They cite the growing gap between rich Northern industrialized countries and poor Southern countries as a 'common crisis' for all nations (Brandt Commission 1983). Reformists point to the irony of a world in which 'international affairs are, notoriously, the area where moral considerations apply least', and castigate social scientists who 'have come to accept different moral criteria for states than for individuals' (Halliday 1994: 236).

Reformism is an even more eclectic school than is institutionalism. It includes feminists, ecologists, various kinds of Marxists and advocates of 'critical theory'. The latter may be 'the most ambitious of all theories, as its ultimate aim is to transform the fundamental nature of international politics and create a world where there is not just increased cooperation between states, but the possibility of genuine peace' (Mearsheimer 1994/5: 14).

Perhaps above all, reformists strive to refute the assumptions and prescriptions of neorealism. Advocates of these two schools tend to talk past one another and even publish in different academic journals. Neorealism is the dominant paradigm for contributors to *International Organization* and, particularly, *International Security*. For perhaps obvious reasons, it is rare to find a neorealist analysis in *The Journal of Peace Studies* or *The Journal of Conflict Resolution*.

One particularly apt complaint of reformists is that neorealism is ahistorical (Walker 1989). Neorealists could not predict and cannot explain the end of the Cold War. By contrast, neo-Marxists, who focus on the political effects of capitalism, insist that the homogenizing pressures of capitalism forced the collapse of the USSR.

Reformists also attack the liberal view of international relations. Many neo-Marxists still see a revolutionary outcome as inevitable as capitalism collapses due to its internal contradictions. Less doctrinaire theorists such as Halliday (1994: 231) argue that 'there is an alternative path which liberal democracy could take: namely, a regression to various forms of barbarism, national and international, via the prevailing of some mixture of capitalist-authoritarian, nuclear, ecological, racist and recidivist trends'.

Reformism is highly normative. Mainstream theorists sometimes generate moral prescriptions for international relations (see Hoffmann 1981; Keohane 1986: 198). But reformists are distinct in insisting that a more humane world requires an end to the existing state system. The reformist strategy is to 'think globally, act locally': international relations can be transformed by revolutionizing domestic politics at the grassroots through non-violence, ecology and social responsibility. Greenpeace's victory in its fight against the dumping of the Brent Spar oil platform in the North Sea in 1995, followed by its high-profile global campaign against French nuclear weapons testing, are good examples of the sort of direct political action that reformists view as potentially transformative.

On one hand, reformists may be accused of utopianism and of offering little of practical use in the day-to-day management of US–EU relations. Mainstream scholars often dismiss reformists as 'advocates of a severely iconoclastic intellectual and political position' (Farer 1977: 130). On the other, the events of 1989–92 have strengthened the reformist argument. Reformism now seems less of a pious and sanctimonious rehash of idealism and a more credible starting point for thinking about how to transform international politics. If nothing else, reformism points to the gap between what exists and what may be possible in an era in which many long-held assumptions about international relations have become irrelevant and outdated. It also highlights how difficult, perhaps impossible, it will be to transform international politics in line with reformist aims without concerted action by Europe and the America.

Chapter 2

The historical setting

Analysis of the post-war history of US–EU relations reveals that collective memories on both sides are surprisingly long. The US has provided considerable moral and political support to the European integration process, but American attitudes have often been arrogant and patronizing. The EU's own development has proceeded in fits and starts. Its inability to speak with one voice on issues extending beyond its most protectionist and insular policies frequently has made it a difficult partner for the US.

This chapter begins with a brief overview of postwar US–EU relations in section 1. The geopolitical earthquake of 1989 is the focus for section 2. Section 3 considers the significance of the Transatlantic Declaration, which marked a historic departure in bilateral relations. Section 4 applies the four theories of international relations to the postwar evolution of transatlantic relations.

1 EUROPE AND AMERICA: 1945–88

The incorporation of Western Europe into a liberal world trading system was a central goal of American foreign policy in the immediate post-war period, after a domestic US political consensus emerged on the need rapidly to rebuild war-damaged European economies. The Marshall Plan pumped US aid worth more than $5 billion into Western Europe after 1947. Under the Truman administration, the US insisted that plans for the use of Marshall Plan funds had to be coordinated through a central authority, the Organization for European Economic Cooperation (OEEC), which brought together representatives of national economic ministries. While the Marshall Plan induced little actual integration of European economies, it did set an important precedent of American support for the broader principle of European unity (DePorte 1986: 134).

The US commitment to Europe was motivated more by pragmatism and strategic concerns than altruism. The Marshall Plan was sold by the Truman administration to a reluctant Congress as an anti-Soviet programme. It was accepted by Congress largely on account of fears that Europe's working classes would fall under the sway of socialist ideals unless its economies were reconstructed quickly. Economic integration was viewed in Washington as the only way to 'kick-start' economic growth in Europe while binding the new Federal Republic of Germany firmly to the West. Above all, European political unity was seen as crucial to collective defence against the Soviet threat.

The Marshall Plan and US support for a strong Europe were in some ways counterbalanced by American insistence on the command structure created for NATO in 1949. Primary operational control over NATO forces and strategy was reserved for American decision-makers. As Krasner (1989: 148) observed, 'for the leaders of Europe this is a peculiar situation, especially given the fact that if deterrence fails it is their citizens, and not those of the United States, that would initially bear the brunt of the suffering'. However, American military superiority and Europe's economic weakness left European leaders with little choice.

The Americans did offer political and financial support to plans for the creation of a European Defence Community (EDC) in 1950. The Eisenhower administration hoped that the creation of a 'European army' would strengthen the European pillar in NATO and allow the US to reduce its forces in Europe. But the EDC was rejected by the French National Assembly in a wave of nationalism in 1954.

Subsequent negotiations on the creation of a European Economic Community (EEC) were more successful and culminated in the signing of the Treaty of Rome in 1957. Again the US actively encouraged the negotiations. The Eisenhower administration calculated that stronger European economies were a prerequisite of a more equal sharing of the financial and military burdens of Western defence. Furthermore, the prevailing economic wisdom of the day was that the 'trade creation' effects of economic growth in Europe would more than offset any 'trade diversion' away from US suppliers due to the Community's new common external tariff (see Viner 1950). Markets would expand for all producers, including those in America.

US views had changed somewhat by the early 1960s. Concerns about the Community's new common external tariff led the Kennedy administration to offer reciprocal tariff reductions to try to guarantee US access to the new Common Market. Kennedy also favoured stronger transatlantic political links. In 1962 he unveiled his 'Grand Design' for a 'concrete Atlantic partnership', based on a 'declaration of interdependence' with a united Europe.[1]

Kennedy's proposal presumed a European unity which clearly did not yet exist. The Community remained divided on most non-trade issues. The Fouchet plan for a wider European 'union of states' which could develop common foreign and defence policies foundered largely due to controversy about its implications for relations with the US. The French President, Charles de Gaulle, rejected suggestions that an Atlantic partnership could be a partnership between equals. His argument was fuelled by the revelation of American plans for a 'multilateral force' in 1962 which assumed total US operational control over all of NATO's nuclear weapons.

De Gaulle's anti-Americanism weakened Kennedy politically when the latter insisted that his Grand Design necessitated US concessions on trade. Congressional rejection of Kennedy's proposal for a 50 per cent cut in US tariffs reflected both suspicions of the Community and scepticism about the President's commitment to defending his country's interests within the GATT. Congress also rejected the State and Commerce departments as suitable candidates for expanded executive trade policy powers and pushed Kennedy to create the new United States Trade Representative (USTR). The USTR was incorporated into the President's own Executive Office, yet remained dependent on Congress's willingness to delegate its constitutional powers over trade policy to the executive (Destler 1986: 17–18).

Still, by any standards the Kennedy Round (1963–8) of the GATT was enormously successful. It resulted in sharp tariff reductions and substantial increases in transatlantic trade. Moreover, the Round left a legacy for US–EU relations in two respects. First, it produced multilateral concessions that would have been unimaginable if the original six EEC member states had negotiated as single entities (Hufbauer 1990: 5). Second, the Kennedy Round yielded little progress on the liberalization of global markets for agriculture, and the construction of the CAP proceeded unimpaired.

The central thrust of US policy towards Europe after the Kennedy Round became one of encouraging the Community to enlarge, particularly to include the UK. Enlargement created the potential for more sweeping liberalization within the GATT, with the Community acting as an institutional lever for opening a larger European market to US producers. UK membership was viewed in Washington as critical for the moderation of protectionist impulses in Brussels, reform of the CAP and Atlantic solidarity.

Close Anglo-American relations were viewed suspiciously by several Community member states, particularly France. The UK's application for membership was vetoed by de Gaulle in 1963 on the grounds that British accession would lead to 'a gigantic Atlantic Community that would be dependent on and be run by America'.[2] De Gaulle continued to resist US dominance of NATO. France unilaterally pulled its forces out of NATO's integrated military command in 1966. A year later, de Gaulle vetoed a second UK application for Community membership.

The mid- to late 1960s were a period of heightened tensions within the Community more generally. De Gaulle protested against moves to increase its supranational powers over budgetary and agricultural policies by withdrawing France from the Council of Ministers in 1965. The 'Luxembourg compromise' was stitched together to coax the French back to the Community table in 1966. It guaranteed member states the right to veto any legislation which impinged on their 'vital national interest' and set no preconditions on what 'vital' meant. The Luxembourg compromise contributed significantly to the stagnation of European integration in the early 1970s. Most policies emerged as the very lowest common denominator that all member states could accept. This period reinforced the impression within the Nixon administration that the Community was not a very important political unit.

In 1970 Nixon reacted to the first US trade deficit since the early twentieth century by condemning the Community and particularly the CAP. In reality, the deficit's primary cause was an overvalued dollar which severely undermined American export competitiveness. In 1971, the US unilaterally abandoned the Bretton Woods system of fixed exchange rates between national currencies, which had been a cornerstone of the postwar liberal trading order. Nixon also abrogated the American guarantee to support the value of the dollar with gold, and slapped a temporary 10 per cent surcharge on all US imports. The American Secretary of the Treasury, John Connally, openly admitted that the measures were taken 'to screw the Europeans before they screw us'.[3] The 'Nixon shocks' were

> deeply disruptive to the postwar economic system. Not only was the content . . . unsettling; [US] rhetoric generated strong doubts in foreign capitals about whether the United States could still be counted on to support the international monetary and trade regimes its leaders had fostered.
>
> (Destler 1986: 39)

The US responded to the ensuing crisis in transatlantic relations by launching the 'Year of Europe' in 1973. The intent of this brainchild of Nixon's Secretary of State, Henry Kissinger, was similar to that of the Bush administration in 1990: to seek agreement on an 'Atlantic Charter' which would commit both sides to more formal and intensive relations.

In the event, the Year of Europe became shrouded in an atmosphere of profound mutual distrust. Kissinger openly argued that US post-war policy had 'assumed, perhaps too uncritically' that European integration served US interests when it was 'clear that many of these expectations are not being fulfilled' (Kissinger 1973: 595). From the Community's perspective, Kissinger's initiative was a blatant attempt to 'subordinate important aspects of developing intra-European cooperation (especially in economics and foreign policy consultations) to American and Atlantic interests' (Kohl 1975: 16).

Kissinger (1982: 153) clearly assumed that US global interests and responsibilities would naturally take priority over the Community's 'regional interests' on any issue which demanded the coordination of Western foreign policies. This assumption was exposed as myopic during the Yom Kippur war of October 1973. The US backed Israel without hesitation. Many European states were naturally more equivocal in view of their dependence on Middle East oil and close trade and cultural links to Arab states. Italy refused the US permission to use its military bases and the UK banned British arms sales to Israel. By the end of 1973, the Year of Europe initiative seemed 'mendacious and absurd' (Grosser 1982: 281).

The global recessions which followed in the 1970s precluded much US–EU cooperation, let alone an Atlantic Charter. EU countries reacted to 'stagflation' – high unemployment and inflation combined with low rates of economic growth – with a range of 'emergency' protectionist measures. The atmosphere within the Community itself turned acrimonious after the accession of the UK, Ireland and Denmark expanded its membership to nine in 1973. A German-backed plan to share European oil stocks was vetoed by the UK in the wake of the discovery of large oil reserves in the North Sea. The German Chancellor, Willy Brandt, threatened to retaliate by delaying the launch of a new Community regional fund on which the UK had relied to compensate for its net EU budgetary contribution and the unfavourable terms of the CAP for UK farmers (George 1991: 194). The period from 1973 until the EU's relaunch in the mid-1980s was a dark age for European integration. Meanwhile the US 'regained its position as the leading power among partners who were unified only when under its direction' (Grosser 1982: 281).

The Year of Europe did, however, push EU member states to design new mechanisms for cooperation in areas where European vulnerability to the vagaries of US policies was high. The Declaration on European Identity of 1973 committed Community states to coordinate their foreign policies within the new European Political Cooperation (EPC) mechanism. Foreign policies remained 'national', but the EPC took as its central principle that no member state would take a position on any foreign policy issue which touched upon European interests without consulting other member states first.

The Werner Report of 1971 reflected new political interest in Economic and Monetary Union as an antidote to the Nixon shocks. Speculative pressures jettisoned the European 'snake in the tunnel' arrangements which sought to keep national exchange rates stable. A revised system included only five EU member states by 1977. At that point, the French President Valéry Giscard d'Estaing and the German Chancellor Helmut Schmidt secured agreement on a new and stronger European Monetary

System (EMS). The EMS created a European Monetary Fund to help control currency fluctuations and a new common unit of account, the European Currency Unit (ECU). As a composite of the value of all EMS currencies, the ECU was viewed as the forerunner of a common European currency. Implicitly, the EMS was an attempt by European states to defend themselves from the effects of US monetary policies which produced an extremely weak dollar and 'exported' inflation as the price of oil climbed in the 1970s.

However, on the security front, Western Europe remained dependent on American security guarantees. The reluctance of national European governments to spend as much on defence as urged or expected by the US unleashed isolationist impulses and scathing criticism of the Community in Congress. Senator Michael Mansfield tabled eight separate amendments to US defence budgets in the early and mid-1970s which mandated compulsory reductions in the number of US troops stationed in Europe. Successive American administrations were able to defeat the proposals only by arguing vociferously that they sent the wrong signal to the Soviets (Smoke 1987: 195).

The Carter administration came to power in 1976 committed to more constructive relations with the Community through 'trilateralism' or closer cooperation between the US, Europe and Japan. New mechanisms for transatlantic consultation were agreed after the EU expressed hope for better relations with the US in the Tindemans report on political union in 1976 (Smith 1984: 25). Substantial US concessions helped to produce a successful conclusion to the Tokyo Round of the GATT in 1979.

But the Carter administration refused to coordinate its expansionary macroeconomic policies with those of European states. Carter's 'locomotive' strategy of encouraging strong industrial states to pull the world economy out of recession was viewed as inherently inflationary in Europe, particularly by West Germany. His administration's abrupt shift from détente to confrontation with the Soviet Union after the invasion of Afghanistan reinforced European perceptions of US volatility (Kahler 1987). More generally, Carter presided over a period of benign neglect of US–EU relations.

The Reagan administration's attitude toward the EU was more overtly hostile. Throughout the early 1980s the administration aggressively criticized a long list of Community policies, particularly the CAP. Trade relations remained on a 'war footing' for most of the 1980s (Ginsberg 1991: 389). In the security arena, most EU governments resisted pressures from strong domestic peace movements and supported the deployment of new US intermediate-range nuclear missiles as a counterweight to the rapid growth of the Soviet intermediate arsenal. Still, the derisory tone of the Reagan administration's European policy was summed up by one of its primary architects:

Many [European] foreign ministers, finance ministers, and other political leaders are woefully ignorant of the nature of the military balance
between East and West. . . . If allied officials had the same access as
their American colleagues to the steady stream of intelligence pointing
to the unrelenting buildup of Soviet military power, they would react
much as Americans have – with concern and apprehension and even
money.

(Perle 1990: 132–3)

Fissures often erupted within the Community itself when the US
insisted on a common European policy on issues such as the Palestinian
question, the Strategic Defense Initiative (SDI) or the war in Nicaragua.
The US applied sweeping trade sanctions to the Soviet Union and urged
the EU to follow suit after the declaration of martial law in Poland in
1981. Several European states argued that trade sanctions were an ineffective method of influencing Soviet behaviour. The Reagan administration
fumed when the Community agreed on a weak compromise which cut
its imports of Soviet goods by a symbolic $100 million.

An outright rupture in transatlantic relations loomed when EU states
signed agreements with the Soviet Union to build a pipeline to channel
natural gas from Siberia to Western Europe. The Reagan administration
argued that dependence on Soviet energy exports would make the Community hostages to Soviet policy and give the USSR increased hard currency holdings which could be used to strengthen its military. In 1981
the US administration barred American firms from participating in the
pipeline's construction, banned the use of US technology, and sought to
apply sanctions to European companies which accepted contracts to work
on the pipeline. European leaders were outraged at what was viewed
as a blatant attempt to interfere in their internal affairs. The Reagan
administration eventually realized it had nothing to gain from pressing
the issue. It quietly accepted the conclusions of a report by the Organization for Economic Cooperation and Development (OECD) which suggested that Community imports of Soviet gas were unlikely to be used as
political leverage by the USSR.

However, a complete breakdown in US–EU monetary cooperation
throughout the period brought relations to their lowest point since the
Nixon shocks (see Cohen 1987). Between 1980 and 1985 the dollar
increased in value by nearly 75 per cent and induced a huge US trade
deficit. The combination of accelerated US defence spending and tax
cuts produced a federal budget deficit which soared to $220 billion by
1986. Interest rates were kept high so that the federal government could
continue to cover its shortfall by borrowing from abroad. Community
governments were forced to raise their interest rates even higher to
prevent massive outflows of European savings to the US. Many European

exporters benefited from the strong dollar, but EU governments feared a protectionist backlash within Congress.

As during the Nixon years, the precarious dependence of European economies on decisions taken by a fundamentally unsympathetic US administration pushed the Community towards closer cooperation. Negotiations on the SEA focused on plans to free the internal market by 1992 (Commission 1985). As the dollar fell rapidly in value, new proposals to give the EU powers in foreign, defence and security policies were tabled. The dollar's decline made it more expensive for the US to maintain its military presence in Europe or to provide foreign aid. European governments were forced to consider the possibility that the transatlantic debate on 'burden-sharing' within NATO would turn nasty, with Congress becoming more reluctant to authorize defence expenditures to defend the European theatre.

In the event, proposals to strengthen the EU's security role posed too many problems for Irish neutrality and were resisted by Denmark and Greece (Corbett 1987: 252–3). However, the Single European Act did mandate closer links between the Community and EPC and did not preclude further development of common defence and security policies. The notion that the EU needed to become a stronger, more unified and more independent actor in international relations was placed firmly on the agenda for future discussion.

2 THE IMPORTANCE OF GORBACHEV

In his analysis of the East European revolutions of 1989, Kumar (1992: 322) observes that:

> Popular rebellions had repeatedly failed. Liberal attempts at reform had been crushed. The dissident intelligentsia was largely impotent. Why did change occur – and change on a scale scarcely dreamt of by even the most hopeful reformer? The answer in a word is as banal as it is inevitable: Gorbachev.

Mikhail Gorbachev's rise to power in 1985 profoundly influenced the EU's internal debate on developing its foreign and security policy role. Previous Soviet leaders had condemned the EU as an 'economic arm of NATO' and an 'organ of West European monopoly capitalism doomed to inevitable destruction' (Nello 1989: 34). Gorbachev, on the contrary, welcomed moves towards greater West European unity in his speech to the 1986 Communist Party Congress. He also argued that the US 'should not expect unquestioning obedience of its allies' as the EU emerged as a new centre of power.[4]

Under Gorbachev, the Soviet Union recognized the EU as a political entity for the first time. His notion of a 'Common European Home' forecast new forms of Soviet-EU cooperation which would be independent of the US. While all Western allies welcomed a modern and progressive-thinking Soviet leader, the Reagan administration suspected that what Gorbachev really wanted was to split the Atlantic Alliance.

Gorbachev's rise to power had an immediate impact on West German foreign policy. The West Germans pushed to normalize their own relations with the Eastern bloc and to 'Europeanize' the Atlantic Alliance by strengthening Franco-German cooperation on security issues. Bilateral projects launched by Bonn and Paris after 1986 included joint support for new EU treaty articles on foreign policy and security, collaboration on a range of weapons systems, the formation of a joint Franco-German military brigade, and discussions on extending the French nuclear guarantee to the Federal Republic. Decision-makers in both France and West Germany seemed unconcerned that such initiatives might not be welcomed by Washington.

The Kohl government played a central role in negotiations leading to the Common Declaration of 1988 between the EU and the Council for Mutual Economic Assistance (CMEA, or the Soviet bloc). The declaration provided a framework for the establishment of diplomatic relations and trade agreements between the two blocs. EU acceptance of the pact was based almost exclusively on political calculations. The CMEA's rigid controls on its internal trade meant that it could not offer any reciprocal trade concessions to the EU without undermining Eastern producers.

By late 1988, the EU had secured a separate agreement with Hungary on trade and economic cooperation. The pact was a milestone on three counts. First, it offered substantial trade concessions to Hungary. It thus gave a signal to other Eastern states that the EU would reward those who took steps towards free markets and democratic institutions independently of the Soviets, as Hungary had done in the past year. Gorbachev appeared to support new links between the EU and CMEA states even if they made it more difficult for the Soviets to control the behaviour of their allies.

Second, the EU pact with Hungary signalled a shift in the power balance between the EU and its individual member states on policy towards the Eastern bloc. Several national EU governments clearly could not have borne the domestic economic and political costs of the concessions made to Hungary acting on their own. The pact showed that EU member states could override domestic political obstructionism in the pursuit of foreign policy goals when they acted in unison.

Third, the agreement showed that the EU had become more independent of the US in its relations with the Eastern bloc. Although the Reagan administration publicly supported the EU's new overtures to the east, it viewed them with apprehension. Traditionally the US had opposed Western trade concessions to the Eastern bloc on the grounds that they dulled incentives for wholesale political reforms. Successive US administrations had criticized the German policy of *Ostpolitik*, or political and economic overtures to the East, when it was not linked to the wider agenda of superpower détente.

But American and West European views of the Soviet Union converged markedly during Reagan's second term (1984–8). He and Gorbachev met in Switzerland, Iceland, the USSR and the US between 1985 and 1988. Even after Reagan shocked and angered EU leaders by nearly agreeing to a total elimination of US nuclear weapons in Europe at the 1986 Reykjavik summit, the intermediate nuclear forces (INF) treaty of 1987 was welcomed by EU states. Gorbachev's announcement in 1988 that free elections would be held within a year to elect members to a new Soviet Congress of People's Deputies, which would replace the old rubber-stamp Soviet parliament, was another milestone.

The importance of the boost which the EU's trade pacts with the CMEA and Hungary gave to reformers in the East cannot be assessed with precision. However, they came at a critical stage prior to the revolutions of 1989. Trade between the EU and the East had been on the rise since the mid-1980s (Nicolaïdis 1993: 202). By the latter part of the decade, the promise of intensified economic exchanges between the EU and the Eastern bloc countries heightened the Union's magnetism and fortified links already established through the Organization for Security and Cooperation in Europe (OSCE). The EU–CMEA declaration gave the EU limited but significant leverage when communist leaders in East Germany, Czechoslovakia and elsewhere faced a choice between repressing street protests or granting concessions to domestic opposition groups in late 1989. For his part, Gorbachev refused to prop up old-line communist governments with Soviet military power in the style of his predecessors.

While the Bush administration hailed the changes in Eastern Europe, by the end of its first year in office it was struggling to develop policies to keep pace. One of few solid guides for US policy was an interagency review conducted in the summer of 1989 which concluded that accelerated political integration within the EU was unstoppable and that US opposition to the process would be both futile and counterproductive. This assessment combined with pragmatic calculations about limits to US fiscal resources led the administration to embrace wholeheartedly the idea of giving the EU responsibility for coordinating Western aid to the East.

At the Paris summit of the Group of Seven (G-7) industrialized nations in July 1989, the European Commission accepted the duty of drawing up plans to channel aid from all twenty-four full members of the OECD to Poland and Hungary. By the end of the year the number of recipients had expanded to include Bulgaria, Czechoslovakia, East Germany and Yugoslavia. A total of $11 billion in Western aid was committed by 1990.

The Commission's task in coordinating export credits, grants, food aid and loan and investment guarantees from so many different sources was daunting. The US endorsement of the Commission's competence was of a sort only rarely extended to it by the EU's own member states.

The endorsement was symbolically potent in the wider framework of US–EU relations. Delors (1989: 10) said it 'provided tangible evidence of a new relationship between the EU and the United States'. It also encouraged EU member states to consider whether links between the Union's external trade policy and its intergovernmental system for coordinating national foreign policies were adequate. The Dutch, Italians and others began to argue that EU policies towards the East – including foreign policies – needed to be made by majority voting instead of unanimously (Pinder 1991a: 5–6). In short, the US decision to give the Europeans primary responsibility for aid to the East began to have an impact in the EU's own internal political debates about its future by late 1989.

3 THE TRANSATLANTIC DECLARATION

The Bush administration's campaign to forge closer relations with the EU was rooted in naked self-interest as well as growing respect for the Union. The EU remained the largest market for US exporters and investment. Delors had come to be viewed in Washington as a generally pro-American voice in Europe. The assignment of the Commission's internal market portfolio to Martin Bangemann, a former German economics minister with established liberal credentials, acted to quell American anxieties about the development of a 'Fortress Europe' in 1988.

Prior to the dramatic events of 1989, the most important development in US–EU relations under the Bush Presidency surrounded the unveiling of a proposed EU directive on banking in the internal market. US banks already held 5 per cent of the EU's total banking assets. American securities and insurance firms anticipated substantial gains from the freeing of the internal market. Concerns arose when the Commission proposed that a 'mirror image' reciprocity test should determine whether banks from any foreign country should be allowed to set up shop in the EU (Commission 1988a). In effect the EU was telling foreign governments, 'we'll treat your banks as you treat our banks'. The proposal set off alarm bells in Washington. A variety of US state and federal laws placed severe restrictions on the geographical and financial activities of all banks and financial firms operating in the US, regardless of their nationality. The EU proposal threatened to place substantial new restrictions on US banks in the internal market.

The Bush administration and the US banking community jointly and fiercely lobbied the Commission to redraft its proposal. Fearing that the issue could poison US–EU relations, the Commission eventually abandoned 'mirror image' reciprocity in favour of a 'national treatment' test for foreign banks. In practice, the revised directive promised not to deny EU market access to banks from countries which gave EU banks the 'same competitive opportunities as are available to domestic credit institutions' (Commission 1989: 2). The EU's line became: 'if you treat our banks as you treat your own banks, we'll treat yours as we treat ours'.

The banking directive provided 'a concrete illustration of the usefulness of protesting early and vigorously any indication of discriminatory intent as the EU moves toward 1992' (Zupnick 1991: 41). A leader of the US private lobbying effort recalled, 'we were both active and lucky, but we got lots of support from the [Bush] administration'.[5] The gravity of the directive for US economic interests reinforced the administration's view that American diplomacy should be reoriented away from bilateral links with individual European states to the EU itself. The White House began to accept the argument that American support for European political unity gave the US more clout in internal debates on new EU policies. Moreover, key US agencies – particularly the State and Commerce departments – urged that more formal and regularized mechanisms for exchange were needed.

Delors clearly supported the idea from an early date. The appointment of Andreas van Agt, a former Dutch Prime Minister and political heavyweight, as head of the Commission's delegation to the US reflected Delors's own desire to upgrade political ties with Washington (Ginsberg 1991: 394–5). During a visit to Washington in April 1989, Delors argued that it was time to 'reassess the relationship. . . . Both partners now have to think about a wider political dialogue, leading possibly to joint action over issues of mutual interest.'[6]

Within a month Bush (1989: 13) floated the idea of 'new mechanisms of consultation and cooperation on political and global issues, from strengthening the forces of democracy in the third world, to managing regional tensions, to putting an end to the division of Europe'. Subsequent events in Eastern Europe accelerated the development of a formal US proposal. Baker's (1991: 5–7) Berlin speech in December urged that the US and EU should 'work together to achieve, whether it is in [a] treaty or some other form, a significantly strengthened set of institutional and consultative links. . . . We want our trans-Atlantic cooperation to keep pace with European integration and institutional reform.'

Baker's speech placed five ideas for intensifying US ties to the EU on the bilateral agenda. First, more regular and intensive bilateral consultations were proposed with a view to preventing economic and trade disputes from festering into political conflicts. Second, Baker recognized the growing importance of the EPC mechanism and urged that its working groups consult with the US on a regular basis. Third, the Americans sought more formal cooperation on environmental issues. Fourth, more input into discussions aimed at developing common European technical standards was requested. Finally, Baker urged closer bilateral cooperation to aid East European economies.

Many in Europe were wary of US intentions. Statements by the Secretary of Commerce, Robert Mosbacher, that the US should be given 'a seat at the table' as an observer in internal EU discussions struck many in Brussels as offensive (Ginsberg 1991: 394). A DG I official later noted,

> His colleagues have probably been kicking him for it ever since because every time since then when the US wants to talk to the Community about something, somebody says, 'ah, it's the old idea of the seat at the table again. We can't possibly accept this'.[7]

In particular, the idea of a formal US–EU treaty found little enthusiasm in Brussels. A formal treaty was viewed by the Commission as too difficult to negotiate, potentially damaging to existing multilateral institutions, and premature in view of the EU's ongoing IGC on political union. The French Foreign Minister, Roland Dumas, claimed that what the Americans really wanted out of a treaty was to expand NATO's role at the expense of the EU.[8]

Yet Delors continued to urge that the EU's political links with the US needed to be upgraded. In his presentation of the Commission's (1990a: 10) programme to the European Parliament, Delors admitted:

> I agree that there is something ambiguous about linking transatlantic partnership with European integration as Mr Baker did. Some member states might interpret it as a deliberate attempt to interfere in our affairs, something which would be unacceptable between two equal partners, the two pillars of the Atlantic Alliance. But it is difficult not to rejoice at the new attitudes emerging on both sides of the Atlantic, the willingness to step up cooperation and prevent the deep relationship between the world's premier powers descending to the level of disputes about pasta and hormones. The bond between the Community and the United States merits better than that.

The urgency of the need for strengthened political contacts with the EU was brought home to the Bush administration in early 1990. EU foreign ministers firmly endorsed the OSCE as a framework for pan-European security and proposed a new OSCE summit without prior consultation of the US. The action reflected a general trend towards common and independent EU positions within the OSCE which were presented to the Americans as non-negotiable.

In February 1990, Bush secured an endorsement from the acting President of the European Council, the Irish Prime Minister Charles Haughey, on an expanded and regularized set of bilateral meetings. The US

President would meet with each President of the European Council during his or her six-month term. Summits of the US Secretary of State and EU foreign ministers would be held twice each year and the Commission would pursue its own meetings with members of the US cabinet (US Mission 1990). The proposal significantly expanded existing mechanisms for consultation.

Previous annual 'round table' meetings between the Commission and the US cabinet had always taken place after the annual NATO summits. When a Commission–US cabinet summit took place in April 1990 in Washington, the 'decoupling' of the meeting from NATO reflected the desire of both sides to acknowledge the growing political role of the EU. A month later Baker met with EU foreign ministers under the EPC mechanism. This meeting was the first time that a US Secretary of State had met his EU counterparts outside the context of NATO or the UN General Assembly. An EPC official suggested that, 'for Baker to sit across the table from 12 ministers who were all speaking to the same brief was quite historic'.[9]

Still, negotiations on the actual content of a joint declaration were dogged by divergent perceptions and agendas. A US-proposed text failed to mention the biannual meetings of the members of the Commission and US cabinet. A DG I official later defended the US negotiators as having 'no hidden agenda. It was just an oversight which stemmed from the fact that they just didn't view meetings with the Commission as very important.'[10] But the incident illustrated that the US diplomatic community remained accustomed to the personalization of political power. Many in Washington faced conceptual difficulties in shifting the focus of US diplomacy from European states to the EU itself.

The Bush administration sought to include a reference in the joint declaration to the Uruguay Round. Commission officials refused and insisted that the text should only refer to broad objectives and the long-term future of US–EU relations. The EU's collective memory of the damage done to European economies by the Reagan administration's monetary policies led the Commission to propose that each side should commit itself to maintaining 'a stable international financial system'. US negotiators refused under firm instructions from the Treasury not to agree to any language which fettered US autonomy in managing the dollar.

The declaration which was finally signed at the Paris meeting of the OSCE in November 1990 was an anodyne one. It formally committed both sides to the measures agreed by Bush and Haughey and bound the US to biannual summits with the Commission. Pledges were made to establish closer scientific cooperation and take joint measures to meet 'transnational challenges' such as international terrorism, the drugs trade, environmental protection and arms control. The common goals listed were unremarkable apart from that of 'reinforcing the role of the United Nations'. Its provisions for strengthening economic cooperation did little more than promise further development of measures already under way (see EPC Secretariat 1990).

The Uruguay Round nearly broke down a few weeks after the declaration was signed. The Brussels GATT conference of December 1990 had been intended to produce a final agreement and mark the end of the Round. But the EU refused to agree to sharp cuts in farm spending and the US blocked agreements on all other issues. Only a last-minute agreement to reconvene the talks in 1991 saved the Uruguay Round from total collapse.

By mid-1992, few tangible results had been achieved which could be attributed directly to the Transatlantic Declaration itself. Yet the intensified dialogue launched by the declaration clearly did much to keep the Uruguay Round alive. After a bilateral summit in April 1991, officials on both sides acknowledged that Bush had heeded Delors's warnings that the USTR, Carla Hills, needed to be reined in to keep the negotiating atmosphere from deteriorating any further. Progress on the agricultural issue accelerated through the latter half of the year.

The fourth bilateral summit under the terms of the Transatlantic Declaration took place in The Hague in November 1991 as a number of crucial 'decision points' approached: the Rome NATO summit to revise Western defence strategy, the Maastricht EU summit and the anticipated conclusion of the Uruguay Round. Bush used the opportunity to urge that 'revitalizing the Atlantic Alliance and building a European Union go hand-in-hand'.[11]

Exchanges at the highest political levels at The Hague clearly touched on substantive, nitty-gritty issues as well as the usual symbolic declarations. Both sides engaged in detailed consideration of difficult dossiers related to the GATT, including agriculture and unilateralism in US trade policy. Bush appeared to respond to the argument of the Dutch Prime Minister, Ruud Lubbers, that tangible gestures were needed to underline US–EU solidarity in advance of the crucial Rome summit of NATO. He agreed to join the EU in imposing economic sanctions on Yugoslavia and cosponsoring a UN Security Council resolution aimed at an oil and arms embargo.

In some respects, the EU almost appeared to accept the Transatlantic Declaration to appease the Bush administration. The declaration allowed Bush to claim that the US still had influence over the political evolution of Europe at a time when this notion had become subject to new doubts. The minimalist content of the declaration was a product of anxieties within the EU that a formal treaty with the US would systematize a relationship between 'a gorilla and twelve squabbling children' in advance of a new EU treaty on political union.[12]

In early 1993, with the Maastricht Treaty ratified and Clinton in office, the Commission identified a range of areas where US–EU cooperation might be strengthened. Hopes of working more closely with a US President who was perceived in Europe as fresh-minded and progressive were dashed quickly. Clinton's National Security Adviser Anthony Lake reportedly confessed that he had never even heard of the Transatlantic Declaration.[13] The Clinton administration paid little attention to Europe or foreign policy more generally during its first year in office. By late 1993, Clinton's ambassador to the EU, Stuart Eizenstat, admitted that some exchanges mandated in the Transatlantic Declaration had become 'moribund'. However, he insisted that the US was 'committed to breath[ing] life into that Declaration'.[14]

The Declaration could be viewed as a symbolic and relatively unimportant Document. Alternatively, it might be seen as a first step in a continuing process of upgrading bilateral relations that could ultimately lead to something like a 'Transatlantic Free Trade Area' or the substantial integration of US and EU foreign policy agendas. These two views probably present a false dichotomy. Ultimately, US–EU relations in the twenty-first century will be determined by wider events in the international system and the evolution of domestic politics on both sides of the Atlantic. The significance of the Transatlantic Declaration is that each side is now far less likely to be caught unaware of the other side's view or of constraints on its actions as events unfold.

4 THEORY AND PRACTICE IN US–EU RELATIONS

The history of US–EU relations shows that the explanatory power of different theories of international relations can change over time and according to circumstances. Theorists naturally tend to use history selectively to validate their arguments. *Neorealism* provides convincing explanations for the Nixon administration's unilateral abrogation of the Bretton Woods system in the 1970s and the Reagan administration's European policy in the early 1980s. De Gaulle's behaviour on issues of transatlantic relations was based quite clearly on neorealist assumptions. EU member states often acted contrary to the goals enshrined in the Treaty of Rome as oil crises, severe recessions and Cold War tensions in the 1970s led them to pursue their national interests as 'unitary-rational actors'.

More recently, the idea that the end of the Cold War could usher in a new era of peace and cooperation has been met with derision by neorealists. With titles such as 'Back to the future' and 'Why we will soon miss the Cold War', neorealists have argued that the end of bipolarity will lead to shifting alliances in Europe (Mearsheimer 1990a, 1990b). The result will be acute instability of a sort reminiscent of the interwar period.

Neorealists assume that the Transatlantic Declaration reflects American self-interest and the need to find new ways to ensure that asymmetric US military power within NATO remains 'fungible' so it can be used to pressure the EU on trade and internal market issues. Ultimately, increased political exchanges between the US and EU cannot ameliorate conflict between them.

> Far from ushering in a period of 'kinder, gentler', and more purely cooperative relations among industrial democracies, the end of the Cold War is likely to mark the dawning of an era of tougher bargaining and greater self-assertion.
>
> (Friedberg 1992: 102).

Critics complain that neorealism is ahistorical. Kratchowil (1993: 66) assails neorealists for assuming that the end of the Cold War could 'simply be treated as one event and dismissed as unimportant for theory building'. Waltz (1986: 329) concedes that 'structures never tell us all that we want to know. Instead they tell us a small number of big and important things. They focus our attention on those components and forces that usually continue for long periods.' However, neorealism failed to predict the 'big and important' transition to a post-Cold War world (Allain and Goldmann 1995).

A separate weakness of neorealism is its failure to take account of a variable which profoundly conditions the way in which states approach cooperation: the information which flows between them. Keohane (1984: 245) argues that neorealism

> is in need of revision, because it fails to take into account that states' conceptions of their interests, and of how their objectives should be pursued, depend not merely on national interests and the distribution of world power, but on the quantity, quality, and distribution of information.

Keohane's argument points to an alternative interpretation of the meaning of the Transatlantic Declaration. *Institutionalists* assume that the potential for bilateral cooperation is much enhanced because information exchange which previously was *ad hoc* is now institutionalized. In the language of rational choice theory, the US and EU moved tangibly closer in 1990 to states of 'perfect information' and 'perfect attention' in their relationship with one another (see Peterson and Ward 1995).

Even if motivated by US self-interest, institutionalists view the Transatlantic Declaration as a response to rising interdependence. Despite emerging as a new centre of power in its own right, the EU's autonomy is naturally constrained by its trade, financial, security and cultural ties to the US. A key determinant of how much influence both partners can wield in global affairs is their ability to foresee developments and ensure predictability in the international system. The Transatlantic Declaration's provisions for more formalized and institutionalized cooperation mean that each partner is in a better position to anticipate and influence future developments in foreign policy which spring from domestic politics on either side of the Atlantic. The effect 'should therefore be to enhance the capacity of both parties to shape and predict the international environment in which they operate' (Devuyst 1990: 24).

More generally, institutionalism helps to explain important features and developments in the evolution of the US–EU relationship over time. Exponentially increasing bilateral trade after 1945 yielded 'unparalleled economic interdependence, entailing mutual sensitivities and vulnerabilities of a degree experienced by no other group of nominally independent parties' (Smith 1984: 1). While US calls for a 'seat at the table' may have been viewed as arrogant, a DG I official argued:

> If you take the more charitable view, the US administration merely was saying, 'the EU does a lot which impacts on our interest, so we ought to have a chance to influence what it's doing'. If you turn that into a reciprocal bringing to bear of influence, then it's simply a reflection of the theory of interdependence and we accept it.[15]

Gorbachev's foreign policy marked a sea-change in Soviet perceptions of the desirability and implications of global interdependence. Speaking to the UN's General Assembly in 1988, Gorbachev observed:

> If we are parts, even if different, of one and the same civilization, if we are aware of the interdependence of the modern world, this understanding should increasingly manifest itself both in politics, and in practical efforts to harmonize international relations. . . . [The world economy] is becoming a single organism, outside which no state can develop normally.[16]

Rising economic interdependence between the EU and Eastern bloc countries was a critical stimulant of developments in Eastern Europe in 1980. Communist governments became more vulnerable to sanctions which the EU could have imposed if popular protests had been met with repression. Moreover, revolutions in the East seemed to depend on the sustained fascination of the West and on 'real-time' coverage of fast-breaking events by new media outlets such as the Cable News Network (CNN). As Brown (1991: 12) argues, 'western television may not have inspired the opposition, but it supplied an audience in the tens of millions. And that audience was vital because it protected them. . . . Blanket coverage prevented blanket retaliation.'

US support for European integration and the GATT process in the early post-war period is perhaps best explained by *liberalism*. The creation of the GATT was possible because of the development of a clear consensus among American internationalists that 'a world open for commerce would be a world at peace' (Destler 1986: 4). The principles of liberalism justified US encouragement of European integration on the grounds that it would make possible multilateral concessions which could not be secured if the EU's member states negotiated individually within the GATT.

Liberalism also sheds light on heightened transatlantic tensions between 1973 and 1988. Each side paid lip-service to liberal principles while pursuing trade and industrial policies which ignored liberal prescriptions. The period showed that governments tend to become more protectionist during times of global recession and that protectionism feeds on itself as trading partners retaliate against one another.

Liberalism re-emerged as a powerful guide for policy in the 1990s. Consolidating liberal democracy in the former Warsaw Pact states meant rapidly incorporating them into the global trading system. Besides eventual EU membership, open Western markets were the most sought-after policy goal of new East European governments after 1989.

For *reformists*, the most crucial security issues are (and always have been) environmental degradation, human rights, nuclear proliferation and poverty in the underdeveloped world. Reformists criticize the US and EU for their obsessive focus on their bilateral trade and military relationships. Meanwhile, global cooperation on far more urgent issues remains unconsummated.

Reformists welcome the unfreezing of bipolarity and attack the neorealist suggestion that bipolarity made for a more stable world. In view of crises over Berlin, Korea and Cuba, US–Soviet relations during the Cold War could hardly could have been described as 'stable' (Goldgeier and McFaul 1992: 490). Each of these crises could have erupted into a major war.

European unity, if not always the EU itself, is viewed by many reformists as a worthy ideal. Vaclav Havel, the dissident-turned-President of the Czech Republic, mused that 'to ponder our return means for us to ponder a whole Europe, to ponder the Europe of the future'.[17] Because it transcends the nation-state, the EU is viewed by some reformists as a possible source of new and innovative initiatives which can be expanded to include other states.

Other reformists take heart in the new emphasis placed on transnational issues in US–EU political declarations. For example, in his address to the US delegation at The Hague summit in 1991, while President of the European Council, Lubbers underlined the need for the US and Europe to work together on issues including 'underdevelopment, overpopulation, mass migration, deterioration of the environment, and human rights'.[18]

Perhaps above all, the reformist paradigm highlights new obstacles to theorizing about US–EU relations or international relations more generally. To illustrate the point, the inability of the West to do much about genocide and horrendous bloodshed in the former Yugoslavia leads Shaw (1994: 168) to argue that 'the politics of war have been transformed, and historic positions outmoded, by the transformations of the international system'. All theories of international relations build on past evidence and events which naturally condition their assumptions. All are meant to describe, explain and predict. But only very rarely do they perform the last of the three functions as well as the first two.

The end of the Cold War has engendered new uncertainties which did not exist during the relatively stable era of bipolarity. The central challenge for US–EU relations is that of maintaining a stable and predictable relationship in a world order which has been profoundly transformed. The challenge for international relations theorists is only slightly less intimidating.

Part II

External and internal transformations

Chapter 3

The new geopolitical reality

Understanding international politics means thinking about the political geography of power: who wields power or influence, where and why? Many classic works in political science have concerned themselves with this question. Mahan (1897) argued that control of the seas was the key to great-power status. According to Mackinder (1904, 1943) the European 'heartland' – the middle of the continental landmass – was the crucial area for any aspiring power to control.

Contemporary students might conclude that such theories are anachronistic. Global communications, economic interdependence and long-range weapons delivery systems make 'geopolitics' seem irrelevant. Major states now compete for knowledge, wealth and the mastery of new technologies rather than territory (see Strange 1988).

However, the demise of bipolarity as the defining feature of the international system led the respective geographical positions of the US and EU states to become more important determinants of their perceived interests. This point was amply illustrated by divergent US and EU actions – and transatlantic tensions – concerning aid to Eastern Europe, the war in ex-Yugoslavia and the Mexican peso crisis of 1995. The US and EU have become potential partners in developing a common agenda on a range of international issues. Yet their interests and actions will never merge into one for the simple reason that a large ocean separates them geographically.

This chapter assesses the implications for US–EU relations of recent geopolitical changes. Section 1 examines the significance of German unification for European integration and US diplomacy. Western responses to wider geopolitical changes in Eastern Europe and the Soviet Union are examined in section 2. The Gulf War and the Yugoslav conflict are considered in section 3. Perspectives on geopolitical change offered by the four theories of international relations are reviewed in section 4.

1 GERMAN UNIFICATION AND EUROPEAN INTEGRATION

After the collapse of communist East Germany in 1989, the accepted wisdom became that:

> The economic integration of Europe will now have to take a back seat to the age-old German question. Until the two Germanys are inevitably united – probably sometime in the mid-1990s – Bonn cannot pursue the planned economic integration with its 11 partners in the European Community.
>
> (Macrae 1990: 16; see also Treverton 1990; Buzan *et al.* 1990)

In the event, Germany unified in less than a year. The pace of European integration was accelerated in the process, as American and wider European positions converged on its desirability as a response to German unification. The US moved to ensure that its relations with both Germany and (especially) the EU were intensified. The New Transatlanticism may be viewed largely as a byproduct of German unification.

The rapid fall of communist regimes in the East in 1989 could have had any number of effects on the European integration process. Thatcher's Bruges speech in September 1988 had argued that the primary goal of European integration should be the extension of EU membership to Warsaw, Prague and Budapest. Many had suspected a hidden agenda to block the deepening of political unity among the EU twelve. However, the notion that EU membership could be used to encourage the reform process in the new Eastern democracies began to appear more sensible and morally compelling by late 1989.

As in many previous debates on the political evolution of the EU, a Franco-German alliance emerged to define the parameters of discussion. The West German Chancellor Helmut Kohl and French President François Mitterrand acted quickly to dispel any notion that the new geopolitical reality in Europe would detract from the pursuit of deeper integration among existing EU member states. Both gave impassioned speeches to the European Parliament in November 1989, urging accelerated completion of the internal market so that a more unified EU could act as the central, secure core around which a new European architecture could be constructed. Kohl sought to calm anxieties about German unification by insisting that it could happen only 'under a European roof' and that the new Germany would 'never again be a threat but a benefit to the unity of Europe'.[1]

The Strasbourg European summit which followed in December 1989 was a watershed in the EU's development. The UK was the lone dissenter when the European Council endorsed the Social Charter of workers' rights, which reflected the principle that states should not compete to attract investment through reduced wages or welfare provisions. EU leaders agreed to launch the European Bank for Reconstruction and Development (EBRD) to promote Western investment in Eastern Europe. They pledged $1 billion in EU aid to Poland and Hungary through the Aid for the Reconstruction of Economies (PHARE) programme. Finally, the summit approved a new round of negotiations with the European Free Trade Association (EFTA) countries to bring them into the internal market and create a 'European economic area'.

A carefully-worded communiqué endorsed German unity in principle and stressed that unification would occur against the backdrop of existing treaties. But Kohl insisted that a genuine political union was needed to accommodate German unity as well as EMU. The summit left open the possibility of a second IGC on political union to run in parallel to the one already agreed on EMU.

The swift economic collapse of East Germany in the first few months of 1990 made early German unification inevitable. Bush pledged cautious US support for Kohl's ten-point plan for achieving it, but was clearly troubled that it did not mention NATO once. The US was left sidelined in debates on how a unified Germany might be accommodated in existing security alliances. In early 1990, the West German Defence Minister, Gerhard Stoltenberg, publicly speculated that German troops outside NATO's command structure might be based in East Germany at some future point. The Bush administration was clearly not consulted on the idea. It feared an adverse Soviet response and loathed the idea of putting German troops outside NATO's integrated command.

Gorbachev initially insisted that unification could occur only if a unified Germany was not a member of NATO. By mid-1990 he had floated ideas ranging from German neutrality to a pan-European security structure based on the OSCE to German membership of both NATO and the Warsaw Pact (Larrabee 1991: 12). All were designed to appease conservative hard-liners within his own government and the Soviet military. None were acceptable to Kohl or the West in general.

Kohl later admitted that it became clear to him in 1990 that 'hardly anyone in Europe wanted German unification'.[2] Nevertheless, he insisted that all debates on how unification would affect foreign states had to proceed with early unification as a given. Crucially, he stipulated that a unified Germany would remain a member of NATO. Kohl's speeches in early 1990 frequently stressed the importance of the US as a geopolitical counterweight to Soviet military power: 'A transatlantic security union is of existential significance for Germans and Europe. Only it can create a true balance in Europe. A look at the map underlines this.'[3]

Initially, Kohl refused to accept the Oder-Neisse line between East Germany and Poland as Germany's permanent Eastern border. As the border had been imposed by Stalin after the war, Kohl argued that only a unified and sovereign German state could accept its permanence. His reticence on the issue produced acute anxieties in the US, the Soviet Union and especially Poland about the implications of unification for German foreign policy.

Throughout 1990 Bush continued to assert that the United States would remain a European power. After meeting Kohl at Camp David in March 1990, Bush stated that as far as the US was concerned, the Oder-Neisse line was permanent and that American and German views were 'aligned' on the matter. The clear message was that the US was ready to support early unification, but not unconditionally.

Kohl quickly agreed to a declaration committing Germany to respect its existing border to the East. He and Mitterrand then issued a sweeping joint declaration on European Union in advance of the Dublin EU summit of April 1990. Although vague on details, it formed the basis for discussions which put a second IGC in motion to consider further EU treaty revisions to deepen political unity.

Meanwhile the West German Foreign Minister, Hans-Dietrich Genscher, issued a statement which urged EU acceptance of the US offer to negotiate a Transatlantic Declaration. Genscher identified a range of political, economic, technological and cultural issues as ripe for bilateral cooperation (Devuyst 1990: 17–18). The Kohl government's assent to both accelerated European integration and an expanded US–EU dialogue was vital in assuring American support for rapid German unification.

At the London NATO summit of July 1990, Kohl finally emerged with a proposal which secured Gorbachev's blessing as well. Kohl agreed to sweeping unilateral reductions in the united Germany's armed forces and subsequently offered close to $10 billion in German aid to the USSR. German troop cuts were codified in the final settlement of the 'two plus four talks' between the 'two' Germanys plus the US, UK, France and the Soviet Union.

German unification and wider geopolitical changes in Europe thus acted to quicken the pace of integration within the EU. A more unified Union became a way to 'bind' Germany into a wider political framework. For all parties concerned – the Americans, Soviets, Poles and other EU states – Kohl's repeated assurances that Germany would seek 'self-containment' within a stronger EU provided reassurance. For France, the continued political and military presence of the United States in Europe began to seem an acceptable and even desirable counterweight to the increased political clout of a united Germany. Geopolitical change in the East made it only logical for the US to focus its diplomatic attention far more on the EU and Bonn than on NATO and London.

Particularly under the Clinton administration, it became clear that if there was to be any 'special relationship' between the US and any individual European country, it would be with Germany (Kielinger and Otte

1993). One of the architects of Clinton's European policy, the Under Secretary of State for International Commerce Jeffrey Garten (1992: 10), argued that Germany was 'too powerful to disappear into a wider European framework'. Nevertheless, German power became a powerful rationale for US support for European integration. Above all, German unification fostered a new consensus in Washington on the idea that the US needed a 'special' relationship with the EU as a whole.

2 THE DEMISE OF SOVIET POWER

Geopolitical calculations were key determinants of Western policy towards the Soviet Union in the period immediately following 1989. Fears of the instability which might follow from a rapid break-up of the USSR led the West to downplay the strong-arm tactics used by Gorbachev against independence movements in Georgia, Armenia and the Baltic republics. A tougher EU line would have undermined the argument of several member states – particularly Germany – that Gorbachev needed Western support to prevent his political and economic reforms from being reversed in a conservative backlash.

The Bush administration's Soviet policy was cautious and non-committal. After Gorbachev acquiesced to the UN's role in the Gulf War, US criticism of Soviet repression in the Baltics was meek. Still, the Bush administration insisted that the US needed to remain militarily prepared for any contingency in the Soviet Union. Weeks before Gorbachev was overthrown temporarily in a coup by conservative Soviet hard-liners in August 1991, Bush argued before Congress that funding for the two most expensive weapons systems in US history, the SDI programme and the Stealth bomber, could not be cut.

The collapse of the Soviet coup within three days rapidly transformed the debate about US Soviet policy. Bush reacted to Gorbachev's reinstatement and the subsequent dismantling of the Soviet Communist Party with a plan for substantial unilateral cuts in the US nuclear arsenal in September 1991. Gorbachev responded within a week by matching the offer and pledging to dismantle even more weapons than had been proposed by Bush.

Bush's offer was motivated by three distinct factors. First, the break-up of the USSR in some form was inevitable after the coup. Bush's proposed cuts reflected serious concern in Washington about the possible erosion of central control over the Soviet nuclear arsenal. It was hoped that Gorbachev would reciprocate quickly before he lost the authority to do so. Second, the President sought to placate Congress by offering the nuclear cuts in exchange for its approval on the massively expensive SDI and Stealth programmes. Third, Bush wished to present himself as a peacemaker with the 1992 election just over a year away.

The details of Bush's plan reflected a wider shift in the focus of US diplomacy in Europe. The proposal's most important element from a German perspective was the implementation of his previous promise to scrap all US land-based short-range nuclear weapons including the Lance missile system. The question of modernizing Lance missiles had caused considerable strain within NATO in 1989. The UK under Thatcher had insisted on their renovation. The Germans resisted on the grounds that their 70–mile range made them useless for any war besides one fought on German soil. Bush had ignored Thatcher's objections and agreed to shelve the issue for a further two years. The subsequent decision to scrap the Lance system altogether showed that Bush was determined to help the Kohl government cope with emerging anti-NATO sentiments in Germany. It provided further evidence of a more German-centred, and less UK-oriented, US policy for Europe.

Close US–German ties on security issues were highlighted again when Genscher and Baker jointly proposed the creation of a North Atlantic Cooperation Council (NACC) as a framework for East European and Soviet participation in non-military NATO activities. The proposal was greeted with consternation in France, where it was criticized publicly as duplicating the work of the OSCE and loathed privately for institutionalizing a security dialogue with the East in a US-dominated framework. However, German endorsement of the plan ensured its acceptance by other European NATO members.

On the economic front, the creation of the EBRD also demonstrated strong German influence over Western policy towards Eastern Europe. Despite its origins as a French initiative, the EBRD's methodology mirrored the strong German view that market solutions had to be applied to Eastern reconstruction. Critics argued that the initial commitment of less than $10 million by Western governments to the EBRD was paltry considering the urgent need for mass capital investment in Eastern Europe. But small capital outlays were accompanied by substantial powers for the EBRD to borrow on capital markets.

The EBRD also revealed a changing balance of power within the transatlantic alliance. The EU and its member states agreed to assume majority shareholder status. The US accepted that the EBRD would be the first international institution with non-European members to adopt the ECU as its official working currency. The ECU offered the practical advantage of being more stable in value than any individual currency including the dollar. More generally, as a European Commission official observed, 'there's a philosophical, almost ideological element behind this as well. The Americans have realized that what they want from the EBRD is to reinforce the point that improvement of conditions in Eastern and Central Europe is essentially a European responsibility.'[4]

The EBRD's first years were rocky: it distributed little actual project funding while paying huge salaries to its directors. Its first head, Jacques Attali, was forced to resign amidst scandal and charges of mismanagement. Yet the total invested by the EBRD in development projects tripled between 1991 and 1993, with private funding increasing from one-quarter to more than half of the total. Nearly all decisions of the Bank were taken by qualified majority voting, a procedure which was unusual for an investment or development institution. By the mid-1990s, the Bank was 'increasingly beginning to drive and focus EU and G-7 Member State policy in the former Soviet bloc' (McMath 1995: 2).

The US strategy of pushing the EU to take the lead in the development and management of Western policy towards Eastern Europe can be traced to the launch of the Group of Twenty-Four (G-24) industrialized nations in 1989. The Commission chaired all subsequent G-24 meetings and became a fierce critic of its members for their slow rates of disbursing aid. Over time, the G-24 began to offer better coordinated aid packages and the Commission's working groups on investment, food aid and so on assumed a central role in designing them. However, conflicting national agendas continued to slow down the delivery of EU aid funds. Money generally flowed to the East far more quickly from national sources via bilateral agreements. G-24 governments continued to give aid on their own terms, and the Commission lacked much leverage in pressing them to increase the amounts on offer.

In particular, the US contribution to the Eastern aid effort was reluctant and often stingy. For example, in late 1991 Bush refused a proposal by US Congressional Democrats to earmark $1 billion from the US defence budget for humanitarian aid to the USSR despite urgent requests from Gorbachev. The European Commissioner for Foreign Affairs, Frans Andriessen, publicly chastised the US (and Japan) for failing to assume a fair share of the aid burden and being slow to deliver on commitments.

Baker retorted that the US had provided more food aid to the Soviet republics than any Western state and announced an international summit on aid to the USSR to be held in Washington in January 1992. Neither EU states nor the Commission were consulted about the idea. It was condemned loudly in Europe as a ploy to divert attention from the US's minimal commitment to the G-24 effort. The flap illustrated the general lack of a unified Western aid policy which could transcend narrow national interests and respond to the true urgency of the situation in the East.

The Western aid effort was also complicated by the pace of events in the East. The break-up of the Soviet Union accelerated rapidly as the Maastricht summit was convened in December 1991. The effect was to juxtapose starkly the simultaneous trends towards integration and fragmentation in Europe. The EU forged agreements on a range of new common policies. Meanwhile Russia, Belarus and Ukraine overrode the objections of an increasingly marginalized Gorbachev, and unilaterally announced the formation of a new Commonwealth of Independent States (CIS), which enshrined their status as independent nation-states. Membership in the CIS was accepted within weeks by eight other former Soviet republics, which joined its founders in rejecting Gorbachev's alternative plans for a more centralized political union under his own executive authority.

The CIS was conceived as an extremely loose club of independent former Soviet republics. It was given no central institutions, apart from its intergovernmental Councils of Heads of State and Government, and no binding decision-making or conflict-resolution procedures. Its formation meant that the Soviet Union was truly dead.

Leaders of CIS republics promised to 'build democratic states ruled by law and to develop relations between them on the basis of mutual recognition of the inalienable right to self-determination, equality, [and] non-interference in each other's internal affairs'.[5] But virtually every issue related to the operation of the CIS, including economic relations, taxation, border controls, citizenship and coordination between state agencies, was left unresolved. The four republics with long-range nuclear weapons on their soil – Russia, Belarus, Ukraine and Kazakhstan – insisted that they were in agreement on joint weapons safeguards. Nonetheless, Western queries about the control of nuclear arms were met with contradictory statements by the leaders of different republics.

The Bush administration's public statements on the CIS revealed its thinly veiled conviction that centrifugal forces in the region were too strong to accommodate any serious cooperation between the newly independent republics in the foreseeable future. Together with the EU, it sought to consolidate the policy levers which the West retained for influencing state-building in the former USSR. The US and EU agreed to act together in extending diplomatic relations to new states in the region. Both recognized Russia as the *de facto* successor to the Soviet Union in the UN Security Council. Joint statements warned that Western aid would be committed to those former republics with nuclear weapons only if they gave speedy and concrete assurances on safeguards.

The short-term prognosis for the region remained bleak. The potential for conflict between different republics increased when most began to form their own armies and military policies in early 1992. Russia and Ukraine clashed in a bitter dispute over control of the Black Sea fleet of the former Soviet navy. CIS weapons were sold on the global market for much-needed cash. Many newly unemployed former Soviet nuclear scientists were tempted by offers from states with nuclear ambitions such as North Korea, Libya and Iraq.

Yet patient Western diplomacy paid off in key respects. Predictably, the CIS became a weak and largely insignificant body, but it maintained a single unified command over the former Soviet nuclear arsenal long enough for agreements to be reached on reducing or consolidating nuclear missiles within Russia. A US plan to transport dangerous and leaking warheads out of Ukraine using covert means was successfully implemented in 1993 under the personal direction of Clinton's Vice-President, Al Gore. Levels of Western aid to the CIS states, and Eastern Europe more generally, remained modest but enough to give the West leverage and influence over the behaviour of states in the region.

It remains difficult to be optimistic about the long-term implications for European security of the break-up of the Soviet Union. Nationalism quickly became a powerful force in Russian domestic politics. The neo-fascist Liberal Democrat Party and its allies emerged as the largest single faction in the Russian Parliament after elections in 1993. Even Yeltsin and pro-Western ministers in his government, such as the Foreign Minister Andrei Kozyrev, insisted that Russia retain the right to police the 'near abroad', or the geographical area of the old Soviet Union. Western pledges – particularly from the Clinton administration – to extend NATO membership to former Soviet bloc countries in Eastern Europe were greeted with disdain across a wide political spectrum in Russia. Despite Clinton's steadfast support for Yeltsin, the Russian President angrily accused the West of provoking a new 'cold peace' at the 1994 OSCE summit in Budapest.

Soon afterwards, Yeltsin apparently yielded to the Russian 'power ministries' of Defence, the Interior and the Secret Service by ordering the Russian army to crush an insurrection in the southern Russian province of Chechnya. The result was a bloodbath: tens of thousands of civilians were killed, many through indiscriminate Russian bombardment of non-military targets. Reports of atrocities committed by Russian forces outraged human rights groups.

However, the geopolitical significance of Chechnya was clear: the real threat to European security was the possibility of Russia's internal disintegration, not external aggression by Russia beyond its borders. The bungled Chechnyan military campaign showed that Russia remained far from being an external threat to any major European state. After the Russian army finally took control of most of Chechnya, the taking of hostages by Chechnyan rebels in the southern Russian town of Buddenovsk appeared to trigger important changes in Russian politics. First, the Russian Prime Minister, Viktor Chernomyrdin – a former communist boss turned market-oriented democrat – negotiated the hostages' release while Yeltsin attended a G-7 summit in Canada. Chernomyrdin's deft handling of the highly volatile crisis established him as a prime candidate to lead Russia for the rest of the 1990s. Moreover, the status of Russia's 'power ministries' appeared damaged by the ill-judged decision to crush the Chechnyan rebellion.

By the mid-1990s, it remained impossible to consider Russia, with its crushing poverty, violent crime and strong neo-fascist parties, a 'stable' democracy. Yet, as Keohane (1994: 239) argues, 'Democracy in Russia is neither likely nor necessary for Western interests . . . moderation is.' In particular, moderation is needed to keep competition for influence between two blocs in the middle of the Eurasian continent – one Christian and the other Islamic – from turning violent. The Christian bloc is apt to be led by Russia, which still wields considerable influence in the region despite its internal difficulties. The Islamic bloc extends from North Africa to Pakistan, with Turkey and Iran vying for leadership. Competition between the two blocs was illustrated by rival attempts to mediate in the dispute between Azerbaijan and Armenia after the break-up of the USSR.

Central Asia is bound to be marked by acute instability well into the next century. Most former Soviet republics in Asia continue to be run by ex-communists. Rapid population increases will exacerbate their already grinding poverty. The ideological and political struggle between fundamentalist and secular Islam in the region shows few signs of abating.

US influence in the region is minimal in the wake of its actions in Afghanistan and the Gulf War, which both fuelled Islamic fundamentalism. The EU has far closer historical, cultural and economic ties to Islamic countries in Eurasia. Its potential to influence the evolving political geography of the region is substantial.

In 1995, the Union took the significant step of offering a free trade agreement to Turkey, the scene of intense conflict between rival versions of Islam as well as between Kurdish rebels and the government. The price of overcoming Greek objections to the EU–Turkey agreement was a promise to begin negotiations leading to an offer of EU membership to Cyprus after 1996. Thus, the EU crossed an important rubicon and opened up the possibility of a much-enlarged future Union taking in European 'micro-states' (i.e. Malta, Slovenia, Lithuania, etc.). The point is that even when the EU manages to wield its potential influence, the price paid to dissident member states is often substantial and the deal struck often makes future unity seem less likely.

The initial effect of the break-up of the Soviet Union on US–EU relations was to push both towards common political and economic responses. The 'unfreezing' of the East–West divide on the security front fed the arguments of those who urged that the EU needed to develop its own independent defence identity (De Gucht and Keukeleire 1991). But geopolitical uncertainty also made NATO's leading role in Western defence less subject to challenge. Despite frequent squabbles, significant US–EU cooperation took place on diplomatic recognition, trade concessions and aid to the former Soviet bloc. In short, the 'Soviet' threat reappeared in 1991–2 in a different permutation but with many of the same effects as before.

Perhaps inevitably, geopolitical change in the East also brought new tensions to transatlantic relations. The US and many EU governments scorned the Kohl government's campaign to recognize the independence of the Yugoslav republics of Croatia and Slovenia in 1991, largely out of fear that it encouraged centrifugal forces in the Soviet Union. The minimal US commitment of aid to the former Soviet Union was loudly criticized by the EU and its member states, which contributed nearly two-thirds of all Western aid to the region after 1989 (Commission 1995d: 28).

Western policy towards Eastern Europe and the former Soviet Union reveals an altered configuration of power within the transatlantic alliance. The new equation features diminished US influence, a more important role for the EU and, particularly, a more independent-minded and assertive Germany. The US and EU may often share a common international policy agenda in a post-Cold War world, but their interests and commitments will often vary, given the new political geography of power in Eurasia.

3 THE GULF WAR AND YUGOSLAVIA

The Bush administration accepted and encouraged EU leadership in the face of the geopolitical changes of 1989–92. The Clinton administration showed considerable deference to its European allies on policy in the Balkans after 1992. However, the notion of a US–EU partnership of equals remains an aspiration rather than a reality. The Gulf War and the Yugoslav crisis showed how the New Transatlanticism is complicated not only by divergent geopolitical interests, but also continued disunity in EU foreign policy and new domestic limits to US international power.

Despite its rhetoric about an approaching era of peace and prosperity, Bush's 'New World Order' speech to Congress in September 1990 was ultimately designed to secure Congressional and popular support for the use of US military force to liberate Kuwait. The speech revealed a dilemma: the US had a vital national interest in the conflict, but was unable to pursue it without support from an international coalition of states. Bush stressed that the United States had become unacceptably addicted to foreign oil imports and budget deficits (US State Department 1990: 3). His speech implied that the US had no choice other than to take military action against Iraq, but that it could afford to do so only by spreading the costs among its allies. For many European leaders, the speech reinforced the twin impressions of declining US hegemony and a continued propensity for Washington to try to make unilateral decisions for the West as a whole.

The EU was unable to develop a consistent or coherent position on the war. Individual member states behaved according to a familiar pattern: they either deferred to US wishes or engaged in selective independent acts which appeared bold but were risk-free because of American leadership. France's attempt at secret and solo diplomacy and German ambivalence were both possible only because the Bush administration was determined to get Iraq out of Kuwait and was willing to expend the resources to do so (Brenner 1991). Intense US pressure eventually convinced all EU member states to support – with words if not deeds – the launching of a ground offensive against Iraq.

Still, in the eyes of the world, the EU's response to the invasion of Kuwait was ineffectual and indicative of its general insignificance when aggression necessitated a military response. The French Defence Minister, Jean-Pierre Chevènement, resigned in protest at French participation in the war. His somewhat sour reflection on Bush's speech was that there was nothing 'new' about a 'New World Order' dictated by the Americans. US analysts concurred that a 'New World Order' simply implied a new 'assertion of American interests and values in the world' (Krauthammer 1991: 26).

The Gulf War experience focused attention on the EU's loose arrangements for coordinating national foreign policies. The EPC system had been gradually strengthened since the early 1970s (Ginsberg 1989; Allen and Smith 1990), but its continued fragility was obvious during the Gulf crisis. The divided EU response became a *cause célèbre* for member states which wished to reform the EPC mechanism – and adopt provisions for majority voting on foreign policy – within the ongoing IGC on political union. According to this logic, the EU could cope with its new external obligations only with more unified foreign policies, particularly after Bush made it clear that brokering a peaceful settlement to the civil war in Yugoslavia was primarily an EU responsibility in 1991.

The Yugoslav war was rooted in complex and historically-ingrained ethnic tensions between Serbs, Croats and Muslims. Arguably, Yugoslavia was always an artificial nation-state, held together only by Tito, the army and a good amount of repression. By 1991, power had been significantly decentralized and Croatia, Slovenia and several other Yugoslav republics had democratically elected governments. Yet Serbia, the largest and most populous Yugoslav republic, remained untouched by the changes which had unseated communist governments throughout Eastern Europe. It continued to be ruled by an old-style leadership which explicitly sought a 'Greater Serbia' incorporating territories inhabited by ethnic Serbs in Croatia and Bosnia-Hercegovina. Meanwhile the democratically elected Croatian government, headed by the demagogic Franjo Tudjman, adopted blatantly anti-Serb policies which inflamed ethnic tensions in Croatia.

When armed conflict erupted in mid-1991, the Bush administration supported the EU's initiative to seek a mandate from the OSCE to negotiate ceasefire and monitoring agreements in Yugoslavia. The first Community effort to mediate a truce initially appeared to succeed. The acting President of the Council of Ministers, Jacques Poos of Luxembourg, triumphantly claimed that, 'This is the hour of Europe, not the hour of the Americans.'[6] The truce fell apart almost immediately, as did countless others after it.

The Community struggled to keep up a united front on the need to preserve Yugoslavia as a unified country. Many EU governments were mindful of ethnic or regional conflicts in their own countries as well as the dangers of encouraging the break-up of the Soviet Union. However, Kohl – with East Germany's recent liberation in mind – pressured his EU partners to adopt EPC declarations which accepted that the Yugoslav republics should be allowed to pursue independence provided it was negotiated peacefully.

The lack of meaningful political control over the Serb-dominated Yugoslav army made a diplomatic solution in the Balkans impossible. Community economic sanctions had little impact beyond subjecting civilian populations caught in the conflict to intensified misery. In Germany, Kohl and Genscher faced severe domestic political pressures to recognize the independence of Croatia and Slovenia unilaterally. The Christian Social Union wing of Kohl's own party overwhelmingly sided with largely Catholic Croatia. A wide spectrum of German opinion, including virtually all German opposition parties, sympathized with the 700,000 ethnic Croatians living in Germany, and took the view that Kohl placed too high a premium on maintaining the EU's unity when Germany had a moral obligation to condemn the Serbs. Throughout the latter part of 1991, only solid resistance from other EU member states, the UN Secretary-General Javier Perez de Cuellar, and the Bush administration kept the Germans from breaking ranks and unilaterally recognizing the independence of Croatia and Slovenia.

The US insistence that any political solution to the conflict had to preserve the territorial integrity of Yugoslavia was reflected in the declaration of the Rome NATO (1991b) summit: 'all attempts to change existing borders through the use of force or a policy of *fait accompli* are unacceptable; we will not recognize any unilateral change of borders, external or internal, brought about by such means'. The Bush administration continued to argue that securing peace in Yugoslavia was primarily an EU responsibility. But, as during the Gulf War, internal EU divisions were contained only because the US insisted on a single European policy which dovetailed with the American one.

Yugoslavia provided ammunition for conflicting arguments in the debate about reform of EPC arrangements. At the Luxembourg summit of June 1991, Kohl urged that the EU needed to adopt majority voting to deal with future and similar issues of foreign policy. The German Chancellor began to hint that he would resort to high-level brinkmanship by asking the Maastricht summit to recognize Croatia and Slovenia, and insisting that a decision be taken by a majority vote. Meanwhile, the British Prime Minister, John Major, urged that the lesson to be taken from the Yugoslav civil war was the opposite: the EPC system worked well in its current form because it helped to maintain an EU consensus on Yugoslavia.

The Italian government feared that squabbling on the issue could derail the Maastricht summit, and moved to support the German position. Italy's Prime Minister, Giulio Andreotti, released a joint statement with Kohl urging that Croatia and Slovenia deserved independence and recognition from the West. Other EU states continued to argue that extending recognition without safeguards for all ethnic minorities in Yugoslavia would spread the war to other republics with Serbian minorities, especially Bosnia and Macedonia. In the event, Yugoslavia was not considered in detail at Maastricht. The summit yielded agreement on plans for strengthening the EPC mechanism to create a Common Foreign and Security Policy (CFSP). Provisions were agreed for majority voting on the implementation of unanimously agreed EU foreign policy initiatives, although it was unclear how they would work in practice.

The convergence of national positions on the CFSP at Maastricht clashed with Germany's unilateral move two weeks later to extend full diplomatic recognition to Croatia and Slovenia. The action was an unprecedented display of German diplomatic muscle which ignored and even taunted US opposition. Kohl called it 'a great victory for German foreign policy',[7] and boldly asserted, 'we won't let ourselves be lectured by others who have hardly raised a finger to support the reform process in Eastern Europe'.[8]

The Yugoslav conflict pointed to three emerging trends in US–EU relations. First, by late 1991 Bonn was determined to lead in the development of Western policy towards Eastern Europe, even if opposed by the US or other EU states. The recognition of Croatia and Slovenia was justified by the Germans as a 'get-tough' policy which would force Serbia into line, but was widely viewed as an emotional response with dangerous ramifications for the peacemaking process.

German unilateralism was partly a response to Kohl's humiliation at Maastricht. Arguably, he gave in on every important issue: a fixed timetable for EMU, a new cohesion fund which increased Germany's net budgetary contribution, and a CFSP conceived as weak and unworkable. Besides, Kohl may have reckoned, the war in Bosnia was 'probably unstoppable anyway' (Krieger 1994: 32, see also Crawford 1994a).

Another explanation was that the Kohl government had begun to believe that Germany's generosity and its allies' relative meanness towards Eastern Europe justified German assertiveness. Germany took in 300,000 refugees from the Yugoslav conflict, compared to France's 58,000 and the UK's 4,000 (Krieger 1994). Other EU states eventually followed the German lead anyway by recognizing the independence of Croatia and Slovenia in early 1992. A dramatic and symbolic visit to Bosnia by Mitterrand in June 1992 occurred after the French President conferred *only* with Kohl among all Western leaders. The deference of its EU partners meant Germany had little to lose from unilateralism.

Second, the Yugoslav civil war illustrated that the role of the UN in conflict resolution was being developed as never before. In 1992 the EU supported a UN decision to send blue-helmeted UN peacekeeping forces to enforce a ceasefire in Croatia after warring factions there appeared to have exhausted themselves. The UN later mounted an impressive and often heroic humanitarian relief operation in Bosnia which saved many lives as the conflict dragged on into 1995. However, Bosnian Serb aggression and the West's lack of will to defend Bosnian Muslims made the UN's mission untenable. The German push to recognize Croatia and Slovenia against the wishes of the UN's Secretary-General showed that Western governments still viewed the UN as a useful and convenient diplomatic tool, but not one which carried more weight than domestic political pressures on foreign policy.

Third, the US hesitated to involve itself in the Balkans. The Bush administration's policy was conservative, reactive and obsessed with preserving Yugoslavia's territorial integrity. Clinton came to power determined to do more for the Bosnian Muslims. In the end, his administration refused to accept the so-called Vance-Owen peace plan in 1993 ostensibly on the grounds that it rewarded the Bosnian Serbs for 'ethnic cleansing' (the murder or mass deportation of Muslims from disputed territories), but also because it required large US ground forces to police the peace.

The Gulf War yielded a different picture: the West was united in so far as the British and French contributed military resources to the campaign and allowed their troops to come under US command when the decision was taken to use force against Iraq. However, Germany (along with Japan) cited domestic constitutional restrictions on the use of its national armed forces abroad to justify its minimal military contribution to the allied war effort. Germany offered almost nothing to diplomatic efforts before the allied military offensive and helped finance the war effort only reluctantly and after considerable US pressure. While Germany's contribution of $10 billion equalled nearly one-third of its defence budget (Krieger 1994: 34), changes in exchange rates and pressure from the political opposition led to unseemly haggling between the US and Kohl governments over how much the Germans had to pay. In the words of one EU ambassador, the inability of the Germans to contribute to allied military actions had 'poisonous and psychologically warping consequences which spill over into other issue-areas'.[9] In Brenner's (1991: 671) judgement, it was 'unreasonable to expect that this state of affairs [could] be left as it is without the allies experiencing a deepening cycle of blame and resentment'.

Comparison of the Yugoslav and Gulf wars suggests a new division of labour based on different US and EU geopolitical interests. The US interest in the Middle East is long established. Its leading role in the Gulf War could be explained as a product of its close ties to Israel, growing US dependence on imported oil and the need for a military response which only the US could provide to get Iraq out of Kuwait.

Yet it remains difficult to imagine that the unique political circumstances surrounding the Gulf War could be replicated in future regional conflicts. Domestic opinion in the US was mobilized in support of the war only with great difficulty and only after Saddam Hussein committed a string of tactical errors, such as seizing US hostages before the war and parading captured and battered Western pilots on Iraqi television. The successful prosecution of the war required a broad international coalition organized within the UN as well as near total acquiescence by its members to the dictates of American policy. The formation of the coalition was possible only because the Soviet Union was on the brink of collapse, China acceded reluctantly, and Islamic states such as Syria, Morocco and Pakistan determined for various reasons that they should join it. Above all, the US was able to justify the costs of the war at a time of severe federal budget constraints because it secured remuneration from German, Japanese and Middle Eastern allies.

The Yugoslav war probably provided a more apt illustration of what the end of bipolarity means. The conflict involved a European country on the EU's doorstep, while America's interest was ambiguous. Particularly when the conflict became localized in Bosnia, it showed how geography matters in US–EU relations. Responding to public outcry after revelations of atrocities in Bosnia in 1993, Clinton first said, 'I think we should act. We should lead. The United States should lead.' Less than two months later, his line became, 'The United Nations controls what happens in Bosnia.'[10]

Geography will remain an important determinant of US and EU interests and responses to political conflict in different regions of the world in the twenty-first century. The EU's role in international relations is bound to be expanded with substantial US encouragement. One upshot is that the EU will be consumed with debates on how it can develop its own military capability as a tool at the service of its foreign policy. The role of Germany will be crucial if it continues to treat Eastern Europe as a special sphere of German influence. The extent to which the CFSP can move the EU towards a truly common foreign policy will be a primary determinant of the Union's ability to handle its new duties. Its record thus far hardly inspires confidence. The Gulf War and Yugoslav

crisis were similar in few respects other than that both revealed a fundamental lack of European unity.

4 THEORETICAL PERSPECTIVES ON GEOPOLITICAL CHANGE

All theories of international relations make assumptions about the implications of geopolitical change. For *neorealists* the distribution of power
between states is inevitably reflected in geopolitics. When the geopolitical
landscape was relatively fixed during the Cold War, any change was viewed
as a threat to the strategic balance between the superpowers. Thus,
western security arrangements constructed in the early post-war period
also remained relatively fixed. The US share of the total costs of NATO
changed only marginally between 1955 and 1985 despite a relative decline
in American economic strength and Congressional pressures to cut the
US troop commitment (Oneal and Elrod 1989).

Neorealism explains change in the international system by reference
to differential growth in the power of its constituent states (Gilpin 1981:
93–6). The demise of communist states in Eastern Europe and the Soviet
Union may be viewed as a product of their relative decline in power
compared to Western capitalist states. Citizens in the East subjected their
own standards of living to comparison with those of Western citizens
and forced political changes leading towards Western-style democratic
capitalism. Neorealists claim that the revolutions of 1989 and after show
that the competitive pressures of the international system produce nation-
states which are internally and functionally similar.

But the events of 1989–92 have ushered in an era in which the structural imperatives of the international system constrain state behaviour far
less than during the Cold War. As Krasner (1989: 158) aptly observes:

> As a description and explanation for state behavior, realism works best
> when the constraints emanating from the international system are
> compelling, a situation that occurs most vividly when territorial and
> political integrity are at risk. Absent such circumstances, the distri-
> bution of power alone will not provide an adequate explanation of
> state behavior. Other factors, such as pressures from within the polity
> and the cognitive mind set of central decision-makers, must be taken
> into consideration.

To illustrate these points, Germany is now less bound by geopolitical
constraints than ever before in the post-war period. It can assert itself in
Eastern Europe with less fear of reprisals from the Russians or a weakening of the US commitment to NATO. Domestic political pressures matter
more now than they did before 1989: witness the effects of popular
German support for Croatian independence and the election of neo-

fascists in Russia. The mindset of key decision-makers has become a more important determinant of Western foreign policies. Spurred by Mrs Thatcher's plea not to 'go all wobbly', Bush became personally determined to use force against Iraq in the Gulf. German unification might not have happened until the mid-1990s had it not been for Kohl's own stubbornness.

Neorealists tend to take a pessimistic view of the chances for enhanced cooperation and harmony between states in a more multipolar world:

> Before assuming that truly collaborative multilateralism will materialize and endure, we must bear in mind that almost every previous multipolar system has begun with optimistic hopes for concerted great-power cooperation and ended in a costly and increasingly deadly great-power competition for predominance.
>
> (Kegley and Raymond 1994: 234)

For neorealists, multipolarity inevitably leads to shifting alliances and instability (Christensen and Snyder 1990; Snyder 1990). Witness new tensions in the closest of all bilateral relationships in Europe: the Franco-German alliance. Gallois (1993) expresses fears which haunt the French right about a new *prédominance allemande* in Europe, with Bonn enlisting the help of Turkey and the Vatican, winning over the US and taking advantage of the goodwill of a cowed EU membership. Most neorealists assert that the emergence of new centres of power is destabilizing, and assume that bipolarity is preferable because 'two great powers can deal with each other better than more can' (Waltz 1979: 193).

The end of the Cold War also poses new challenges to other neorealist assumptions. Neorealism teaches that different kinds of state power are fungible, but the ability of US military strength to compensate for its relative economic decline is subject to new doubts. States may remain the essential actors in international relations, but the US and others have come to view the EU as an island of geopolitical stability in Europe and thus worthy of increased support and attention.

Institutionalists accept that more complex international power structures have arisen as a result of geopolitical change, but observe that pre-existing institutions have persisted and adapted. Nye and Keohane (1993: 118) argue that instead of reappraising the institutionalist strategies that it had followed for forty years, the US reinforced and adapted them to a new geopolitical reality. The creation of the European Community in the 1950s may have been been a product of Cold War fears. New doubts have arisen about the inevitability of closer European unity. However, the EU remains the most important and developed of all regional institutions in the world. More generally:

Institutionalist theory advances two major predictions: first, levels of international cooperation are often suboptimal, owing to the lack of appropriate international institutions, and, second, cooperation is more likely to occur within preexisting international institutions because institutions are cheaper to maintain than create.

(Haggard and Moravcsik 1993: 284).

In short, the institutionalist recipe for stable and peaceful geopolitical transition is Western leadership combined with stronger international institutions.

One of the main criticisms of institutionalism is that its focus on international cooperation leads its proponents to ignore the domestic sources of state behaviour. For their part, institutionalists try to account for this link by stressing the need for intense exchanges of information between states if relations between them are to be secure. Former Warsaw Pact states must adopt open polities to attract Western investment, become integrated into the global trading system, and generally inspire the trust of Western states. Keohane (1984: 258) argues that:

Governments that close off their decision-making processes to outsiders, restricting the flow of information about their true preferences or likely future actions, will have more difficulty providing high-quality evidence about their intentions than their less tightly organized counterparts, and will therefore find it harder to make mutually beneficial agreements.

Institutionalists are hopeful that the end of communism in Eurasia will open the way for heightened cooperation between states because information about states' likely future actions will become more readily available. However, they do not claim that increased cooperation will arise spontaneously. Institutionalists caution that heightened interdependence can lead to new conflicts as the assumptions which underpinned past patterns of cooperation suddenly become outdated (Buzan 1991: 41–4). They insist that political leadership is required in order for new power structures to emerge peacefully in the wake of rapid regime changes such as the demise of the Warsaw Pact and the unification of Germany. Interdependence must be managed.

Different strands of institutionalist theory prescribe different methods for managing heightened interdependence. Regime theorists insist that the answer is strengthened international institutions. The EU should cross the rubicon of making all foreign policy decisions by majority vote. NATO remains a useful deterrent to aggression in the short term, but must outgrow its legacy of US dominance and extend membership to former Warsaw Pact states. Institutionalists generally support the OSCE, but want it to be transformed into a treaty-based organization which places stronger obligations on its members. Meanwhile, the UN must be reformed internally before it can take on new responsibilities in the areas of peacekeeping, arms control and environmental protection.

Hegemonic stability theorists argue that strengthened international institutions may be desirable, but they cannot compensate for weakened US leadership in a multipolar world. These theorists tend to take a dim view of the EU's ability to become a politically united power in Europe. Some suggest that Germany has the potential to be a hegemon in Europe but doubt whether this is politically or practically feasible (Buzan *et al.* 1990: 215–18). Others argue that 'Germany has been forced by circumstance and self-interest, if not by design, to seek a hegemonic role in Europe', but conclude that German methods mostly will involve 'chequebook diplomacy' in the pursuit of relatively benign economic goals (Sperling 1994: 92). Many American analysts argue that only the US has the power to ensure that the geopolitical transformation of Europe is peaceful (see Nau 1990; Nye 1990; Nye and Keohane 1993). A corollary of this argument is that NATO must be preserved, if also reformed.

Theorists concerned with 'epistemic communities' stress that intense interactions between experts who share values and are concerned with specialized issues can constitute critical 'managers' of interdependence. Three bilateral US–EU working groups formed in 1994 on foreign policy coordination, Eastern Europe and international crime yielded mixed results. Still, they are precisely the sort of epistemic communities which can lay the groundwork for broader initiatives at higher political levels.

Liberalism often seems the 'odd theory out' in assessing geopolitical change. Geopolitical analysis is anathema to liberals because it leads to an obsession with 'spheres of influence' and political manoeuvrings which disrupt free and open trade. Geopolitics would be irrelevant in a perfect world of free trade between states.

Yet liberal principles have lurked behind Western policy responses to geopolitical change in Europe. The EBRD's methodology reflects the notion that the economic reconstruction of the former Eastern bloc must be market-led. The catchphrase 'trade not aid' has become internalized by US and EU policy-makers as well as those within international organizations such as the International Monetary Fund (IMF) and the World Bank.

On the one hand, the EU's effort to open its markets to East European producers after 1989 was bitterly contested, and revealed considerable Western reluctance to eliminate trade barriers. On the other, as Nicolaïdis (1993: 243) observes:

> Given the relatively depressed state of western economies at the time, a plausible argument can be made that western governments acting bilaterally may not have been able to justify concessions to their con-

stituents short of the traditional use of multilateral obligations as scapegoats.

While the EU's trade agreements with Eastern Europe and Western aid programmes were by no means generous, they were at least informed by the liberal principle that desirable political changes could be prompted through expanded trade links and open Western markets in sectors where the new democracies could compete.

For *reformists*, the geopolitical changes of 1989–92 proved that the Western doctrine of deterrence of the Soviet threat was rooted in meaningless dogma (MccGwire 1986). In the words of a leading reformist:

> The Cold War was not about an ideological or inter-systemic conflict at all – this was the myth of the Pentagon, the KGB and odd people such as myself who tried to say so – but about a *pas de deux* of two hegemonic systems. Each pretended to rival the other, but in fact used the pretence of conflict to hold down their own people, make money out of useless military production, and so on.
>
> (Halliday 1994: 230)

The 'people's revolutions' in Eastern Europe were welcomed but entirely predictable for reformists because communist regimes denied their citizens fundamental human rights, political freedoms and decent standards of living. Many reformists bemoaned the subsequent failure of 'the Western peace movement and progressive forces' to instigate a 'reciprocal process in the West to match the decomposition of Cold War ideological controls in the East' (Thompson 1990: 144).

Reformists direct their fiercest criticism at Western governments for their uncertain and glacial response to geopolitical change after 1989. The Bush administration stood by Gorbachev despite his 'divide and rule' strategy which provoked considerable bloodshed in Georgia, Armenia and the Baltic states. The West, and the US in particular, woke up to the danger of civil war in the ex-Soviet Union only after 90 per cent of Ukrainians had voted for independence and the Soviet Union was declared legally dead in 1991. The Clinton administration stubbornly supported Yeltsin despite his penchant for authoritarianism and Russia's brutal invasion of Chechnya. Reformists were left asking whether having a Democrat in the White House made any difference to US foreign policy.

During the Gulf War, reformists bemoaned 'the UN's failure to maintain its independence and its evident willingness to allow itself to be shamelessly manipulated as a vehicle of US foreign policy and geopolitical ambition' (Falk 1991: 14). The EU was criticized for engaging in its own brand of geopolitically-inspired power politics in the region. Reformists noted with disgust the lifting of EU sanctions against Iran in 1990, which allowed Tehran to purchase weapons from EU producers anxious to find new export markets with the end of the Cold War in sight (Ehteshami *et al.* 1991: 268). For reformists, the West's fetishiz for geopolitical 'stability' exacerbates problems such as global arms trafficking and the denial of human rights by fundamentalist governments.

Reformists are scathing in their criticism of Western leaders for their narrow-minded and weak leadership in the face of recent genocide or humanitarian tragedies. The EU's inability or refusal to intervene in Bosnia fuelled pessimism among reformists about the value or desirability of European integration. Reformists argued that, 'Bosnia was, by any standards, a dismal, indeed criminal, failure of the "international community" to uphold its professed goals and values' (Shaw 1994: 183).

Theorists of all stripes could agree that two geopolitical changes with profound ramifications for international politics are now irreversible: German unification and the collapse of the Soviet empire. These changes permanently altered the political geography of power in Europe, put US influence on European affairs into question, and forced a fundamental reconsideration of American internationalism.

The geopolitical changes of 1989–92 also ushered in a period in which US and EU interests in international affairs showed signs of diverging as never before during the post-war period. The new situation was summed up well by Clinton's first Secretary of Defence, Les Aspin. A thoughtful but tragic figure, Aspin was purged after US 'peacekeepers' were ambushed and killed in Somalia, shortly before he died in 1995. For Aspin, the Cold War world of good guys and bad guys had given way to a complex, fluid world of 'grey guys'.[11] A world without a clear common enemy made US–EU partnership more difficult to create, if not impossible to imagine.

Chapter 4

The domestic politics of US–EU relations

Traditionally, political scientists tended to assume a clear division between foreign and domestic policies. Foreign policy-making was an elite activity monopolized by a 'political class': a 'small, privileged caste of government officials, former government officials, professors, think-tank denizens, and journalists' (Tonelson 1991: 37). Domestic policy-making was marked by a far more diverse set of interests competing in a far more open polity. Domestic and international politics thus were viewed as separate domains, particularly by international relations theorists.

These neat distinctions have blurred. The US political class must contend with a larger, more aggressive and pressure group-based collection of interests which seek to influence the foreign policy process. The move to a 'common' foreign and security policy (CFSP) has combined with pressures to eliminate the Union's 'democratic deficit' to create similar pressures in the EU.

This chapter begins by exploring the meaning and implications of the 'democratization' of US foreign policy in section 1. Section 2 examines how domestic politics in the EU's member states constrain its policy process, and particularly the construction of the CFSP. Section 3 considers how domestic political inputs into US–EU relations are managed. Section 4 examines the role ascribed to domestic politics by the four theories of international relations.

1 DOMESTIC POLITICS AND US FOREIGN POLICY

The politics of 'fair trade'

Trade has been the most important dimension in transatlantic relations since the founding of the original EEC. The US constitution grants Congress exclusive powers to regulate commerce with foreign nations. Many of these powers were delegated to the executive through the creation of the US Trade Representative (USTR) in 1962, but power over trade policy shifted back to Congress in the 1970s. Post-Watergate reforms decentralized Congress and made it more accessible to special interests. Meanwhile, trade doubled as a share of total US economic output, from 13 per cent in the 1970s to 27 per cent by the mid-1990s. The number of US producers vulnerable to foreign competition increased in the process, with firms in the industrial strongholds of the Democratic Party coming under particularly strong pressure.

The domestic consensus which allowed the US executive to seek free trade and 'treat trade policy as a component of US international leadership' gradually fell apart (Destler 1986: 30). The trend was accentuated as the American trade deficit increased. Of 782 trade bills introduced in Congress in 1985–6, no less than 248 were judged by Yoffie (1989: 113) to be fundamentally protectionist.

The Reagan administration was one of the most protectionist in United States history. The percentage of US manufactured imports subject to non-tariff barriers (NTBs) grew from 20 to 35 per cent during Reagan's first term alone (Tyson 1988). In the event, increased protection of US producers in industries ranging from semiconductors to steel to motorcycles had little impact on the US trade deficit, which peaked at close to $160 billion in 1986. As the Uruguay Round began, American negotiators were urged to take aggressive and defensive positions by an ill-tempered and Democrat-controlled Congress, many of whose members believed the US had 'given too much away' in previous GATT Rounds (Destler 1986: 42–5).

The Omnibus Trade and Competitiveness Act was passed by Congress in 1988. Its notorious 'Super 301' clause mandated that trade sanctions be applied to any foreign country which showed a 'consistent pattern of import barriers and market distorting practices'. The executive was required to act against 'unfair' traders unless it could explain why retaliation was not in the national interest.

The launch of the 1992 project towards the end of Reagan's second term led many in his administration to view the EU as a potentially positive force for economic liberalization. More favourable attitudes in the upper echelons of the administration were not, however, replicated in Congress or within the USTR and Commerce Department. A DG I official recalled:

> People in the higher reaches of the administration turned quite suddenly pro-EU. But these people overreacted in the eyes of people lower down in the agencies and especially in the eyes of Congress. That contributed to the 1988 Trade Act.... We found that people lower down in the bureaucracies seemed allied with certain people in

Congress who were not at all sympathetic to the argument that European integration was good for US interests.[1]

For EU policy-makers, it became more difficult to identify a single 'American view' on most issues of foreign policy, particularly those concerning trade. The 1988 Trade Act was less a Reaganite bow to protectionism than 'a partisan affair . . . something like a Democratic party economic program dealing comprehensively with "competitiveness" ' (Nivola 1990: 236–7). The Bush administration sought a GATT deal, while Democrats returned to the theme of 'fair trade' as the 1992 election campaign drew nearer. Bill Clinton promised tougher action than any taken by previous presidents against US trading partners. After his election, Clinton created a new National Economic Council, a sort of National Security Council for 'economic security' issues. He then threatened to ditch the so-called 'Airbus accord' and reopen a long-running US–EU dispute over subsidies for aircraft production.

In early 1993, Clinton surprised many observers by declaring that 'open and competitive commerce will enrich us as a nation'.[2] Risking considerable political capital, Clinton secured Congressional passage of the NAFTA and Uruguay Round agreements. However, his administration was thrown on the defensive after 1994 by a new hostile Republican majority in Congress, which demanded aggressive action to shrink the country's yawning trade deficit. In early 1995, Republicans told Clinton's USTR, Mickey Kantor, that they did not want a 'level playing field' but rather one tipped in America's direction.[3] This period confirmed that divided government in the US tends to bring more protectionist trade policies (Lohmann and O'Halloran 1994).

Another force for pluralism (or even confusion) in US foreign policy stems from the differing interests of different types of firms. Large US multinationals tend to invest in the EU, while smaller firms are usually restricted to exporting goods 'made in America'. American companies with plants and other investments in the EU notched up total European sales of over $740 billion in 1991 while the value of US exports to the EU was less than $100 billion. As Hufbauer (1990: 24) noted:

> Out of such comparisons emerges a simple but compelling observation: for the great majority of large American firms, the business climate inside Europe, and their place in the European economic scheme, have become far more important than their exports to Europe. . . . From all this follows the proposition that, to the extent that the US government responds to the interests of the US business community, it will be more concerned about operating conditions within Europe than export opportunities to Europe.

The proposition is probably *too* simple. Large sales by US-owned multinationals with investments in the EU meant that maintaining open access to the EU's market for US foreign direct investment (FDI) was a priority for both the Bush and Clinton administrations. By contrast, the US trade deficit remained far more worrying for Congress because it symbolized the declining fortunes of smaller export-dependent manufacturers which were localized in Congressional constituencies.

In short, US trade policy inevitably reflects rivalries between Republicans and Democrats, and the executive and Congress. The 'American view' of European integration is also a product of these rivalries. Neither is monolithic or even very coherent.

Controlling the foreign policy agenda

Trade issues became 'core' foreign policy issues in the 1980s. In the process, US executive autonomy declined as policy became subject to new challenges from Congress. In particular, the costs of American internationalism became more closely linked with domestic economic conditions in the country's political discourse. A widening swathe of Congressional and public opinion began to blame problems at home on the Bush administration's neglect of the economy after 1989.

After US victory in the Gulf War, Bush's approval rating, at nearly 70 per cent, was higher than that enjoyed by any other president so late in his term in the history of polling. But Bush's popularity was both superficial and fleeting. A series of polls taken six months later indicated that less than half of Americans voters wished to re-elect Bush. About two-thirds thought that he did not devote sufficient attention to domestic issues.[4]

The severity of the US recession of the early 1990s was reflected in a decline in median income and in the lowest rate of job creation since the 1930s. During previous recessions, the federal deficit had been small enough to use loosened fiscal policy to stimulate the economy. This time, the deficit reduction package of 1990 effectively precluded reflation, let alone new programmes to deal with inner-city decay, homelessness, declining educational standards or the drug epidemic.

Bush was criticized for going abroad and neglecting the economy even as the transatlantic summit at The Hague in November 1991 yielded progress on the GATT negotiations and concerted action on Yugoslavia. The White House responded to growing evidence of a prolonged recession by cancelling Bush's long-planned trip to Asia, which had already been postponed once during the Gulf War. Fresh polls put Bush's approval rating lower than any other post-war President (except Gerald Ford) at a similar stage in his first term.[5]

When Bush finally did visit Japan in January 1992, his administration took the extraordinary step of including in the delegation representatives of US industries which had pressed the government hardest for protection against Japanese imports. Weak Japanese concessions and Bush's collapse from illness at a state banquet made the trip a political disaster. Bush went on the offensive immediately afterwards by urging the EU to dismantle its 'iron curtain' of agricultural protectionism. The clear intent was to distract attention from one foreign threat to another. However, the damage had been done: one could argue that the Clinton era really began during Bush's trip to Japan.[6]

Clinton was elected largely on the strength of his promise to focus on domestic, not foreign, policy. He managed to portray his Asia policy as more successful than Bush's, even though Japan and China accounted for more than half of a rising US trade deficit by 1994. The Clinton administration staked out tough positions in disputes with Japan on auto parts and with China on intellectual property rights in 1995. In both cases, the US was able to claim victory despite conceding much from its original bargaining position. In neither did the US speak with one voice. Many American auto parts manufacturers opposed Clinton's sabre-rattling in view of plans by all major Japanese car-makers to expand US production, thus increasing purchases of US-made parts and creating American jobs. Even as the US was threatening China with economic sanctions in the intellectual property rights dispute, its Energy Secretary, Hazel O'Leary, was dispatched to China to seek huge energy contracts for American suppliers.

More generally, the Clinton administration put more resources into commercial diplomacy than any US administration in history. In 1993, Clinton played an active and personal role in securing a $6 billion aircraft contract from Saudia Arabia for Boeing and McDonnell-Douglas. The Commerce Department was transformed from a sleepy backwater into a thrusting focal point for 'high intensity advocacy' of US trade interests. Its new 'war room' featured inter-agency groups who monitored and often intervened as US producers sought foreign deals. The Clinton administration claimed that the federal government had a hand in $46 billion worth of foreign deals that helped create or save 300,000 jobs in 1994 (see Peterson *et al.* 1995).

Still, Republicans in Congress targeted export promotion funds for cuts as part of their effort to 'reduce government' after 1994. The Commerce Department was even threatened with extinction. This period illustrated a wider point about US foreign policy: the executive's ability to control the agenda had been eroded, primarily because the 'balance of power between the executive and legislature shift[ed] with the Cold War's end' (Maynes 1990: 7).

The problem of the US President's lack of leverage is not just one for Clinton, even if his 43 per cent of the popular vote in 1992 revealed his uniquely weak grassroots support. In the 1990s, unlike the 1970s or even 1980s, the US executive had far less 'pork' (bridges, dams, military contracts) to distribute to its Congressional supporters. Most candidates for Congress raised most of their own campaign funds. It mattered to few whether Clinton campaigned for them (many hoped that he would not). Clinton's initial foreign policy approval ratings were generally poor (Rielly 1995: 16), thus encouraging Congressional 'micro-management' of US foreign policy. Clinton found that 'the old sense of party discipline was gone. A President had no sanctions' (Drew 1994: 266). More generally, Clinton found that US foreign policy had been pulled 'into the maelstrom of American politics' (Mann 1990: 29).

A new isolationism?

The American political class confronted two fundamental challenges in the 1990s: adapting to a redefinition of 'national security' and maintaining public support for United States internationalism. The gap between perceptions of US political leaders and the public at large widened on a range of questions related to the country's role in the world. In 1995, 72 per cent of ordinary citizens thought that reducing illegal immigration was a 'very important' goal of US foreign policy, compared with only 28 per cent of elites. Only one in five members of the general public favoured increased US aid to Eastern Europe compared with over half of elites (Rielly 1995: 15,32).

Advocates of a 'new isolationism' in US foreign policy sought to capitalize on this gap in perceptions:

> Internationalism . . . has led directly to the primacy of foreign policy in American life and to the consequent neglect of domestic problems. . . . [We must] begin to think in terms not of the whole world's well-being but rather of purely national interests. . . . American foreign policy has been conducted with utter disregard for the home front largely because it has been made by people whose lives and needs have almost nothing in common with those of the mass of their countrymen.
>
> (Tonelson 1991: 37)

Neo-isolationism was fuelled by the recession, the federal budget deficit, and pressures created by the latter for higher taxes and federal spending cuts. The reality of new limits to US resources was well understood within the Bush administration. It extended a 'begging bowl' to Germany, Japan and others for help in paying for US intervention in the Gulf War. Its minimal contribution to aid for Eastern Europe reflected declining public support for US foreign aid. One Congressional insider observed, 'no one wants total isolationism, but the "America first" idea brings together all people, all spectrums'.[7]

When Republican majorities took control of Congress in 1994, foreign aid became a prime target for budget cuts. The almost obsessive focus of Republicans on the issue was motivated by opinion polls which suggested that pluralities of Americans thought that foreign aid accounted for 20–30 per cent of the US federal budget, when the actual figure was about 1 per cent. Ultra-conservatives such as Jesse Helms, the chair of the Senate Foreign Relations Committee, likened foreign aid to 'throwing money down foreign rat holes'. Clinton's National Security Adviser, Anthony Lake, responded with a tough attack on Republican 'new isolationists'.[8] Still, it was clear that Clinton stood to win very few votes with his position on the issue.

The inevitability of growing public support for a neo-isolationist US foreign policy was not clear. A clear majority (69 per cent) of Americans appeared to believe that the US should continue to 'take an active part in world affairs'. This percentage was lower than during peak periods of Cold War tension but higher than in the 1970s or early 80s (Rielly 1995).

It is also arguable whether there was anything 'new' about the new isolationism. In many respects, the US has always been and remains an insular society. Fewer than 3 per cent of its people travel to foreign countries other than Canada or Mexico each year. Mann (1990: 13) insists that the US public has always been 'deeply sceptical of substantial and extended American involvement abroad'.

More generally, US political culture – the values, feelings and beliefs about politics that most Americans share – reflects a fundamental tension between the competing values of democratic government and a credible foreign policy. The former implies open competition between a wide range of interests. The latter requires executive autonomy to set goals and pursue them consistently (Destler 1985: 344). What was different about the 1990s was that geopolitical change, declining US fiscal resources and the increasingly fuzzy division between domestic and foreign politics accentuated this tension as never before in the post-war period.

The democratization of US foreign policy

Whatever the true strength of neo-isolationism in US public opinion, American foreign policy has become significantly 'democratized': that is, subject to more effective pressures from a wider range of interests. The policy agenda is now more difficult for the political class to control. The foreign policy process has become more indistinguishable from the domestic policy process.

The upshot is that any initiative to deepen cooperation with the EU or any other foreign state raises suspicions about fettered US autonomy. Witness the rhetoric of Patrick Buchanan, Bush's Republican challenger in 1992, on the eve of the Maastricht summit: 'In Holland today, a Conservative Prime Minister is being pressed to lead the mother of parliaments into yielding up to bureaucrats in Brussels what generations of British soldiers have fought to preserve. We must not allow that to happen here.'[9]

A return to the US isolationism of the 1930s is impossible because 'advances in military technology and the progress of economic integration have long since removed the insulation from the rest of the world that geographical distance used to provide' (Gaddis 1990: 102). Yet new constraints have been placed on the development of a joint US–EU policy agenda. Any President who seeks a more unified security alliance in Europe, joint leadership of the WTO or expanded cooperation on 'new' foreign policy issues, such as environmental protection or international crime, stands to encounter obstacles that did not exist during the Cold War. If anything, the democratization of foreign policy creates new pressures for US withdrawal from its NATO commitments, more protectionist American trade policies, and aggressive unilateralism more generally.

2 DOMESTIC POLITICS AND EU POLICY-MAKING

Three factors make it difficult to compare the impact of domestic politics on American and European foreign policy-making. First, and most obviously, the EU is not a 'state'. In many respects it operates as a 'two-level game' (Putnam 1988, 1993; see also Sandholtz and Zysman 1989; Peters 1992). Policy outcomes are a product of bargaining between domestic political actors at the national level as well as between member states at the EU level. Yet even this model crudely simplifies. The EU is the most complex political system in the world.

Second, the EU lacks a 'common' foreign policy in all but name. Particularly in view of the EU's failure as a mediator in the former Yugoslavia, few would have termed the CFSP a success by the mid-1990s. Despite fresh arguments for a move towards majority voting for *all* foreign policy decisions (see Commission 1995b), the CFSP seemed destined to remain a product of the narrowing of differences between distinctly national foreign policies.

Third, the EU has undergone frequent and important changes since the 1980s. The future institutional development of the EU is an open book. Whatever its future, political scientists have much work to do to conceptualize the 'domestic politics' of the EU and identify the factors which determine the CFSP.

Domestic politics, external trade policy and 1992

After the deadline for the 1992 project passed, the internal market was, in theory, complete. However, the EU had yet to make a range of decisions related to the internal market. The choices made promised to have wide implications for the Union's external trade policy and its relations with the US.

The 1992 project was a highly political endeavour. The Commission and pro-integrationist member states put substantial effort and resources into promoting 1992, European unity and the internal market as ideas which appealed to a wide cross-section of European governments, industrialists and peoples. Initially, the selling of the 1992 project appeared to be one of the most successful marketing campaigns in history. Over time, the project – and the EU more generally – lost much of its lustre as the recession of the early 1990s hit. Promises of future economic growth and job creation through economic liberalization rang hollow when measures to achieve them often made the pain of the slump even worse.

During its formative years, the EU was primarily concerned with lowering tariffs between its member states. The 1992 project was mostly about abolishing non-tariff barriers (NTBs) to trade. Tariffs are relatively 'transparent:' they are quantifiable, visible to trading partners, and have effects on trade which are relatively easy to gauge. NTBs are difficult to quantify, more visible to some trading partners than to others, and have effects which are open to dispute (Yannopoulos 1990). Removing them is almost always politically contentious.

NTBs tend to increase the costs of both domestic production and imports in equal measure. Removing them may benefit foreign (non-EU) producers as much as, or even more than, domestic ones. Thus, while the completion of the internal market was forecast to increase the EU's overall trade surplus, a net loss of more than $4 billion was predicted for the EU's trade balance with the US (Cecchini *et al.* 1988: 98; Hufbauer 1990: 22–3). The actual effects of the single market programme on the Union's external trade balances are open to dispute. However, the importance of the EU as a market is not. Even low projected economic growth rates for the EU in 1996 meant the creation of a new market the size of Taiwan's (USTR 1995b).

In the longer run, two extremely controversial elements of the 1992 project will go far towards determining its actual effects on trade with the US: the liberalization of EU public procurement and the elimination of national import quotas. The Commission has fought a long battle with member states to create an internal market for public procurement, but little meaningful competition exists in many EU public markets. The amount of public spending that *could* be opened up to competition was worth as much as 10 per cent of the Union's GDP by 1993, but inter-EU trade in public markets still accounted for less than 0.2 per cent of GDP (Commission 1993).

Telecommunications have been a key focus of the Commission's efforts since 1987. Traditionally cosy relationships between national equipment suppliers and public telecommunications authorities produced fragmented markets for expensive capital products such as central office switches. 'National champion' producers dominated European domestic markets, with the only meaningful competition coming from non-EU firms (see Table 4.1).

Table 4.1 Market shares for central office switches in Europe in 1986 (per cent)

	France	Germany (FRG)	Italy	UK	Denmark	Sweden
ITT (US)	0	35	30	20	10	0
CGE/CGCT (France)	100	0	0	0	0	0
Ericsson (Sweden)	0	0	21	15	90	100
Siemens (FRG)	0	65	0	0	0	0
Italtel (Italy)	0	0	49	0	0	0
Plessey (UK)	0	0	0	35	0	0
GEC (UK)	0	0	0	30	0	0

Source: adapted from Lodge (1990: 307)

As the Commission sought to create a single market for public procurement, it was pressured by EU member states to restrict the access of non-EU suppliers. A 1990 directive on public procurement in telecommunications and other big-ticket public products contained a 'Community preference', or built-in discrimination against foreign suppliers. The EU's 'Television Without Frontiers' directive in 1989 contained provisions for reserving a majority of EU transmission time for TV programmes of European origin. The US response to both directives was outrage.

The procurement issue remained volatile for three reasons. First, powerful domestic interests in EU member states benefited from time-honoured patterns of 'nationalized' public procurement. National champions lobbied hard for protection from large, globalized American firms.

Second, on the US side a range of 'Buy America' laws, particularly at the level of the individual states, often prohibited public purchases of non-American products. On no other issue was the independence of the individual states from the federal government a greater source of tension in US–EU relations. The Clinton administration declared that Washington was 'traditionally opposed' to 'Buy America' laws, but Jean-Paul Benoit of the European Parliament (EP) expressed the widespread European view that the Clinton administration was 'playing the autonomy of the federal States well' on the issue.[10]

Third, the wide gap between US and EU positions on procurement threatened to block progress towards a more general GATT deal to conclude the Uruguay Round. After arguing for years about whose procurement markets were the least open, the US and EU hit upon a unique solution in 1993. The results of an independent study of public markets on both sides underpinned a deal which went beyond anything that could be agreed in the GATT. The US and EU pledged to observe strict reciprocity in procurement: the total value of Union contracts open to bids from America would be identical to the value of US contracts open to EU bids. The deal was in some ways a testament to the ability of the US and EU to develop innovative solutions to problems in their relationship.

Another problem which demands creative solutions is an equally divisive element of the 1992 project: the elimination of national import quotas. The Single European Act mandated the abolition of Article 115 of the Rome Treaty, which allowed member states to restrict imports from non-EU states if they caused 'economic difficulties'. Quantitative restrictions applied by member states at the national level obviously could not be sustained if internal frontiers were to be eliminated. Still, the Commission was pressured to replace national quotas with EU-wide quotas.

A fragile agreement was reached in 1991 on the ultra-sensitive issue of an EU-wide quota on Japanese automobile imports, as national quotas maintained by France, Italy, Portugal, Spain and the UK had to be disbanded. A key issue was the treatment of cars made by Japanese-owned 'transplants' in the US and then exported to the EU. After personal lobbying by James Baker, the French stopped insisting that US-manufactured Hondas and Toyotas should be considered 'Japanese' when EU-wide quotas came into effect. Yet a USTR official remained sceptical about whether the deal would hold:

> It seems to me that autos are just too controversial a subject in Europe for that one to just slide along quietly . . . I think it is entirely conceivable and well within the ambit of Commission thinking to some day try to argue that cars produced by transplants in the States should be considered Japanese cars.[11]

The deal could easily fall apart if European automobile producers lose market shares rapidly – which appears likely – after all EU import restrictions are eliminated in 1998. The EU is the world's largest market for cars and the stakes are high.

The public procurement and import quota cases illustrate a more general point: the hype surrounding 1992 could not obscure the reality that economic liberalization creates economic losers, such as national telecommunications producers and auto manufacturers, as well as winners. 'Diffuse' public support for European integration obviously becomes difficult to sustain when politically powerful national producers lose market shares, reduce workforces and focus the blame on Brussels. Supporters of a *non* vote in the French referendum on Maastricht in 1992 found it easy to foment an anti-EU backlash at a time of deep recession, as did Euro-sceptic French parties in the 1994 EP election. Conservative

French governments, particularly under the Gaullist President, Jacques Chirac, can be expected to defend French interests robustly at the EU level in the late 1990s. Somehow, the French and their partners must nurture diffuse support for the EU, satisfy the demands of entrenched domestic economic interests *and* maintain the internal market, without discriminating against US producers. How well the Union manages this balancing act will go far towards determining the state of US–EU relations in the twenty-first century.

The politics of EMU

Economic and monetary union (EMU) emerged at the top of the EU's agenda after 1988. It became the Union's most ambitious and contentious goal. Put simply, EMU means the creation of a single European currency, Central Bank and monetary policy. The potential economic gains from EMU are threefold.

First, a single currency would be more economically efficient than fifteen or more national ones. In the early 1990s the Commission estimated that the EU was wasting $10–14 billion per year, or 0.5 per cent of the Union's GDP, on needless economic activity associated with exchange rate uncertainties and currency transactions (Emerson 1991: 468).

Second, a single currency would promote increased trade and lower prices. Additional cross-border trade would be encouraged as EU industrialists no longer worry about exchange rate fluctuations and become more certain of the value of future receipts for current transactions. A widespread assumption is that a new European Central Bank would hold down inflation in the style of the German Bundesbank.

Third, EMU would provide European industries with advantages in international competition. European producers would benefit because the costs of currency exchange would be reduced as more trade with non-EU states was carried out using a European currency. EU banks could offer more funds for investment since they would need to hold reduced reserves of non-EU currencies previously used to intervene in currency markets.

An important catalyst in the EMU debate came when member states agreed in 1988 to ban all restrictions on capital flows in the EU within five years. The decision produced fears – later realized – that the limited reserves and loose rules of the existing EMS would be inadequate to keep exchange rates stable after the free movement of capital became a reality. A plan unveiled by Delors in 1989 for moving to EMU in stages was so vague as to spark a new debate about how the transition should be managed.

The debate was transformed when Kohl made a firm pledge in 1990 to try to achieve EMU by the end of the decade. Kohl insisted that Germany would accept a treaty-based commitment to EMU only if a separate treaty on political union was agreed simultaneously. From this point, the momentum behind a new treaty which incorporated both EMU and political union was unstoppable.

The Maastricht Treaty's section on EMU reflected the broad outlines of the Delors plan, but in many respects was more ambitious. Between 1996 and 1998, finance ministers and the European Council would decide by a series of weighted majority votes which members were ready to join a full EMU and when it could be launched. A nascent European central bank, the European Monetary Institute, would be created to handle overall monetary policy and scrutinize national fiscal policies. It would even have powers to fine states which ran large budget deficits. A single currency was foreseen for 1999 at the latest.

At the Maastricht summit, Kohl secured agreement on five 'convergence criteria' which any member state would have to meet before joining EMU. The criteria required strict discipline on national inflation and interest rates, annual budget deficits, total public debt and stable exchange rates. In response to a sceptical German public which feared losing the Deutschmark and Bundesbank, Kohl insisted that the criteria matched 'anything we have in Germany'.[12]

At the time, it was difficult to explain why southern member states accepted the convergence criteria. Italy and Spain met only one of the five criteria and Greece and Portugal met none. These states seemed to be 'no-hopers' for EMU with the first vote on entry only five years away. Yet poorer EU states had begun to look at monetary union as a device to justify harsh remedial economic policies to their domestic publics. Most sought to end their addictions to high inflation and public spending, and to make their producers more competitive in the internal market. The strategy revealed the potent symbolism of the 'European project' for states seeking to modernize, compete and remain full partners in its construction. It also pointed to the critical need of governments in these states to sustain diffuse support for the EU at home when the price of European unity was considerable economic pain.

Serious new doubts about the credibility of plans for EMU arose when the EMS was beset by the first in a series of currency crises in 1992, prior to the French referendum on the Maastricht Treaty. Finally, in August 1993, member states succumbed to signals from currency markets and reconstructed the EMS as a much weaker mechanism which was much less likely to facilitate a smooth transition to EMU. The more defective their carefully planned architecture for EMU began to appear, the more European leaders sought to vilify external forces. The French President, François Mitterrand, blamed international currency speculators and proposed a global tax on currency transactions. The Major government blamed the German Bundesbank for not defending the pound on 'Black Wednesday', when it had to be withdrawn from full membership of the EMS.

For his part, Kohl singled out the US policy of 'benign neglect' of the value of the dollar as a deliberate attempt to undermine plans for a single European currency. While Kohl's charges were both paranoid and incredible, they illustrated clearly how fragile yet forceful the EMU project was as a symbol of the EU's success or failure. They also hinted at how the EMU project could become a new source of tensions in US–EU relations.

Eastern Europe and internal security

Geopolitical change in Eastern Europe had numerous effects on the internal politics of the EU. One of the most important was new concern about the prospect of economic refugees flooding the EU from the former Warsaw Pact states. In Germany, the rise of anti-immigrant violence in 1991 became one of the most intractable problems associated with unification. Kohl proposed a domestic political solution: changes in Germany's post-war constitution, the Basic Law, so that the state would no longer be required to accept all applications for asylum and to feed and house all applicants during a lengthy examination process. The proposals were blocked by opposition parties in the German Parliament.

The Kohl government thus backed plans for EU external border controls and a common asylum and immigration policy. Controversially, the Germans urged that decisions on 'internal security' issues should be made by majority voting. As it became clear that several other member states would not accept the proposals, the Germans took a variety of steps to let East European governments know that they risked losing economic aid unless they cooperated in deterring economic migration to the West.

The internal security 'pillar' eventually agreed at Maastricht only mandated closer intergovernmental cooperation outside the legal confines of the Community. In the short term, it did not solve the immigration problem for EU governments. Nearly all faced pressures to tighten controls as unemployment increased in the recession of 1991–2, and then fell only marginally as the economy recovered. Polls showed that about half of all EU citizens thought the Community was populated by too many immigrants (Commission 1992: 63–5). In France, Jean-Marie Le Pen's National Front swung an alarming number of voters – nearly 30 per cent according to some polls – behind its racist and xenophobic programme. In Belgium, the ultra-nationalist Flemish Bloc increased its vote exponentially and led all parties in large Flemish cities such as Antwerp. About half a million immigrants applied for asylum in the EU annually in the 1990s, or twice as many as in any year before 1985.

The magnetism of the EU for those facing poverty and political unrest will not soon diminish. After 1989, the choice for EU governments became either a common EU policy on immigration or tougher national border controls, which threatened to restrain the free movement of citizens while erecting new barriers to trade. More generally, the Union faced powerful incentives to develop common policies on a range of issues related to Eastern Europe. The furious row which ensued after France blocked proposals in 1991 to open EU markets to East European agricultural producers was indicative. The incident generated ill will in the East and caused considerable upset in Washington before the French eventually relented.

Table 4.2 East and West European labour costs (manufacturing sector, $ per hour in 1993)

West Germany	24.9
Belgium	21.0
EU Average	15.1
UK	12.4
Portugal	4.7
Slovenia	2.8
Hungary	1.9
Poland	1.4
Czech Republic	1.2
Slovakia	1.2
Romania	0.7

Source: adapted from PMI (1994: 21)

New competition from the East threatened to split the EU along North–South lines in the absence of agreements at a high political level to support fledgling economies and the democracy-building process in Eastern Europe. Even Portugal, which had the lowest manufacturing labour costs in the EU, found its producers overmatched by low-wage competition from Eastern Europe (see Table 4.2). In short, the EU's trade, economic aid, internal security and foreign policies are uniquely inseparable in its relations with Eastern Europe.

The domestic politics of European Union

The negotiations surrounding the Maastricht Treaty illustrated clearly how domestic political conflict feeds into EU bargaining. Traditionally, support for European unity has been strong in Italy. In 1991, its government pushed hard for a strong commitment to EMU as well as for new common policies on industry, consumer protection, health, education and assistance to poorer regions.

Above all, Italy's government sought to use the Maastricht summit to distract attention from its acute domestic political problems. The impression of Italian leadership at the EU level became a way to divert attention from calls for domestic constitutional reform and the dismantling of the spoils system upon which mainstream political parties had built their power bases. Support for the governing Christian Democrats and Socialists evaporated as the Lombard League, an upstart regional movement, notched up stunning electoral gains by accusing Rome of misgovernment and 'milking' the prosperous North to subsidize the underdeveloped South. Within a few years, both the two main Italian negotiators at Maastricht, the Prime Minister Andreotti and the Foreign Minister, Gianni de Michelis, faced serious corruption charges. Their longstanding and fervent support for European unity tainted the EU in the minds of many Italians. By late 1994, the Italian government included the anti-EU and neo-fascist National Alliance as well as Umberto Bossi, the leader of the Lombard League, who memorably declared that a 'multi-cultural society is hell' (see Eatwell 1994).

Domestic politics in France also were transformed by Maastricht and its aftermath. François Mitterrand tried to use the Maastricht summit to help rescue the French Socialist Party from its chronic decline in opinion polls. Mitterrand claimed that the agreement on the internal security pillar was a European solution to France's immigration problem. A new Treaty reference to the West European Union (WEU) as an 'integral part of the development of the EU' was presented as a diplomatic victory for France, whose troops remained outside NATO's integrated command.

In the minds of many French voters, the EU and the Maastricht Treaty both became associated with Mitterrand himself, who played a major role in the Union's development during his fourteen years in office. After Danish voters rejected the Maastricht Treaty in June 1992, Mitterrand put the Treaty before French voters in a referendum designed to demonstrate the strength of popular support for the EU in France. The plan backfired with near-disastrous results: many of the 49 per cent of French voters who voted *non* were expressing their distaste for Mitterrand as much as their opposition to the Maastricht Treaty.

Compared to Italy or France, support for European unity has always been weak in the UK. The Major government had to be particularly mindful of British public opinion at Maastricht with a domestic election only months away. Polls taken in late 1991 suggested that 58 per cent of Britons opposed a single currency and 63 per cent were against a 'political union'.[13]

Major returned home with a British 'opt in' clause on EMU, modest increases in the powers of the EP and Commission, and a bizarre agreement allowing the UK to 'opt out' of social policies which were mandatory for other member states. His claim that the outcome of the summit had been 'game, set and match to Britain' strengthened him domestically as he led his party to victory in the 1992 UK general election. However, by end of the year Major faced political humiliation when his economic policy was undermined by a sterling crisis and the British pound had to be withdrawn from the EMS. Deep splits opened up within the UK Conservative Party between nominally pro-EU and fiercely 'Euro-sceptic' factions. As his popularity ratings sank lower than those of any other UK Prime Minister in history, Major (1993: 27) took tough anti-EU positions, insisting that the Union had to remain 'a union of sovereign national states'.

In Germany, Kohl was pressured by cross-party consensus on the need to increase the EP's powers and make the EU a true parliamentary democracy. With support from the UK and smaller member states, the French resisted the German agenda. Kohl settled for new EP veto (or 'co-decision') powers on a range of EU policies, including those related to the single market. Although he tried to portray the Maastricht Treaty as a good result for Germany, support for the EU – and particularly for EMU – declined sharply in Germany.

German enthusiasm for empowering the EP and creating a 'federalist Europe' more generally stoked a wider debate about the nature of the EU as a political system. The EP remained weak, the Commission unelected, and the Council of Ministers a secretive cabal. The EU's general lack of democratic legitimacy became a more urgent concern as the Union's powers increased (Pinder 1991b; Williams 1991). In Austria, where a resounding 'yes' to EU membership was recorded in a 1994 referendum, fewer than 40 per cent of Austrians said they would vote the same way in 1995. It became difficult to imagine that diffuse support for European unity could be maintained if the EU continued to accrue powers without becoming a more open, democratic political system.

Part of the problem was that much of the 'European project' – to create a more united, richer and powerful EU – seemed utopian without further transfers of national powers to Brussels. As Marquand (1994: 19) argued, 'the nation-states of the Union have already surrendered too much power to supranational institutions to implement it on the national level, while the institutions of the Union will continue to be too weak to implement it on the supranational level'.

Another problem was the EU's inability to meet the high expectations of the US and the rest of the world. During the Cold War, at least for Hinsley (1989: 1), the EU was the 'loosest of loose confederations', lacking all the basic attributes of a sovereign state. After 1989, external pressures pushed the EU to consider developing these attributes – a single foreign office, intelligence service and military – but all were still years away from existence.

Even if the EU still lacks a 'common' foreign policy, it does nevertheless stand for something in international affairs: the consolidation of democratic government in Europe. In the eyes of the world, and particularly Washington, 'Europe is, indeed, becoming recognizable as a polity even if it is not a sovereign entity. It is a polity characterized by universal agreement that the price of admission and of continued membership is constitutional democratic government' (Ullman 1991: 145–6).

Yet the EU is highly *undemocratic* in many respects. The new internal security and CFSP pillars give it more scope for developing common positions in areas ripe for cooperation with the US. But they give the Commission and EP no genuine powers to scrutinize policies hatched between governments meeting in secret. The pillars illustrate the continued propensity of European governments to pool resources without pooling accountability.

The undemocratic nature of the EU is part of a wider problem. After 1993, European citizens actually expressed more dissatisfaction with the way that democracy worked at national than at the EU level (Shackleton 1994: 7). Popular attitudes towards the Union at least remained stable: 57 per cent of EU voters still expressed a 'positive feeling about membership' (Commission 1995c: 3). It is perhaps worth recalling Milward's (1992) insight that the Community was originally created to 'rescue' weak, insecure and war-ravaged national states and to make them more legitimate and effective. The same trick might work today, if the end of the Cold War had not had the apparent effect of making European citizens less tolerant of diversions from democratic ideals.

It remains difficult to democratize the EU because it is characterized by a distinctive type of multi-level bargaining (Peterson 1995). Putnam's (1988: 434) model of 'two-level games' is apt: 'on occasion ... clever players will spot a move on one board that will trigger realignments on other boards, enabling them to achieve otherwise unachievable objectives'. National governments often use the EU to 'Europeanize' domestic problems and make them less intractable. This strategy allows governments to shift the policy-making process from the national to the EU level, where domestic political pressures are weaker and do not constrain as much.

Foreign policies became 'Europeanized' in significant respects from the early 1970s. The European Political Cooperation (EPC) mechanism was created to allow member states to 'coordinate' their foreign policies within a closed circle of EU foreign ministers far removed from domestic politics. Compared with the US foreign policy process, the EPC allowed less input from a far narrower set of interests.

More recently, the ability of governments to use the EU to 'hide' from domestic political pressures has eroded. After Maastricht, it became obvious that governments in a number of EU states – France, Ireland, Germany and, especially, Denmark – had failed to build a solid domestic consensus in support of the Treaty. For his part, Kohl was forced to grant the German *Länder,* or individual states, new powers to co-determine key aspects of German EU policy to ensure ratification of Maastricht by the *Bundesrat,* the German upper house of Parliament, where the *Länder* are represented. Florian Gerster, the Minister for Europe from Rhineland-Palatinate, argued that, 'we are no longer talking about German foreign policy, but European domestic policy'. The Social Democratic leader of Hesse, Hans Eichel, insisted that in future 'European politics will be seen as domestic rather than foreign politics'.[14]

Most EU policies remain a product of bargains between national elites. Polls in 1995 showed that only 17 per cent of Europeans were even aware that another intergovernmental conference was planned for 1996 (Commission 1995c: 2). Yet an expanded number of EU bargains have increasingly perceptible impacts on the social and economic lives of ordinary citizens. The ability of EU governments both to justify this system of policy-making and to sustain diffuse support for the European project became subject to new doubts in the 1990s. The EU risked undermining its image as a guardian of democratic government in Europe by leaving the 'democratic deficit' largely untouched at Maastricht.

In debates about the EU's future, ardent federalists argued that, 'we should never forget: whole peoples can be rallied around symbols' (Gazzo 1991). Throughout the post-war period, EU elites often used the symbolic force of European unity to legitimize policies they could not otherwise 'sell' at home. Declining popular support for the ideal of European unity generally and the EU specifically in the 1990s made this ploy less viable.

In foreign policy, the EU has clear incentives to present a single, unified face to the rest of the world in the twenty-first century, if for no other reason than to cooperate with, rather than kowtow to, the Americans. But foreign policies inevitably touch on sensitive questions of national sovereignty and identity. A CFSP made in isolation from European citizens is unsustainable for very long.

3 MANAGING DOMESTIC POLITICAL INPUTS

As the line separating foreign from domestic policy has blurred, US and EU elites have had to cope with a wider array of pressures being brought to bear on foreign policy. Asserting political control over an expanded number of domestic agencies which now have an interest in foreign policy has become a particularly challenging task. The management of domestic political inputs into US and EU foreign policies has become a more crucial prerequisite of stable bilateral relations.

The Bush administration came to office determined to control the US foreign policy-making machinery. The choice of Baker as Secretary of State reflected Bush's determination to subject the State Department to firm political direction and overcome its tendencies towards 'elitism, aloofness and arrogance' (Dumbrell with Barret 1990: 102). As Baker had served in a variety of key posts under Reagan and had managed Bush's election campaign, his political weight and access to the President were unchallenged. The State Department kept a firm grip on policy towards the EU.

The picture under the Clinton administration was less clear-cut. On the one hand, Clinton's Secretary of State, Warren Christopher, was primarily a Middle East specialist with relatively little knowledge of Europe. His access to the President was limited by Clinton's focus on domestic policy. On the other, Clinton's first ambassador to the EU, Stuart Eizenstat, was a Washington insider and political heavyweight. His fingerprints were perceptible on Clinton's first speech on European soil, which declared that, 'the new security must be found in Europe's integration . . . [I] assure you that America will be a strong partner in it'.[15] The appointment in 1994 of Richard Holbrooke, a respected and experienced diplomat, as the head of the State Department's European desk gave greater coherence and predictability to American EU policy. One of Holbrooke's deputies insisted that, 'this administration has been more supportive of European integration than any since Kennedy's'.[16]

However, the administration's control of the foreign policy agenda became tenuous after Republican majorities took over Congress in 1994. By mid-1995 Dole had made good on his longstanding threat to seek a Congressional vote to abrogate the UN arms embargo on the former Yugoslavia. In a rare show of European unity, all fifteen EU member states condemned the action on the grounds that it unilaterally imposed a misguided US 'solution' in the Balkans. Clinton could do no more than threaten a veto that Congress appeared capable of overturning. More generally, Bosnia illustrated Putnam's (1993: 71) maxim that 'credible international threats must also win domestic approval'. The Bosnian Serbs could ignore Western threats for most of the war, safe in the knowledge that there was no domestic consensus for substantial US involvement.

On the EU's side, the CFSP remained an amalgam of national foreign policies. The Union lacked a 'foreign ministry' and the EP had little influence over the CFSP. However, the Commission's management of the Union's external trade policy made it an important player in US–EU relations, particularly given the EU's lack of a Council of Trade Ministers. DG I often found itself caught between national tendencies towards free trade and protectionism. If the EU had any strategy for the Uruguay Round, it was unclear precisely what it was (Pelkmans and Murphy 1991).

Still, the Commission attracted admiration in Washington and other foreign capitals for its willingness to face up to Mediterranean EU countries which lacked liberal trade policy traditions (Sandholtz and Zysman 1989: 126). In particular, DG I pressured member states to acknowledge that the CAP was no longer worth defending if it meant the breakdown of the Uruguay Round.

Ironically, there is no analogous, integrated US agency for managing domestic political inputs into trade negotiations. As Vernon (1989: 9) argues:

> Americans place a high value on the diffusion of bureaucratic power and on the participation of the public in policy-making. At the same time, they prefer an international economic environment that is open – and stable. American negotiators, in consequence, are supported by a fragmented decision-making structure that was never designed to shape and implement foreign economic policies.

The EU's own behaviour has been conditioned by the frequent inability of the US executive to deliver on its trade policy commitments (Grieco 1990). To illustrate the point, the 1988 Trade Act was the product of over forty Congressional subcommittees, most of which were lobbied intensely by sectoral trade interests. Of course, mandates given to DG I by EU member states prior to trade negotiations are products of hard bargaining between national interests. But US trade policy is often even more events-driven and politically-derived than EU trade policy.

The Transatlantic Declaration was accepted by the EU largely because it was viewed as a means for ensuring that the Union was consulted prior to the emergence of new US trade legislation in Congress. As a US State Department official put it, early consultation 'doesn't really help on long-standing issues like Airbus and agriculture'.[17] However, an 'early warning system' at the sub-cabinet level, unveiled in 1994, facilitated a 'somewhat quieter dialogue' on thorny issues such as procurement and FDI.[18]

The Transatlantic Declaration committed the US administration to two cabinet-level 'round table meetings' with the Commission each year. While these meetings did not always take place or were 'outflanked' by meetings held at a higher political level, the number of bilateral 'panels of experts' expanded considerably. For example, US enthusiasm for the creation of a Joint Task Force on Biotechnology was a product of a long-running bilateral dispute over an EU ban on exports of American beef treated with growth hormones (Peterson 1989). The Bush administration hoped the Task Force would conclude that the ban was a desperate measure designed to cope with the EU's domestic beef surpluses rather than a product of legitimate consumer safety concerns. A Commission official claimed,

> It was [the USTR Carla] Hills' idea to set up the biotechnology group to be a political group which the US could use to beat the EU over the head. But the scientists within it were outraged by the idea and hijacked it. They just wanted to talk about biotechnology research.[19]

A separate Joint Consultative Group (JCG) on Science and Technology was created in 1990. It became a 'useful channel for discussing, in an informal framework, important subjects which it would not be possible to treat as effectively in a broader, more public setting' (Commission 1991a: 7). Agreements were reached within the JCG on exchanges between partners in the EU's collaborative JESSI project and the US Sematech project, both of which were engaged in extremely expensive R&D to develop the next generation of computer chips.

DG I officials contended that such low-key exchanges were 'the iceberg of which the tip is the ministerial meetings set out in the Transatlantic Declaration'.[20] Increased exchange between experts created a web of joint dialogues which were depoliticized and removed from domestic pressures. They became potential facilitators of broader agreements at higher political levels.

In foreign policy, joint exchanges after 1990 established a 'culture of cooperation', despite the absence of a formal treaty. A diplomat with considerable experience of the EPC claimed:

> We've become very open toward the US about our agendas and the [EU] Presidency now briefs the US after all the major meetings. We also brief other countries but the usual pattern is that most of the other countries are taken as a group and the US is briefed separately. . . . Our relations with the US are on a different plane. But that's not the sort of thing one would formally say.[21]

Despite stronger bilateral relations, American expectations of the EU often remained unmet. Europe's disunity in foreign policy was usually a consequence of the inability or refusal of EU governments to buck domestic public opinion for the sake of a common European policy. Examples included Belgium's refusal to sell arms to the UK during the Gulf War and Germany's unilateral recognition of the independence of Slovenia and Croatia. The EU's behaviour during the Gulf War and the Bosnian conflict fuelled isolationist impulses in Congress. The argument became: 'The EU is richer and stronger now. Why should we help them when they will not help themselves?'

The degree to which Western foreign policies have been 'democratized' is easily exaggerated. Usually, foreign policies are products of bureaucratic competition more than outcomes of open domestic political debates. For some, the sharper focus of the US Congress on domestic problems during the Clinton years 'reinforced the inherently elitist nature of foreign policy-making' (Latter 1994: 6–7). Arguably, the CFSP made it easier for EU governments to 'hide' from domestic pressures when they made foreign policy. In the 1990s, as before, pressure groups and public opinion remained important, but rarely decisive factors in foreign policy-making (Eichenberg 1989; Risse-Kappen 1991).

Still, there is no denying that foreign policy perceptions and processes have changed radically since 1989. The Transatlantic Declaration was mostly a response to new geopolitical uncertainties following the demise of the Warsaw Pact. It may also be viewed as an attempt to systematize US-EU relations and thus counterbalance the democratization, and increased volatility, of Western foreign policies in a post-Cold War world.

4 DOMESTIC POLITICS AND INTERNATIONAL RELATIONS THEORY

The primary level of analysis for most theories of international relations is the international system as a whole. The focus of neorealism on systemic factors means that 'sub-systemic' factors – the domestic political forces which shape state preferences – are considered theoretically irrelevant. Neorealists claim that the internal characteristics of states 'drop out' and have little or no effect on their behaviour as international actors:

> Neorealism cuts itself off from theoretical insights by assuming that the preferences of states are derived from location (placement) of the state within the international structure. This structural assumption relieves neorealism of the burden of constructing state preferences from the bottom up, from the preferences and political processes of domestic agents and groups.
>
> (Caporaso 1996: 33)

Neorealists feel exonerated by the EU's recent setbacks and particularly by the apparent derailment of EMU. But they have difficulty explaining why the Union acts with more unity on some issues than others. For many neorealists, the EU is an international organization like most others, not a political system in itself. The 'domestic politics' of European unity – the extent to which governments may appeal to diffuse support for the EU – does not matter in neorealist terms. More generally, neorealists deny that regional integration in Europe has led to a 'domestification of inter-state relations', which in turn makes the international system a bit less like anarchy, a bit more like a constitutionalized domestic polity (Caporaso 1996).

Neorealist assumptions lurk behind the arguments of US isolationists and unilateralists. The former urge that the US must 'accept today's anarchic system of competing nation-states as a given ... US national interests can and must be distinguished from the interests of the inter-national system itself and from those of other states' (Tonelson 1991: 38). One member of the House National Security Committee confesses to being 'a unilateralist in a planning sense: we should not depend solely on coalitions because our friends today may not be our friends tomorrow'.[22] Waltz (1993: 79) muses that 'one may hope that America's internal preoccupations will not produce an isolationist policy. . . . But I would not bet on it.'

Perhaps the most frequent criticism of neorealism is that it is ahistorical. The neorealists' stubborn insistence that domestic politics do not matter makes them vulnerable to the charge that they cannot explain the profound changes of 1989–91:

> Given that international change resulted from the reconstitution of the domestic political systems rather than from systemic factors – *vide* the importance of human rights and democratization leading to a new 'civil society' in Eastern Europe – neorealism had no conceptual apparatus for understanding the nature, scope and direction of change.
>
> (Kratochwil 1993: 63)

Just as neorealists tend to downplay 'sub-systemic factors', the preoccupation of *institutionalists* with international regimes has meant that 'the role of domestic factors [has] slipped more and more out of focus' (Putnam 1988: 431). Institutionalists tend to overestimate the ability of national leaders to bargain with a free hand in international institutions. The bargaining position of the Bush administration within the Uruguay Round was tightly constrained by pressures from Congress and by domestic pressure groups. As a corrective, 'the two-level game approach is not a purely "bottom-up" theory of the domestic roots of foreign policy, for the leader acts with some degree of autonomy. Foreign policy in this view is not constituency driven, but it is constituency constrained' (Putnam 1993: 71).

Institutionalists also tend to assume that political leaders can ignore or override domestic political pressures and change perceptions of the 'national interest' to reflect a more interdependent world. To illustrate the point, the portion of total world exports sold by American corporations in the late 1980s was nearly identical to the portion which they sold in 1966. The difference was that US firms exported far more from operations abroad. Yet US domestic political debates focused on the national trade deficit and the unfair practices of foreign states, not the benefits of an open global system of FDI or the changed behaviour of US firms. Few attempts were made to explain to consumers why buying a Honda helped to reduce the US trade deficit more than buying a Pontiac Le Mans (Reich 1991: 134).

Institutionalism does provide a theoretical base for explaining the move to more institutionalized US–EU relations. The Transatlantic Declaration reflected the need to cope with new uncertainties and more powerful domestic political inputs into foreign policy-making. Institutionalists who focus on 'epistemic communities' stress the importance of new bilateral panels of experts working on specialized issues such as biotechnology, agricultural liberalization or R&D. They help to 'depoliticize' transatlantic relations by forging practical bargains in settings which are removed from domestic political pressures.

However, institutionalists may be criticized for failing to appreciate the domestic political difficulties of managing US–EU relations. Particularly on trade issues, the power of Congress and the individual US states gives rise to a system which 'shortchanges broader interests at the expense of narrower ones, and stalemate becomes more common' (Putnam 1993: 80). The politics of EU external policy may be characterized as a *three-level game* which takes place simultaneously at the global, EU and national levels. The EU's disappointing performance as an external actor is predictable for Putnam (1993: 80), because 'at each stage, the risks posed by veto groups or weak leadership rise exponentially'.

If some institutionalists blithely assume that market pressures can be subordinated to politics within international regimes, *liberals* often assume that politics can be subordinated to markets through free trade. All that is required is political commitment to liberal principles (Humphreys 1990). Yet political leaders clearly cannot nullify protectionist pressures simply by citing economic theories which show that free trade is a positive-sum game.

The naivety of liberals about domestic politics contains a lesson for US and EU policy-makers. Placing bilateral relations in a vacuum where domestic political groups are powerless is impractical and counterproductive. A US State Department official explains:

> You can't say that in the interest of the long-term relationship you won't take action you'd otherwise take on trade issues because over the long haul that's going to ruin and undermine the domestic consensus for the relationship. We'll be viewed as not standing up for our trade rights. So we actually don't trade off trade concessions today for stronger political relations tomorrow that much. The more democratic your system is, the more difficult it is to make that trade-off.[23]

The primary value of liberalism is its insistence that an expanding international economy based on open trade regimes is a prerequisite for stable political relations between industrialized states. A breakdown of the Uruguay Round would have wreaked havoc on US–EU trade for which no amount of agreement on other issues could have compensated. Liberalism points to the reality that bilateral partnership is impossible without relatively open bilateral trade.

The *reformist* axiom of 'think globally, act locally' explicitly links international political outcomes with domestic political action (Alger and Mendlovitz 1987). Reformists argue that transnational threats such as environmental degradation, terrorism and drug trafficking are treated as 'domestic' or 'national' problems, if they are treated at all, when they are in fact shared by many governments and peoples. The reformist's critique of the state is implicit in Halliday's (1994: 237) lament that a 'world of nations' is taken for granted by international relations theorists and foreign policy-makers despite its 'ethical weakness, and nefarious consequences'.

Reformists view national sovereignty as an increasingly artificial and meaningless construction. Yet Western foreign policies guard it jealously. They thus produce piecemeal, ineffectual responses to global problems such as diminishing natural resources through bilateral initiatives, weak intergovernmental compromises or the use of military force. Reformists claim that the 50 per cent increase in US domestic dependence on foreign oil in the 1980s made the Gulf War inevitable (Wald 1990).

Reformists are leading critics of the EU's democratic deficit. Many view the EU as an 'executive committee' which helps the European elite to manage its affairs. They ask:

How long will Euro-proletarians, Euro-professionals, Euro-consumers, Euro-environmentalists, Euro-feminists, Euro-regionalists, Euro-youths, or just plain Euro-citizens tolerate such a 'benevolent' hegemony before demanding a greater voice and vote in the governance of their common affairs, and a greater reliance on public authorities to redress the inequities of private exchange?

(Schmitter 1992: 400)

Reformists insist that Western governments must nurture domestic support for international solutions to global problems. Many viewed the 1992 Rio environmental summit as a litmus test for Western foreign policies. The EU's Environmental Commissioner, Carlo Ripa di Meana, argued for a binding agreement on reducing carbon dioxide (CO_2) levels, the main cause of global warming. Member states resisted proposals for a common EU energy tax on the grounds that it would give competitive advantages to foreign producers. Attempts by the Clinton administration to seek a US energy tax in 1993 ran aground due to Congressional resistance. The only answer for reformists is a global energy tax, but such an initiative remains unthinkable because Western leaders lack the will to convince their domestic publics that it is necessary.

Reformists tend to assume that the democratization of foreign policies is an inherently good thing. Some fail to appreciate that domestic politics and public opinion often act to generate aggressive and uncooperative national responses to foreign events (see Klingberg 1983; Wittkopf 1987). The idea that foreign policies can be based on some type of international morality may be criticized as both ethnocentric and unworldly. However, reformists are on strong ground in arguing that US and EU foreign policies must actually stand for something, such as democratic principles, human rights or environmental protection, if they are to inspire and sustain popular support in a post-Cold War world.

To summarize this chapter, the most glaring weakness of international relations theory, as a body of knowledge, is its inability to cope with the vanishing line between domestic and foreign politics:

> States, as 'decision-makers', are the scene of political conflict that often proves inconclusive.... They are not ... unified and single-purpose decision-makers. State policies are likely to be ambivalent on most issues, and international agreements consist of a complex mixture of cooperative and conflictual behavior.
>
> (Underhill 1994: 24)

US–EU relations cannot be understood without appreciating the growing impact of domestic politics on Western foreign policies. Bilateral cooperation requires policy-makers on both sides who understand the domestic political constraints under which their opposite numbers operate. One team of scholars concludes that many international crises have been exacerbated because political leaders 'only occasionally attempted such assessments and when they tried they did pretty miserably' (Snyder and Diesing 1977: 516). More intensive exchanges between the US and EU in the wake of the Transatlantic Declaration have the potential to head off crises which spring from the exigencies of domestic politics.

More generally, Western leadership in global affairs requires popular support for foreign policies which are seen as promoting peaceful, prosperous and constructive international relations. The US–EU alliance may be better able than any other existing alliance of international actors to defuse the most critical threats to international peace and stability. But ordinary voters need to be shown that the game is worth the candle.

Chapter 5

Trade and monetary relations

Transatlantic economic relations will have crucial implications for the international economy as a whole in the twenty-first century. The power of the Europe and America to dictate the international trade agenda has declined, but the active support of both remains a 'minimum requirement for a viable trading system' (Baldwin 1988: 1). EMU could lead either to intensified coordination of bilateral monetary policies and increased global economic stability, or to 'system friction' as each side pursues its own domestic monetary agenda.

Even if they have become 'core' foreign policy issues, trade and monetary questions remain subject to far more varied and intense domestic pressures than what diplomats call 'straight' foreign policy issues, such as relations within NATO or with Russia. Joint US–EU actions facilitate mutually rewarding economic exchange, but governments on both sides must respond to powerful, diverse and often competing domestic imperatives.

This chapter begins by tracing the recent evolution of US–EU trade and monetary relations in section 1. The Uruguay Round of the GATT is the focus for section 2. Section 3 examines the implications for bilateral relations of the economic challenge posed by Japan. The assumptions of the four theories of international relations on trade and monetary questions are contrasted in section 4.

1 KEY ISSUES IN TRADE AND MONETARY RELATIONS

Transatlantic trade or monetary disputes can only be understood in the context of the broader state of bilateral political relations at the time they take place. The legendary 'chicken war' of 1962–3 involved very low volumes of trade but was a microcosm of heightened tensions after the creation of the CAP. In the mid-1960s, de Gaulle responded to US plans to monopolize NATO's nuclear strategy by ordering French banks to sell vast amounts of dollars in order to undermine the currency's value.

Squabbles over trade and monetary issues have been most acrimonious in times of global economic downturn. During the period of the Nixon shocks or the recession of the 1980s, macroeconomic and monetary policy coordination broke down, thus provoking trade imbalances and atmospheres of mutual recrimination. In particular, the tensions of the Reagan years resonated for long afterwards. His administration's single-minded focus on lowering inflation and increasing national defence spending allowed little room for policy coordination with EU governments. US macroeconomic policy stimulated rates of domestic economic growth which were far higher than those in Europe. Foreign investors rushed to take advantage of superior American growth at a time of tight US monetary policies. The combined effect was to force up the value of the dollar.

Thus, US exports became less competitive and the trade deficit mushroomed. The US balance of trade with the EU shifted from a surplus of $14 billion in 1981 to a deficit of nearly $23 billion by 1986. Despite European protests that the bilateral deficit was a direct result of Reagan's economic policies, the period brought substantial actual and threatened increases in US trade barriers (McCulloch 1988).

Tensions eased somewhat after 1985. With the overall US deficit in decline (see Table 5.1), the Trade Act passed by Congress in 1988 was less protectionist than many in the EU and elsewhere had feared. It also delegated to the US executive – where the EU carries far more weight – substantial powers to design its own strategy for the Uruguay Round (Spero 1989). Trade relations improved after 1990 when the US actually recorded a surplus *vis-à-vis* the EU.

Table 5.1 US trade balances 1986–94 (current $ billion)

	1986	1988	1990	1991	1992	1993	1994
Total	−142	−117	−95	−67	−85	−116	−151
With EU	− 23	− 10	6	17	9	−1	−8

Sources: Harrison (1994, 1995); USTR (1995a)

In retrospect, it was clear that the 1988 Trade Act's Super 301 clause marked a distinct shift in US trade policy. Previously, post-war American policy had been based on the principle of 'generalized reciprocity': the notion that a level playing field should be sought across a full range of sectors through multilateral negotiations and common rules of process. Super 301 reflected a new emphasis on 'specific' reciprocity: singling out individual US trading partners who engaged in unfair trade in specific sectors. US trade policy became rooted in the assumption that 'trade is fair when the outcomes are balanced, and outcomes – not process – are the core of discussion' (Sandholtz and Zysman 1989: 124). Super 301 was designed as a political weapon to be used in trade diplomacy.

Super 301 may have helped to extract some concessions from Japan, as reflected in 'framework agreements' on US–Japanese trade in 1994. However, recent evidence suggests that the broader Section 301 of the 1974 Trade Act, which was amended by Super 301, generated only $4–5 billion in additional US exports in the first half of the 1990s (Bayard and Elliott 1994). Super 301 almost certainly changed the composition more than the volume of US exports. The primary culprit for the national trade deficit was the federal budget deficit: this, not trade policy or unfair practices by US competitors, kept levels of American savings and investment low.

Many gloomy forecasts about the dire consequences of the US trade and budget deficits failed to come true. Economists noted that the combined value of all US debt would fall as a share of total GDP as long as the country's economy continued to grow (Eisner 1986). But 'feel-good' analyses of the twin deficits obscured the root causes and long-term consequences of US debt. Before he joined the Clinton administration, Reich (1991: 265) argued that:

> There is nothing terribly wrong with being indebted to foreigners – so long as the borrowings are invested in factories, schools, roads, and other means of enhancing future production. In fact, taking on debt for these purposes is preferable to maintaining a balanced budget by deferring or cutting back on such investments. Debt is only a problem if the money is squandered on consumption.

The 1980s were a decade of enormous consumtive squandering in the US. Investment fell from 8 to 5 per cent of American GNP. US domestic savings dwindled from a post-war average of 6.5 per cent of GNP to less than 3 per cent. The twin deficits reflected a consumption binge financed largely by borrowing, and marked by a huge inflow of goods and capital from abroad.

For their part, EU countries suffered from 'capital flight' as European investors took advantage of high US interest rates and consumption-led economic growth. Low levels of European investment heightened the severity of the 1981–2 recession in the Union. From the EU's perspective, the 'Eurosclerosis' of the period was largely a consequence of US macroeconomic and monetary policies. European governments faced up to the hard reality that their economies could be hostages to decisions made in Washington over which they had little influence. The experience contributed to renewed political interest in moving towards a full EMU.

Disentangling the US interest in EMU is difficult. On one hand, EMU could reduce the role of the US dollar as an international unit of exchange or 'reserve currency', and empower the EU in negotiations on monetary policy coordination. The dollar's post-war status as a reserve currency gave the US unparalleled opportunities for expanding its global economic, political and military influence because close relations with the US brought foreign states the most commonly accepted unit of international exchange. It also made other nations more tolerant of American balance of payments deficits since these acted to pump money into the international economy that could be used by any country for foreign exchange. These advantages would come under threat if a common European currency emerged as an alternative reserve currency.

On the other hand, large American MNCs would be advantaged by a single currency. The value of sales by US firms with direct investments in Europe is far higher than the value of US exports to the EU. American multinationals with European assets would benefit, as would all who do business across borders in Europe, from a single currency.

Like the 1992 project itself, EMU is a highly political project which is perceived by many of its advocates as a litmus test of Europe's will to unite. The creation of the internal market accelerated European political integration because increased trade required harmonized regulations and strengthened powers for EU institutions. EMU has the potential to propel the development of a true political union. Not only does it promise a single monetary policy, central bank and an EU which speaks with one voice in international monetary diplomacy. Perhaps more importantly, the advantages on offer to member states which are part of a single currency give the EU an important means of disciplining violators of its rules (Pelkmans 1995).

The political symbolism of EMU is well-understood within the State Department. However, the Treasury Department takes a different and decidedly dim view of EMU:

> We're not concerned that much about EMU and ultimately we want greater economic growth in Europe. . . . But there is a US concern about the fiscal drag of EMU, and the large amounts needed for redistribution or convergence in order to make it work. We see an analogy with German unification, which put things out of whack for quite a while. And we also see a pretty simple trade-off between a single currency and lower unemployment.[1]

The latter point is supported by economic evidence: higher taxes and spending cuts needed for member states to meet the convergence criteria could cost up to 1.5 million jobs (Barrell *et al.* 1995). The unanswered question of how non-participant EU states would relate to those which *did* join a single currency led the EU to launch a study in 1995 to assess the potential damage to the economies of member states left 'out in the cold'.

EMU also has the potential to strain transatlantic relations. The early 1990s saw the US adopt a policy of benign neglect of the dollar, even 'talking it down' at several points, to try to stoke a domestic economic revival. One effect was to exacerbate tensions within the EMS (Smith and Woolcock 1993: 103). In short, the US cannot remain agnostic about EMU.

By the same token, friction is never entirely absent from US–EU trade relations. In 1995, after the US trade balance had deteriorated again, the USTR launched a fresh Section 301 action targeted at the EU's controversial regime for favouring banana producers in former European colonies. More generally, trade relations remained complicated by lingering uncertainties about the actual effects of the 1992 project on transatlantic trade.

A good example is product standards and testing. The principle of 'mutual recognition' of national standards, which became a central cornerstone of the internal market programme, prompted considerable concern in the US. Under this principle any product made in the EU could be sold throughout the internal market if it satisfied the standards of any single member state. Thus if beer made in France satisfied French standards, it could not be excluded from the German market even if it did not conform to seventeenth-century German laws on the purity of ingredients. Since mutual recognition implied a minimum level of harmonization of national standards, fears arose that EU standards would become stricter and discriminate against US exporters (Zupnick 1991).

In 1989 the US Secretary of Commerce, Robert Mosbacher, made his famous request for 'a seat at the table' in European standards-setting, most of which took place within the intergovernmental forum of CEN/CENELEC. A representative of CEN/CENELEC recalled:

> Mosbacher was frank, almost brutally so. He said, 'We want to be in.' We told him that was impossible. We did say we could develop a procedure for notification, but one that was not just for the USA, but was open to the rest of the world. We developed a mechanism for that, and in the end, they came away very pleased.[2]

The mechanism gave the American National Standards Institute (ANSI) input into European standards development. ANSI reciprocated by allowing European representation in its own discussions on new standards. Mosbacher declared that the arrangement 'was open and transparent' and that it 'at times, allowed literally a seat' for US interests.[3] Yet standards remained a source of transatlantic tension. The US government did little to ensure that national standards regimes kept up with market developments or that the country's industry respected agreed international standards (Woolcock 1991: 92–110).

From the EU's point of view, the standards issue was typical of a general schizophrenia in American trade policy. The Bush administration insisted that the Union had to adopt 'specific reciprocity', and liberalize its markets in sectors such as telecommunications, as the US had done in the

1980s. In others, such as banking, the US demanded that the Union extend 'national treatment', and treat American banks the same as European banks, even though the American market was far more heavily restricted than the EU's (Commission 1991c: 66–71).

When US trade policy appears schizophrenic, it is usually due to interest-group politics or institutional rivalries (or both) in Washington. The USTR must constantly watch its back in trade negotiations to ensure that what is agreed is not torpedoed by Congress. In contrast, even if EU member states try to keep it on a short lead, the Commission is subject to far less legislative scrutiny or industrial lobbying compared with the USTR (Woolcock 1990; Pelkmans and Murphy 1991; Wallace 1992).

These differences helped to explain the respective priorities of the US and EU for the Uruguay Round. The Union wanted an agreement which could bring European producers benefits across a wide range of sectors over the long term. Meanwhile, the Bush administration needed to deliver 'more dollars in the cash registers of US exporters' (Woolcock 1991: 23), and to do it quickly.

2 THE GATT

The Uruguay Round was the most ambitious in the GATT's history. It sought to develop rules-based, mandatory regimes for resolving trade disputes across a far wider range of sectors than had ever been subject to international rules before. From an early stage in the Round, it became clear that its outcome would have critical implications for the future of the global trading order.

The importance of the Uruguay Round for transatlantic relations was almost impossible to overestimate. The US and EU had often clashed with great acrimony within the GATT. After the EU became a full member in 1960 nearly one-third of all unfair trade disputes mediated by the GATT stemmed from complaints brought by the US or EU against the other (Hudec 1988).

The Union's primary goal in the Uruguay Round was to stop the drift towards unilateralism in American trade policy. EU exports to the US remained far more broadly based than American exports to Europe, which were dominated by a few products such as agricultural produce and aircraft. The EU pushed for broad agreements to subject far more sectors to stricter GATT rules. New regimes were sought on trade in services, public procurement, intellectual property rights (covering patents and standards) and public subsidies to domestic industries.

Problematically for the EU, the 1992 project touched on many of these same issues. Its provisions for liberalizing the internal market often went beyond what was required under the pre-Uruguay Round rules of the GATT, thus leading to a sort of 'unilateral disarmament' (Woolcock 1990:

7; Kreinin 1991: 70–1). For the United States, the importance of the Uruguay Round was accentuated as it became clear that its outcome could either reinforce the Union's commitment to liberalization or encourage it to design new barriers to US access to the internal market.

The Uruguay Round fuelled scepticism in Washington about the ability of the EU to implement the 1992 project without bowing to protectionist pressures. The GATT secretariat roundly criticized the EU in 1990 for its heavy reliance on anti-dumping measures, or penalties imposed on countries accused of expanding their export market shares by selling goods below their cost. The Union's reticence on agriculture acted to undermine its relatively liberal stance on other issues as the Round proceeded.

By late 1991 the US had given much ground on its original ambitions for the Round. The GATT's Secretary-General, Arthur Dunkel, tried to force the pace of negotiations by giving delegates a clear deadline by which draft agreements on services, patents and most other key issues needed to be tabled. The deadline passed with no drafts submitted. One diplomat observed, 'Everyone is waiting for agriculture.'[4]

The agricultural dispute had been festering for years. The US showed considerable leadership in helping to create a relatively open post-war international trade regime. However, rules were often bent to protect US farmers. For example, the United States exploited loopholes in GATT rules in the mid-1950s and imposed import quotas on sugar, cheese and beef. Such actions were cited often by EU trade negotiators when the CAP was criticized by the Americans (Destler 1986: 32).

Still, the damage done by the CAP to American agricultural exports was unambiguous. Each enlargement of the Union acted to lower sales of US farm goods to Europe. For example, the EU bought 21 per cent of all American agricultural exports in 1985, but only 15 per cent by the early 1990s (Harrison 1994: 5). The US continued to run a small, perennial trade surplus with the EU in agriculture. But the Union persisted in spending nearly ten times more than the United States on export subsidies, which acted to oversupply markets, drive down global prices and reduce the incomes of American farmers. The US insisted that the elimination of all CAP subsidies would raise the American surplus in agricultural trade by more than $6 billion (USTR 1991: 67).

The Bush administration worked hard to isolate the EU on agriculture in the Uruguay Round. A solid alliance was forged with the 'Cairns group' of other agricultural exporters such as Canada, Argentina and Australia. The US even secured informal assurances from Japan that it would relax its longstanding import restrictions on rice once a US–EU agreement was secured. The period showed that the US would not hesitate to work with other trading partners to try to persuade or force the EU to accept the American trade agenda.

Several EU member states – particularly France – firmly rejected cuts in agricultural subsidies of the magnitude demanded by the US. While the Commission pushed hard for lowered CAP spending, it allied with the French in arguing that it made little sense to hold an agreement on trade in services hostage to US farming interests. Trade in services was worth far more than agricultural trade and accounted for about a quarter of total world trade by the early 1990s (Drake and Nicolaïdis 1992: 37). Basic telecommunications services alone were worth as much as $320 billion per year. Free trade in this sector had the potential to promote increased cross-border trade in a wide range of service industries such as banking (Sapir 1988).

A deal on services became the EU's highest priority. In particular, it pushed hard to have telecommunications included in a wider services agreement. The US position was that publicly owned European telephone companies should be covered by a new GATT code, but that US telephone companies, such as regional 'Baby Bells', should not. A USTR representative explained,

> The degree to which telecoms is included depends on the extent of the commitment made to the liberalization of telecoms services by our trading partners. . . . We'd prefer to have telecoms services in a general services agreement. But we're not going to put it in if nobody else is opening their markets to the degree that we have.[5]

US stubbornness on telecommunications and other trade issues reflected the need to satisfy a Congress which had become predisposed to 'fair trade' principles, and sceptical of the entire GATT process (Woolcock 1990: 14). By 1991, the Commission appeared to realize that it was staring the death of the Uruguay Round in the face. The Commissioner for Agriculture, Ray MacSharry, submitted proposals for substantial (in some respects radical) reform of the CAP. The MacSharry Plan formed the basis for discussions within both the EU and the GATT over the next year.

Meanwhile, significant progress was made in the long-running dispute over subsidies to the European Airbus programme. A tentative settlement emerged in 1992 that led the US to drop a complaint it had prepared to bring before the GATT. The agreement showed that the US and EU could solve a very complex dispute at a sensitive point in the GATT process.

By this time, intensive contacts between the Bush administration and the Commission appeared to put a GATT deal within reach. In a letter to Delors, Bush proposed a new compromise between the US and EU positions on agriculture. A month later, EU national farm ministers approved the most far-reaching restructuring of the CAP since its origins. Although watered down from MacSharry's original proposal, the plan promised price reductions of nearly 30 per cent for cereals and 15 per cent for beef and poultry.

No settlement to the Uruguay Round was possible without a complex package deal between the US and EU which embodied almost countless compromises across a wide range of issues. Balances had to be struck between the views of a dizzying array of specialized agencies and domestic economic interests on both sides. No deal was possible without brokering at the very highest political levels. These circumstances acted to heighten the importance of more intensive US–EU political interactions in the wake of the Transatlantic Declaration.

To illustrate the point, the Clinton administration became distracted by its domestic battle to ratify NAFTA in late 1993, and essentially stopped negotiating within the GATT. Amidst fears that the US had lost interest in a GATT deal, a meeting held under the terms of the Transatlantic Declaration on 1 November brought together the EU's Trade Commissioner, Leon Brittan, with Delors, Christopher and the USTR, Kantor. It yielded critical progress on the GATT and was a milestone on the road to an eventual settlement to the Uruguay Round.

When states negotiate with one another, the most important discussions usually take place at lower bureaucratic levels on technical, nitty-gritty details. Representatives of leading agencies such as the Commission and USTR tend to play down the importance of high-level summitry and broad political declarations. However, officials from both, working on the front line of the GATT negotiations, admitted that transatlantic summits, such as the 1991 meeting in The Hague, were crucial in pushing the Uruguay Round towards resolution:

> That meeting in the Hague was very helpful. . . . From our standpoint, we knew that Bush was very much personally involved in the Round. . . . But our feeling was that The Hague summit did engage Delors to a degree we felt he had not been engaged, particularly on agriculture. We knew we'd get nowhere on the issue without the personal engagement of Delors.[6]

> The reason that meeting was so useful was because it was timely. The Uruguay Round had just been discussed within the G-7 and the EU was already moving on agriculture. But it's true that the trade dossiers were considered in more detail at The Hague at higher political levels than ever before. . . . That meeting did a lot to 'deconstipate' the whole process.[7]

No outcome to the Uruguay Round was ever going to be a panacea for US–EU relations. The price demanded by Congress for its approval of the GATT Treaty was a series of measures which put the American commitment to the new World Trade Organization (WTO) – the post-

Uruguay Round successor to the GATT – into question. The GATT's conflict resolution procedures operated on the basis of unanimity, thus allowing any side in a dispute to block any punitive measures. By contrast, parties to the WTO agreed to try to maintain consensus, but to opt for majority decisions when unanimity was impossible (see Devuyst 1995).

Congressional Republicans, led by Senator Robert Dole, voiced alarm about the threat posed to US sovereignty by the WTO, and initiated a debate which in some respects resembled Europe's struggle to ratify Maastricht. In exchange for Congressional approval of the WTO, the Clinton administration agreed to a range of safeguard clauses, including the creation of a panel of US judges to review all WTO decisions. If the panel – popularly known as the 'Dole commission' – found that the WTO had acted arbitrarily against American interests in three cases, Congress could instruct the President to withdraw the US from the WTO.

Clinton administration officials downplayed the importance of the concessions. A senior USTR adviser insisted that 'the process will be managed at the highest political level. We'll make sure that the Dole Commission only looks at very "big" issues.'[8] Yet, in the trade row over car parts, the US threatened Japan with unilateral sanctions which were almost certainly illegal under WTO rules. Trade experts lambasted Clinton for a trade policy which threatened to do 'grave and lasting damage' to the WTO (J. H. Jackson 1995).

The stakes were higher by this time because the Uruguay Round had freed more trade than any previous GATT deal in history. The WTO offered extended coverage of trade rules and stronger and more efficient dispute settlement procedures. From the EU's perspective, one of the most important outcomes of the Uruguay Round was that more Section 301 cases were likely to be submitted to the WTO dispute settlement process. Two possible, though not certain, effects were that the WTO's credibility in the United States stood to be enhanced if it sanctioned retaliation against unfair trade practices, and that the general unilateralism of US trade policy would diminish.

In this context, an early show of EU commitment to the WTO was critical. The Union had a clear interest in encouraging the development of a strong body of WTO 'case law'. More generally, it was hard to imagine a US–EU partnership without a strong and authoritative WTO.

3 MEETING THE JAPANESE CHALLENGE

In terms of both trade and investment flows, the US and EU's economies are far more interlinked than is either with Japan's. By the mid-1990s annual transatlantic trade was worth more than $210 billion. US trade with Japan was worth less than $160 billion and EU–Japanese trade barely reached $85 billion (Commission 1994: 310–13; Harrison 1995). Crucially, transatlantic trade remained relatively balanced. Despite its huge volume and disputes over specific products such as bananas, the overwhelming majority of US–EU trade took place without incident (see Commission 1995d).

In contrast, trade with Japan remained highly politicized and emotionally charged in both the US and EU. The perceived need of each to take a tough line with Japan often spilled over into US–EU trade relations. For example, the long and acrimonious row over the EU's ban on hormone-treated beef affected only about $100 million in annual US exports. However, the US refused to dismantle retaliatory sanctions against the EU for fear that Japan might be encouraged to backpedal on its commitment to open its market to imports of American beef.

The US and EU often found it difficult to aim measures at Japan without upsetting transatlantic trade and investment. The point was illustrated clearly in the debate on FDI in the US. The total global value of FDI expanded by nearly 30 per cent annually in the late 1980s. One effect was that a higher share of US businesses became controlled by foreign investors. By 1990, about 10 per cent of non-financial US corporate assets were owned by foreigners, five times more than in the late 1970s (Kudrle 1991: 397–8).

Congress reacted with alacrity. The Exon-Florio provisions of the 1988 Trade Act required the President to investigate any foreign purchases of American assets which affected 'national security', which the Trade Act left entirely undefined. After the Exon-Florio rules lapsed in 1990, political support for new restrictions was fuelled by Japanese purchases of Universal Studios, the Rockefeller Center, Columbia Records and the Seattle Mariners baseball team.

Yet more than half of all foreign investment in the US remained European in origin (Harrison 1994: 1). The total value of US acquisitions by British interests alone was more than double that of Japanese purchases. The EU had good reason to be outraged about proposed new restrictions on FDI in the US. The share of the domestic American workforce employed by foreign companies was relatively low: only about half the German and British shares, and a third that of France (Graham and Krugman 1989). Ford and General Motors continued to invest heavily in the EU and controlled more than one-fifth of the EU's automobile market (Zupnick 1991: 34–8).

The US is both the world's leading 'source' and 'host' country for FDI. The net benefits for the US of an open global system with as few restrictions as possible on FDI are substantial. The Commission (1995a: 23–4) is keen to point out that European-owned companies employ about 3 million US workers and tend to offer higher salaries: more than 20 per cent above the American average. Moreover, the volume and direction of exports is highly dependent on patterns of FDI: about one-third of US exports to the EU are a consequence of American investment in Europe (Harrison 1994: 1).

The total flow of FDI between the US and EU was worth more than $410 billion in 1993, compared with about $100 billion between the US and Japan (see United Nations 1994; Commission 1995d). Only $20 billion passed between the EU and Japan and nearly all of it went in one direction. Japanese investment in Luxembourg alone was higher than total EU investment in Japan (Lehmann 1993: 126).

The EU remained the most important market in the world for US investment abroad, attracting more than 40 per cent of the total. The income of American firms operating in Europe was more than ten times the income of American firms in Japan (Harrison 1994: 1,8). The 1992 project and particularly the liberalization of EU public procurement prompted large European investments by US firms which wanted to sell in the internal market and compete for huge public contracts (Winters 1991b: 368). In short, restrictions on FDI mooted in the US threatened to work against the grain of countless private, market-based investment decisions and do significant damage to bilateral economic relations.

By 1995, the issue had attracted enough political concern to generate a dialogue on investment within the OECD. Discussions focused on minimum investment levels needed before foreign firms could be treated as domestic firms, the repatriation of profits and other restrictions on FDI. However, the dialogue was marred by US scepticism about whether the Commission was really serious about eliminating restrictions on investment in the Union. For better or worse, the view that the Commission could be counted on to push EU member states to adopt liberal economic policies was less widely held within the Clinton administration than the Bush administration. Kantor insisted that discussions on investment rules should take place within the OECD, not the WTO where the Commission wielded more power. Somewhat paradoxically, France, which maintained more restrictions on FDI than most EU states, supported the proposal to discuss investment rules within the OECD so that the EU's fiercely liberal Commissioner for Trade, Sir Leon Brittan, could be kept on a shorter lead. The investment issue illustrated how internal EU divisions continued to complicate transatlantic relations.

The point was also illustrated in the EU's economic diplomacy with Japan. Between 1987 and 1989, the Union abolished national import quotas on over 130 Japanese products, before tackling the ultra-sensitive issue of Japanese auto imports. Initially, the EU Commissioner for Industry, Martin Bangemann, shocked member states by tabling a politically unthinkable proposal for nearly complete liberalization of the EU's auto market after 1992. An eventual compromise hinged on a larger EU-wide quota for Japanese imports in exchange for substantial opening of Japan's market, to be followed by full liberalization of the EU's market after

1998. The so-called 'Elements of Consensus' agreement is 'deliberately vague and ambiguous' and 'politically fragile': whether or not it holds without the EU opting for further protectionism remains an open question (Mason 1994: 450).

More generally, EU–Japan relations are usually one step short of acrimony. Delors's response to a bid in 1990 from the Japanese Prime Minister, Toshiki Kaifu, to revitalize political relations with the EU was indicative:

> We can only welcome this approach and trust that the new structures for high-level consultation between Europe and Japan will be more effective than the old. But I would repeat what I said to Mr Kaifu on this, namely that we feel very disappointed. . . . They cannot expect the West to apply the principles of openness and free trade indefinitely while these are denied to Western companies in Japan.
>
> (Commission 1990a: 10)

In the event, an EU–Japanese declaration in 1991 amounted to a weak statement of good intentions about freeing bilateral trade. Within months, Kaifu had been ousted by his own Liberal Democratic Party, which abhorred his proposals for cleaning up Japan's electoral system.

Yet sweeping reforms of Japan's political system were in place by the mid-1990s. Hopes arose in the West that the interests of consumers would be better represented in Japanese politics, and thus barriers blocking access to Japan's market, as well as obstructionism by its powerful bureaucracy and MNCs, would die away. Patient cajoling by Brittan and the EU, as well as domestic changes in Japan, led the EU's trade deficit with Japan to fall by nearly a fifth after 1993.

However, the US trade deficit with Japan rose to $55 billion in 1994, up from about $40 billion in 1991. The dollar's weakness and a powerful yen meant that Japan's surplus was declining in yen terms (if not dollar terms), with its imports increasing at a rate of more than 20 per cent per year. With Japan's population ageing rapidly, the trade surplus was expected to continue to fall as its progressively larger older population spent more and saved less. Regardless, Japan-bashing remained popular in the US. The Clinton administration's unabashed pursuit of 'managed trade' with Japan was loudly criticized by Brittan, who feared that EU producers would lose out. Meanwhile, a new assertiveness in Japanese trade policy was exemplified by the insistence of Tomiichi Murayama, Japan's Prime Minister, that the Americans had 'lost the argument' in the 1995 trade row over cars.[9]

The comment reflected a general sentiment in Japan that barriers blocking American access to its market were a relatively unimportant factor in the US trade imbalance. Japanese tariffs were low and most of its NTBs were gradually being lowered or eliminated (Ponnuru 1995).

On the other hand, Western economists could cite abundant evidence to suggest that the Japanese market was far less responsive than Western markets to changes in market forces such as currency fluctuations (Prestowitz 1988; Hufbauer 1990; Woolcock 1991). A simple conclusion emerges from such contrary evidence: both the US and EU must approach their trade deficits with Japan as *structural*, as problems deeply rooted in the structures of their domestic economies, as well as Japan's. One effect could be to push the US and EU towards joint action on a range of trade issues.

A good example is technological competitiveness, which became the subject of intense debate on both sides of the Atlantic in the mid-1980s. After enjoying a $20 billion surplus in high-tech trade in 1976, the US recorded its first deficit ($2.3 billion) in 1986. Small surpluses in subsequent years became deficits again by the mid-1990s. For many analysts, the root of the problem was that nearly $40 billion out of a total US R& D effort of about $70 billion continued to be spent on military research even after the end of the Cold War.

European competitiveness in high-tech industries eroded even faster. By the mid-1980s European producers controlled only about 10 per cent of the global market for basic technologies such as computer chips. Japanese firms claimed nearly half. The EU responded by creating the Framework programme to subsidize collaborative R&D projects between firms from different member states in a wide range of sectors. Its annual budget grew to reach more than $3.2 billion by the mid-1990s.

Meanwhile the intergovernmental Eureka programme, originally a French response to SDI, included more than twenty European states and funded 'near market' R&D projects which could not be funded by the EU due to its rules on competition. Eureka grew to rival the Framework programme in size (Peterson 1993b; Sharp and Peterson 1996). Many collaborative R&D projects in Europe resembled those organized in Japan by its Ministry of International Trade and Industry (MITI). For the EU, at least, the rising share of trade accounted for by high technology and the willingness of other governments, especially Japan's, to promote their domestic industries led to a merging of trade and technology policies. Between 1985 and 1990, nearly 40 per cent of all EU anti-dumping actions concerned electronics, with most directed against Japan or one of the Asian 'tigers'.

While the EU mimicked Japanese methods, the US under Republican administrations rejected them. In the 1980s, aggressive trade actions under Section 301 were taken against Japan over computer chips, supercomputers and satellites. But the Bush administration resisted pressure from Congress and the Commerce Department to use the military budget to fund more research into 'dual-use' technologies, or ones with civilian and military applications (Yudken and Black 1990). Critics of government intervention in high-tech industries argued that the secret of Japanese success was not MITI or trade barriers, but stiff competition, low taxes and inflation, a high savings rate and a strong educational system (Ponnuru 1995).

By contrast with the US, the EU and its member states channelled enormous subsidies – a total of more than $3 billion in the 1980s for computer chips alone – to collaborative research projects. The Commission supported several with comprehensive industrial policies designed to prepare markets for products being developed with the help of EU subsidies. For example, EU governments used Eureka to subsidize the development of hardware employing a European (non-Japanese) technical standard, needed for the next generation of 'high-definition' television (HDTV). The Commission provided funds to European TV producers so that 'software' (TV programmes) would be made using the European standard. The Commission also brokered an agreement on the 'Television Without Frontiers' directive, which reserved a majority of EU transmission time for programmes of European origin (Peterson 1993c). In Europe, an EU industrial policy for HDTV was a logical response to the Japanese challenge in a key industry of the future.

However, television programmes remained among America's leading exports to Europe, generating nearly $2 billion per year in royalties. Bush's USTR, Carla Hills, condemned the EU's policy as 'blatantly protectionist and unjustifiable'.[10] The leader of the EP's delegation to the US House of Representatives claimed he had 'never seen the US delegation so united around a single issue'.[11] The controversy showed how EU industrial policies designed to confront Japanese competition nearly always had impacts on US trade interests (see Kreinin 1991).

The assumption that the Bush administration would be the last 'holdout' against a stronger US industrial policy was validated when Clinton was elected in 1992. The US Office of Science and Technology Policy was empowered to coordinate actions which promoted technological advance across all departments and agencies. The National Science and Technology Council, a cabinet-level committee chaired by Clinton himself, controlled budgets and maintained a strategic overview. Even in the face of general fiscal austerity, the US began to put far more money into EU-style research consortia (Sharp 1995). Vice-President Al Gore's personal advocacy of the National Information Infrastructure programme to develop 'information superhighways' showed that 'old taboos [were] increasingly being regarded as outdated, or simply brushed aside without comment' (Gaster and Bradshaw 1993: 52).

Meanwhile, many US and EU firms were forming strategic alliances, particularly in sectors where the EU funded research or restricted access to its market. Even before the projected Euro-standard was abandoned, both Philips and Thomson were involved in two separate US projects to develop a separate HDTV system. Many US television producers began working collaboratively with European partners to skirt restrictions imposed by the 'Television Without Frontiers' directive (Kreinin 1991: 63).

The Commission remained keen to develop new collaborative US–EU projects. Yet as a DG I official admitted:

> It is one of the most delicate areas because it is very difficult to construct a convincing argument for collaborating in the technological areas with the US and not doing it with the Japanese. The tendency then is to say in principle 'it's just European and we won't collaborate with anyone,' and you draw up regulations with that in mind. At the same time, you say that this is a very open regime and we'd like to collaborate with everyone. And in practice you try and work it so you collaborate with the US and not the Japanese.[12]

The record of the EU's collaborative programmes has been modest. Arguably, the 1992 project has diminished incentives for EU firms to collaborate because the single market sharpens intra-EU competition and makes it easier for firms to sell across frontiers without collaborating (Kay 1991). Even so, several forces have conspired to create new incentives for *transatlantic* collaboration. One is the globalization of corporate strategies. US and European firms which want access to each other's markets often find that collaboration is the easiest way to get it. Investment flows across the Atlantic blur US and EU corporate identities. The arguments for restricting EU-funded collaborative schemes to European firms have become largely untenable.

A second force for US–EU collaboration is the rising cost and complexity of technologies in sectors such as computer chips, defence technologies and automated manufacturing. Innovations in these sectors are usually a product of 'multi-technological' advances, resulting from collaboration between firms working in different areas of technology. The end of the Cold War led the US to loosen restrictions on the licensing of dual-use technologies which previously were classified for security reasons. The result was wider opportunities for collaboration between US and European firms.

Above all, the only option for many US and European firms hoping to compete with large, integrated, cash-rich Japanese competitors was to collaborate on expensive and complicated R&D into basic 'building block' technologies. The imperatives for transatlantic collaboration were particularly strong in sectors such as automobiles, electronics and robotics where American and European producers were increasingly overtaken by their Japanese rivals. Warren Christopher's (1995) call for intensified transatlantic cooperation in information technology was indicative of the fact that the US, 'more than any other advanced capitalist country ... has based its economic strategy during the information revolution on military technology and military competition' (Carnoy *et al.* 1993: 11). More generally, the Clinton administration became convinced that more was at stake than just 'economic security', defined narrowly:

> The best technologies vital to military security are found in global commercial markets; autarky and a narrow focus on military R&D in the face of the globalization of commercial high technology production and exchange severs the state from the fruits of technological innovation.
>
> (Crawford 1994b: 26)

One effect of increased US–EU industrial collaboration is to push governments on both sides to harmonize their rules on competition. The EU's powers in this area – the regulation of mergers, industrial collaboration and state aid to industry – have expanded since the 1980s. The Union's rules-based approach resembles US competition policy far more than do the approaches of its individual member states, which typically use their competition policies as instruments of industrial policy. Stronger EU powers over competition policy thus help to facilitate common US–EU actions. By 1995, a bilateral Competition Agreement had been agreed which mandated close policy coordination, thus sending a signal to Japan to change its meek, even collusive approach to state aids and anti-trust policy. One senior USTR official described competition policy harmonization as 'the new frontier' of transatlantic economic relations.[13]

The Japanese challenge gives the US and EU clear incentives to cooperate with one another on competition policy, technology and trade issues. However, relatively low rates of Western economic growth and the rise of new economic competitors have combined to diminish the power of the US and EU to set the international economic agenda. The decline of the West's economic dominance might have unambiguously heightened incentives for transatlantic cooperation, were it not for the emergence of alternative partners, such as the Cairns group on agriculture.

Moreover, trans-Pacific trade was worth 50 per cent more than transatlantic trade by 1993. The Clinton administration thus sought to invigorate the Asia-Pacific Economic Cooperation Forum (APEC). It became a way to prise open fast-growing markets in Asia, as well as a weapon for persuading the EU to give ground in the Uruguay Round. At the Jakarta summit in 1994, APEC's eighteen member states agreed that all trade barriers between them would be abolished by 2020, and by 2010 in the case of industrialized countries such as the US and Japan. However, no agreement could be reached on trade in services or agriculture. It seemed unthinkable that the US Congress would agree to remove all barriers to imports from China and other developing Asian countries ten years before they opened their own markets to US imports. Rivalries between the US, Japan and China for leadership of the Pacific Rim make a coherent Asian economic bloc difficult to imagine (Betts 1993/4; Friedberg 1993/4).

The future political significance of APEC rides largely on the issue of how those outside the Pacific Rim, such as the EU, will be affected by trade liberalization in Asia. Most APEC members wish to maintain the principle of 'open regionalism', with no increase in discrimination against outsiders. Others – South Korea, Australia, Singapore and, especially, the US – want EU access to APEC to be conditional on reciprocal measures to open its markets (Richardson 1994).

Without prejudging APEC's future, alliances in a globalized economy are likely to remain fluid in the absence of overarching political agreements. For example, the EU had little choice but to seek new allies when the US unexpectedly withdrew its offer to grant increased access to its market for financial services in 1995. In a clear sop to 'fair trade' principles, the United States denied MFN status to countries which failed to offer sufficiently generous terms to US firms. The EU's response was to forge an alliance of states with relatively modern economies – including APEC members such as Japan, South Korea and Hong Kong – which promised to offer greater access to their markets. Attempts to persuade the US to join in were unsuccessful. The EU thus managed to secure at least a limited deal on financial services, but barriers remained to transatlantic trade and investment in the sector.

The financial services negotiations appeared to validate the warning of Clinton's Under Secretary of Commerce, Jeffrey Garten, that the US and EU needed 'to invest at least as much time and energy in the development of a new economic architecture as we are doing in the restructuring of NATO. . . . We have no time to lose.'[14] It was hard to deny Garten's logic given two new, essential features of international relations in the mid-1990s: the lack of a clear security threat to encourage Western solidarity on economic questions, and the rise of new potential alliances (other than the transatlantic one) on specific economic issues. The Japanese economic challenge was a daunting one, but the new 'glue' it provided to US–EU relations was sometimes rather weak.

4 TRADE AND MONETARY RELATIONS IN THEORY

Neorealist assumptions underpin the arguments of US advocates of 'fair trade' who insist that American trade interests must be defended aggressively and unilaterally. They see little scope for common US–EU actions in pursuit of a more open global trading order, and reject the notion that 'free trade is necessarily good and protection is necessarily bad. Both policies represent legitimate options that the United States should employ depending on the prevailing state of the US economy and the international trading system' (Prestowitz 1988: 322). For neorealists, capitalist states will always be natural rivals regardless of any political ties which link them in alliances (Hart 1992).

Neorealists view the EU as a strategic alliance between 'unitary-rational' states capable of modest levels of cooperation in response to common threats. Its abilities to achieve EMU or resist national pressures for protectionism are viewed with profound scepticism. Neorealists also deny that much US–EU cooperation is possible on trade and monetary issues. Waltz (1993: 59) argues that: 'economic competition is often as keen as military competition, and since nuclear weapons limit the use of force among great powers at the strategic level, we may expect economic and technological competition among them to become more intense'.

Neorealists are surely correct to assume that trade disputes will continue to complicate US–EU relations, even given the creation of the WTO or political agreement on some type of 'new economic architecture'. *Institutionalists* agree that 'interdependence in the world political economy generates conflict' (Keohane 1984: 243). But they part from neorealists in insisting that rising economic interdependence promotes a convergence of interests on trade and monetary issues. For example:

> The net effect of the large-scale presence of US multinational firms in Europe, combined with the newer but now about equally large presence of European multinationals in the United States, is likely to be one of softening the intensity of conflicts.
>
> (Graham 1991: 201)

Increased interdependence also means that governments are losing autonomy as they seek to achieve their trade or macroeconomic policy targets. The logical response for institutionalists is the creation of new mechanisms – such as the US–EU Competition Agreement – in which policies are coordinated and targets are set and pursued jointly. Keohane (1984: 13) argues that international regimes often '*empower* governments rather than shackling them' by making it more likely that their economic policies will succeed.

Stronger regimes also promote stability in the international economy. Institutionalists view economic stability as a collective good which serves the interests of all governments (Stein 1982; Artis and Ostry 1986; Taylor 1987). They note that economic interdependence often has unanticipated consequences. States must cooperate to cope with crises which arise from them. To illustrate the point, institutionalists would link Mexico's economic crisis in 1995 with China's extraordinarily rapid rate of economic growth. The large US trade deficit with China was mostly a consequence of imports of Chinese-made consumer products – watches, textiles, games, footwear and toys – which the US would otherwise buy from Mexico (Allen 1995). The peso crisis led to discussions on designing new mechanisms within the IMF and G-7 to anticipate and head off such crises.

Institutionalists tend to share with *liberals* an abhorrence of all forms of protectionism. Liberals go further to argue that the effect of EU anti-dumping measures or the refusal of the US to throw open its telecommunications market is to confound the law of comparative advantage and misallocate economic resources. 'Fair trade' advocates are denounced for their tendency

> to apply intuitive standards of fairness to international commerce much as is done to the domestic economy. In doing so one risks vitiating the entire rationale for international trade: that nations trade with one another because transactions based on their differences can enhance mutual welfare, often regardless of whether they are 'fair'.
>
> (Nivola 1990: 251)

Liberals thus attack the idea that ' "rules" should be replaced by a "result-oriented" strategy *vis-à-vis* Japan' (Kreinin 1991: 67). The endorsement of 'fair trade' principles by social scientists is viewed as pandering 'to the politicians' worst mercantilist instincts' (Winters 1991b: 76).

Liberalism often seems politically naive. Few of its advocates appreciate how difficult it is to shift power away from domestic groups by preaching the virtues of free trade, given the political imbalance between those who benefit from protectionism and those who lose. As Destler (1986: 3) observes,

> It is an imbalance in *intensity* of interest and, as a result, in political *organization*. Producers and workers threatened by imports tend to be concentrated, organized, ready and able to press their interests in the political arena. Those who benefit from trade are diffuse, and their stake in any particular trade matter is also small.

Liberals also have few answers to the problem of 'market failures' or instances when free markets do not produce efficient allocations of economic resources. The US would have a monopoly on civilian aircraft production if European governments did not pour large subsidies into Airbus. EU member states – particularly France and Italy – argue that the Japanese will monopolize markets for many strategic technologies unless the EU pursues interventionist policies such as the Framework programme to 'flank' the freeing of the internal market. In short, neither the US nor the EU could ever manage to ignore political pressures for intervention in their economies as liberals urge them to do.

Whatever its failings, liberalism does point to the self-defeating logic of protectionism and the political dilemmas that it creates (see Olson 1982). When governments give in to the protectionist demands of one group, they act to legitimate the demands of other groups, particularly those who are dependent on the first group for components or materials. For example, the price of US steel rose when American steelmakers successfully lobbied for protection in the 1980s. This meant that the domestic automobile manufacturers paid up to 40 per cent more for steel than did foreign car makers, thus leading to calls for greater protection from Japanese imports (Reich 1991: 72).

Liberals also highlight the difficulty of achieving 'fair trade' and designing rules to ensure it. They lament the increasing tendency for US trade policy to be determined by 'micropolitical' pressures (Nivola 1993). One result is that 'dumping is whatever you can get the government to act against under the anti-dumping law'.[15] EU anti-dumping rules are no less arbitrary.

The Bush administration embraced liberal principles far more than did the Reagan administration. Such principles (as well as naked self-interest) informed US arguments for reducing agricultural protectionism in the Uruguay Round. Liberals attacked Clinton's trade policies as 'incoherent' and prone to treating 'trade problems almost completely in terms of domestic constituencies' (Lavin 1993: 29–30). Yet Clinton's legacy in foreign policy will be elevated his successful advocacy of NAFTA, the WTO and APEC.

Liberalism also inspired the 1992 project and the evolution of the EU's external trade policy, as illustrated by reform of the CAP and the gradual opening of the EU's auto market to Japan. Widespread acceptance of liberal principles spurred the political relaunch of the EU after the mid-1980s more generally. While protectionist pressures in sensitive industrial sectors will not wither away, 'it is just as plausible to argue that the [EU's] new self-confidence has allowed more, not less, liberal trade policies in these areas' (Winters 1991a: 372).

The *reformist* critique of liberalism centres on the environmental costs of free trade and economic growth. Reformists applauded GATT proposals in 1992 to penalize countries which engaged in ecologically damaging trade practices. Liberals countered that new trade-related environmental measures would lead to 'micromanagement of world trade on a scale hitherto undreamed of' (Glover 1994: 284). In the event, the liberal view prevailed: member states determined that environmental protection and trade should be linked only after a successful conclusion to the Uruguay Round.

Such arguments are anathema to reformists, who insist that environmental degradation should be the most immediate and urgent concern of all international institutions. Reformists insist that trade and environmental protection must be viewed holistically with wider North–South issues. They point to World Bank estimates that $75–100 billion in annual investments are needed before LDCs will be able to stabilize and reduce their pollution emissions (Tran 1992). Greens in the EP criticize the methods chosen for CAP reform on the grounds that lower prices drive small farms out of business and mean 'more industrialized farming, more damage to the environment – and more surpluses'.[16]

Neo-Marxists argue that the imperatives of global capitalism act to push environmental degradation and underdevelopment lower on the agendas of Western countries (Gill 1990). Other reformists see growing economic interdependence as a potential lever for new international agreements on environmental protection. Restrictions on the use of ozone-destroying chlorofluorocarbons (CFCs) in manufacturing is a case in point. The large EU states resisted American proposals to reduce CFC levels until the US threatened to restrict access to its domestic market to those who did not accept them. Fearing for its export industries, Germany broke with France and the UK on the issue. The eventual result was the Montreal protocol of 1987 which was seen by some reformists as a model for future international agreements (Young 1991: 290–1).

Reformists of all kinds worry that economic nationalism in the wake of the recession of the early 1990s has pushed environmental protection lower on Western political agendas. The rise of protectionism in Europe combined with the EU's democratic deficit stokes fears that:

> The mountains of paper, the hours of talk, the agitated comings and goings of self-important personages will be so much spitting in the wind; that, while preserving the forms of a supranational Community, the reality of European life will be one of beggar-thy-neighbor attempts to sneak competitive advantages in an ever-more cut-throat world economy, accompanied by increasingly raucous chauvinistic drum-beating and deepening national rivalries in politics as well as economics.
>
> (Marquand 1994: 18)

More generally, as resources are depleted and the earth's population increases, the need for another historic revolution, as important as the earlier ones in agriculture and industry, becomes more urgent. This 'third' revolution must focus on sustainable development and environmental protection. It obviously requires international cooperation. Yet reformists argue that existing international institutions are not up to the task. For example, the Final Act of the GATT, which created the WTO, mentioned the goal of sustainable development and the need to protect and preserve the environment. However, the WTO's delegates and secretariat are specialists in trade law and economics, not the environment. They cannot be expected to make credible judgements about which environmental problems justify global rules (Glover 1994).

More generally, reformists tend to view the WTO with scorn. Speaking before the Senate Foreign Relations Committee, the US consumer protection guru, Ralph Nader, asserted that:

When historians look back on this period . . . either they will focus on it as a moment in which Congress resisted the anti-democratic WTO or they will view it as the moment in which Congress ceded authority to safeguard the interests of this country to this new autocratic international body.[17]

The four theories reflect very different assumptions and thus offer competing explanations for state behaviour on trade and monetary issues. Still, theorists of all stripes agree that these issues have become more important determinants of US–EU relations. Most would share three further observations about trade and monetary policies. First, they have become more politicized at the same time as their importance for US and EU foreign policies has heightened.

Second, the unilateralism of US policies on trade and FDI points to the general decline of American international power. The fact that the volume of US assets owned by foreigners has increased relative to the country's investment abroad 'can plausibly be interpreted as yet another manifestation of declining US economic hegemony' (Kudrle 1991: 399). One might concur with advocates of 'fair trade' that 'with America in relative decline the real penalties resulting from liberalism and openness have been exposed' (Prestowitz et al. 1991: 130–1).

Such penalties can be minimized if a global trading system can be constructed which more closely reflects the relative openness of the US economy. The Uruguay Round agreement promised to increase US exports by $19 billion and create 265,000 jobs by the turn of the century (Schott and Buhrman 1994). One plausible way for the US to compensate for the decline in its ability to dictate the terms of global trade is through stronger partnership with its most reliable and 'open' allies, above all the EU.

A third observation follows from the first two. Managing bilateral trade and monetary conflicts is hard work and requires constant negotiation and compromise at multiple levels. Active attempts at the highest political level are needed to balance a complex array of issues and interests. Disputes will inevitably occur and their resolution must be sought via processes which are viewed as fair on both sides. A healthy, functioning WTO and intensive bilateral exchanges at all levels must be viewed as prerequisites of US–EU partnership in the 1990s.

Chapter 6

European security after the Cold War

In military terms, the defence of Western Europe during the Cold War was a relatively straightforward matter of coordinating national defence policies under US leadership to deter Soviet aggression. In political terms, the loss of sovereignty demanded by NATO's integrated military structure and different perceptions of the nature of the Soviet threat inevitably caused tensions within the Atlantic Alliance. However, NATO's members were conditioned to assume that the US would normally take the initiative on policy and then push European states to 'form up' around it (Walker 1991: 129). The East–West divide muted political differences within NATO and acted to unite US and European foreign policies more generally.

The new geopolitical reality makes risks to European security less easy to define. The resiliency of the American commitment to European security has become subject to new doubts. The EU has found it difficult to avoid debates about whether it needs its own independent security identity.

This chapter analyses changing US–EU relations on questions of European security. Section 1 explores how geopolitical change has altered perceptions about European security. Section 2 reviews political responses to the perceived need to reform existing security structures. Section 3 analyses the key institutional issues in the emergence of a new 'security architecture': the reformulation of NATO and the development of a European defence identity. In section 4, explanations, predictions and prescriptions are culled from the four major theories of international relations.

1 ADJUSTING TO THE NEW GEOPOLITICAL REALITY

Only with hindsight was it clear how much the imperatives of the Cold War had acted to fuse the United States and Europe together within NATO. De Gaulle's ardent desire to avoid French dependence on US security guarantees led him to withdraw French forces from NATO and develop France's own nuclear deterrent. Yet successive American administrations provided covert technical assistance to the French nuclear force. In exchange, the French agreed to coordinate their military plans with NATO in the event of a European war (Ullman 1989). Such arrangements were a consequence of a clear, common threat to European security which no longer exists. The potential for discord within the Atlantic Alliance has clearly increased.

At the same time, the demise of the Warsaw Pact prompted a convergence of views about the nature of the EU's foreign policy interests. In late 1989, Delors began to argue that the economic prosperity generated by the single market gave the EU new external responsibilities in Eastern Europe, the less developed world and Asia (Delors 1989, 1990). On the American side, the idea that the EU should assume global – not just regional – responsibilities was supported and even promoted by a US administration, essentially for the first time.

The change in US attitudes was rooted in budgetary pressures as well as the political relaunch of the EU. In 1990 the Bush administration proposed that the Commission become a 'deputy coordinator' for an aid operation for Central America and the Caribbean modelled upon the G-24 effort for Eastern Europe (Barber 1990; Zoellick 1990). EU member states demurred from committing themselves to regional initiatives beyond their geopolitical sphere of interest, but redoubled their efforts to assume a leadership role in developing a collective Western response to events in Eastern Europe.

The instinctive reaction of many EU states to the demise of the Warsaw Pact was to focus on 'institutionalizing' what was then the Conference on Security and Cooperation in Europe (renamed the OSCE in 1994). The OSCE offered the advantage of bringing together all European states – from the Soviet Union to the Vatican – plus the US and Canada. Created following an EU initiative, it ensured a European role in superpower détente after the signing of the Helsinki Accord in 1975. Despite US suspicions that the OSCE would legitimize Soviet control of Eastern Europe, the Ford administration agreed to participate in exchange for a Soviet commitment to begin negotiations on Mutual and Balanced Force Reductions (MBFR) in Europe.

The OSCE became a forum for inconspicuous diplomatic negotiations on a range of human rights and troop levels issues. For political dissenters throughout Eastern Europe, the Helsinki Accord legitimized demands for guaranteed political rights and 'provided the intellectual basis from which to attack and erode the official system' (Syme and Payton 1992: 88). The MBFR talks yielded little, but a number of concessions were obtained from the Soviets on human rights, culture and trade (Tsakaloyannis 1989: 243–5).

After the Berlin Wall fell, a debate emerged between advocates of a pan-European security organization based on the OSCE and those who

insisted that NATO's leading role in European security should be preserved. The Germans in particular argued that the development of the
OSCE process was a way to compensate the Soviets for the demise of
the Warsaw Pact. The argument found supporters not only in Europe but
also among US analysts (Safire 1990; Albright 1991; Treverton 1991:
97–101) and even members of Congress (DeConcini and Hoyer 1990).

The Bush administration realized that developing the OSCE process
was essential if talks on reducing conventional forces in Europe (CFE)
were to bear fruit. By 1990, original CFE targets for reducing armaments
had to be altered to accommodate both the increased cuts in German
forces promised to Gorbachev and the absence of a single Eastern negotiating authority after the death of the Warsaw Pact. Only the OSCE
brought together all relevant parties.

At the landmark Paris summit of November 1990, a CFE treaty was
signed which substantially reduced levels of key categories of military
equipment held by both the Warsaw Pact states and NATO. The Charter
of Paris mandated the creation of a small, permanent OSCE secretariat
in Prague as well as new 'conflict resolution' procedures to be coordinated through a central office in Vienna. Perhaps most importantly, the
Charter committed all signatories to respect the 'ethnic, cultural, linguis-
tic, and religious identity of national minorities' (Greene 1992: 150).

The OSCE's greatest strength was its inclusiveness. However, the advantages of its wide membership were mirrored by its greatest weakness.
With unanimous decision-making procedures, any member could veto
any proposal. In 1991, the USSR blocked an attempt to invoke OSCE
procedures to halt Soviet military intervention in the Baltic republics.

A good illustration of the US position on the OSCE came when James
Dobbins (1991), Bush's ambassador to the EU, contrasted the 'geographi-
cally-defined' membership of the OSCE with the 'common values' shared
by all members of NATO. Critics accused the Bush administration of
treating the OSCE as little more than a 'mail drop' to exchange information on troop reductions (Walker 1991: 138). The European Commission along with the French feared that strengthening the OSCE would
hinder EU efforts to develop its own security competence. Strange bedfel-
lows with the Americans, they agreed that the OSCE should remain
a rather toothless and decidedly intergovernmental organization with a
small secretariat. The expansion of the OSCE in 1992 to include the
former Soviet republics, many of which lacked any previous experience in
international diplomacy, weakened arguments for its institutionalization.

The OSCE nevertheless remained a suitable forum for monitoring
human rights and force reductions. The US came round to the view that
the OSCE was at least a useful means for encouraging the EU to take a
more active role in security matters, as was demonstrated when the Union
secured an OSCE mandate in 1991 to mediate in the Yugoslavian civil

war. In 1992 the OSCE adopted a 'unanimity minus one' rule to make actions possible when any member state clearly or persistently failed to meet its OSCE commitments. After the break-up of both the Soviet Union and Yugoslavia, the OSCE undertook useful preventive diplomacy in Georgia, Ukraine, the Baltic states, Kosovo and Macedonia. Rarely in the headlines, the OSCE specialised in:

> unspectacular, low profile activities. Nevertheless, they are important in providing early warning of rising tension, in demonstrating outside interest and thereby possibly dampening signs of violence, and in bringing the various parties together.
>
> (Lunn 1993: 63).

The Germans continued to be the strongest Western advocates of the OSCE. Because it facilitated linkages of political, social, military and economic aspects of security, it was considered by the Kohl government to be 'the only solution with any prospect of permanent success' among the various institutional options for maintaining European security (Kinkel 1992: 4). Moreover, the OSCE facilitated linkages across existing security institutions. It incorporated all members of NATO and the WEU as well as all permanent members of the UN Security Council except China. The OSCE thus could claim a leading role in any scheme of 'interlocking institutions' to guarentee European security.

Ultimately, fifty-three OSCE member states signed the Charter of Paris, but Serbia did not. The Charter mandated that, in case of conflict between members, the use of force to punish aggressors was not an option. Unsurprisingly, the debate about the future of European security structures moved on to focus on the relative merits of revamping NATO, developing a more independent European security and defence 'identity' (ESDI), or seeking a synthesis between the two.

The debate permeated internal EU discussions about its future evolution and membership in the early 1990s. Political support grew for the the development of a European military capability through the WEU which could be put at the service of the EU's foreign policy. The WEU had lain largely dormant after its origins in 1948, when it was created ostensibly to monitor the pace of German rearmament. Moves at Maastricht to try to close the gap between the divergent memberships of the EU and WEU were indicative of new interest in strengthening organic links between the two, ultimately leading – in the view of most EU members – to full merger (see Table 6.1).

The ambition to create an ESDI soon became linked to discussions about the EU's enlargement. EFTA states traditionally had viewed Union membership as a threat to their neutrality on East–West issues. Yet, in a post-Cold War world, the meaning of 'neutrality' became obscure. By 1992 formal applications for EU membership had been submitted by

Table 6.1 Memberships of the EU, WEU and NATO (1996)

	EU	WEU	NATO
United States			X
Canada			X
Iceland			X
Norway			X
Turkey			X
Denmark	X		X
Greece	X	X	X
Belgium	X	X	X
France*	X	X	X
Germany	X	X	X
Italy	X	X	X
Luxembourg	X	X	X
Netherlands	X	X	X
Portugal	X	X	X
Spain	X	X	X
United Kingdom	X	X	X
Ireland	X		
Finland	X		
Sweden	X		
Austria	X		

Note: * French forces remain outside NATO's integrated military command.

Austria, Sweden, Switzerland and Finland, as well as non-EFTA members Cyprus, Turkey and Malta.

By the mid-1990s the list of actual or expected applicants expanded to include nearly all of the former members of the Warsaw Pact (outside the USSR), with others such as the Baltic and former Yugoslav republics certain to follow. In particular, Poland, Hungary, the Czech Republic and Slovakia argued that they deserved early membership by virtue of their geographical proximity and efforts to reform their economies and polities in line with Western urgings. Political leaders from the so-called Visegrad Four countries, as well as their ethnic supporters in America, insisted that the West had a moral duty to admit them to its institutions, particularly the EU and NATO.

Political commitment to further enlargement of the EU continued to vary considerably among its current member states. The UK and Denmark favoured 'widening' the Community quickly. France, Italy, Spain and others remained sceptical about enlarging the Union without steps to 'deepen' integration among its current members first. Germany looked both ways, urging that the Union should be deepened and widened simultaneously.

Eventually, the debate about the merits of widening or deepening became moot under the Danish EU Presidency of 1993. At the Copenhagen summit, a consensus emerged on the principle that new applicants should be offered membership as long as their economies were strong enough to avoid implosion of the kind East Germany would have suffered were it not for huge capital transfers from the West after unification. In 1995, a tacit Greek veto on an EU free trade agreement with Turkey was lifted in exchange for a commitment to begin accession negotiations with Cyprus within six months of the end of the Union's 1996 intergovernmental conference. It was widely assumed Germany would insist that its neighbours among the Visegrad Four – Poland and the Czech Republic – should start accession negotiations at the same time. Ultimately, a Union with as many as twenty-five members and its own defence and security arrangements by the end of the century seemed plausible.

EU enlargement is a key issue for transatlantic relations. In many respects, US interests are served by expansion of the Union. An EU which represents all of Europe is a potentially stronger and more effective partner to the United States. Most of the American political class believes strongly that the EU has a moral obligation to spread Western values and wealth to Eastern Europe. US opinion can be expected to become impatient and ill-tempered quickly if enlargement negotiations are delayed because current member states blackmail each other and new applicants.

However, the Gulf War and then the Yugoslav conflict reinforced US doubts about the EU's ability to achieve the internal cohesiveness it needs to play a global role commensurate with its economic and political weight. Further enlargement of the EU's membership is almost certain to exacerbate the problem. Moreover, US support for EU enlargement cannot be unconditional due to trade concerns. Reform of the CAP is a prior condition for unmitigated American enthusiasm for EU enlargement on political grounds: the accession of Spain and Portugal brought the US and EU to the brink of a trade war due to losses suffered by American agricultural exporters (Devuyst 1995: 7).

Perhaps above all, concerns persist in Washington about the security implications of a widened EU membership and its possible effects on NATO. The Maastricht Treaty gave all EU member states the right to join the WEU, but with ambiguous reference to 'conditions to be agreed'. Some EU Member States, notably the UK, took this to mean that new WEU members should also join NATO. By 1992 the Bush administration had begun to view the WEU with suspicion and as a potential rival to NATO. The Maastricht Treaty contained a commitment to ensure that WEU policies were compatible with NATO, in a clear attempt to try to allay US fears. But its effect was to create a new potential link between EU enlargement and NATO security guarantees. Eventually, EU enlargement might induce a parallel expansion of the WEU. The nightmare scenario for the US would be an implicit extension of US-backed NATO security guarantees to new members of the EU/WEU in a process over which NATO – and the US itself – might have little influence or control.

Compared to its predecessor, the Clinton administration showed itself to be far more relaxed about an emergent ESDI. At the Brussels NATO summit of 1994, Clinton spoke with enthusiasm about a stronger WEU with closer links to Eastern Europe, and even the possible use of NATO assets by the WEU. The communiqué of the Brussels NATO summit contained seven references to a 'European security and defence identity', five to 'the European pillar of the alliance' and eight to the WEU (see Peterson 1994a). By contrast, in a customary swipe at Clinton's foreign policy, an advisor to Republican Senate majority leader Robert Dole argued:

> An ESDI hurts, it is non-constructive. One possible effect of strengthening the WEU is to weaken the [Atlantic] alliance. . . . The US has bridged differences between the Greeks and Turks, and between other European countries. Who will do it if not the US?[1]

Clearly, any foreseeable US administration will wish to maintain political leadership of the Atlantic Alliance regardless of the pace or extent of EU enlargement. The United States remains a 'European power' primarily through its leading role within NATO. However, consensus has developed within the EU on the notion that Europe must develop its own defence identity as part of its drive towards political union. Views may be converging on both sides of the Atlantic about the Union's proper role in international affairs. But the readjustment of European security structures has the potential to generate considerable acrimony, testing the durability of the transatlantic alliance.

2 A EUROPEAN SECURITY IDENTITY?

The American commitment to European security was symbolised by the stationing of 320,000 US troops in Europe as late as 1989. However, many US divisions sent to the Gulf in 1991 were not redeployed in Europe. Combined with planned reductions, the result was a reduction to 260,000 troops by late 1991. By the Brussels NATO summit of 1994, Clinton was reasserting the American commitment to European security by guaranteeing only that a minimum of 100,000 US troops would be maintained in Europe as long as he was President.

In the short term, even massive cutbacks in US troops and weaponry will yield only a modest 'peace dividend'. American isolationists who want to let NATO 'slide into obsolescence' (Kristol 1995) make the exaggerated claim that the 'savings achievable through troop cuts could provide much of the financing that a domestic-revitalization strategy would need'

(Tonelson 1991: 48). The decommissioning of troops is typically a long, drawn-out and expensive process.

However, the US fiscal commitment to European security remains substantial. The Reagan-era build-up sharply increased the asymmetry between the US and European contributions to NATO, which subsequent budget cuts on all sides did little to erode (see Table 6.2). In the long term, pressures to reduce the US financial and manpower commitment to European defence are likely to be irresistible.

Table 6.2 US and European NATO member defence expenditures ($ billion)

	1980	1990	1994
US	138	306	283
NATO Europe	113	185	172

Source: NATO (1991c); UK Ministry of Defence (1995)

Despite the EU's obvious need to take on more of the security burden, the Gulf War fuelled the conviction, widely-held in Washington, that NATO should not be undermined by a hasty effort to create a common European defence. It reinforced the notion that the UK – which immediately and fully supported the US decision to use force – remained the crucial linchpin of the Atlantic Alliance. Meanwhile, the French, whose attempts at unilateral diplomacy were kept secret even from their EU allies, remained unreliable and insecure (Brenner 1991: 673).

After the Gulf War, the EU sought to re-establish its unity by launching an EPC initiative for an internationally protected 'safe haven' for Kurdish refugees fleeing retributive attacks by the Iraqi army. The plan was announced at the Luxembourg European summit in April 1991 but could only be implemented in a substantially adapted form under US leadership. The EU could do little when US military protection of the haven was removed within months. The incident underscored the EU's incapacity to implement its own security initiatives.

The crisis in Yugoslavia erupted soon afterwards. The rapid and unanimous endorsement of an EPC plan to mediate in the dispute contrasted sharply with the EU's delayed and divided response to the Soviet invasion of Afghanistan in 1979, a reaction which had enraged the Reagan administration. Yet successive EU arbitration efforts in Yugoslavia failed, and gave way to a somewhat desperate exploration of options for strengthening the Union's ceasefire monitoring operation. In September 1991 EU foreign ministers formally invited the WEU to submit plans for actually sending troops to Yugoslavia. The WEU offered proposals covering a range of options from sending armed escorts to accompany EU monitors in Yugoslavia to committing up to 50,000 troops in a full-blown military enforcement operation. While the Benelux countries, France, Italy and

Germany all leaned towards some type of action, the UK categorically opposed it.

In the event, renewed fighting made WEU intervention implausible as there was no peace to keep. Continuing political divisions within the EU precluded any WEU label for the European troops sent to Croatia in early 1992 as part of a UN peacekeeping force, after combatants there appeared to have exhausted themselves. The outbreak of even worse violence in Bosnia later in the year produced more of the same: much rhetoric and posturing by European governments, but only limited and ineffectual actions by the EU as a whole. For example, after EU foreign ministers unanimously condemned Serbian aggression in Bosnia in 1992, the Greek Prime Minister, Constantine Mitsotakis, visited Belgrade and appeared to legitimate a new Serb-dominated rump Yugoslavia which the EU refused to recognize. Mitsotakis also repeatedly vetoed EU recognition of Macedonia in response to domestic fears in Greece that the new state might develop territorial ambitions threatening the Greek region of the same name. More generally, the Gulf War, the Kurdish crisis and the Yugoslav conflict all underlined the EU's inability to wield its collective power in international affairs.

Meanwhile, after his election in 1992, Clinton appeared to consider foreign policy to be, at best, a relatively low priority and, at worst, a distraction from his domestic agenda. US policy became driven by events, the media and public opinion. In response to appalling reports of Serb atrocities in Bosnia in 1993, Clinton sought European support for a 'lift and strike' policy: lifting a UN arms embargo which disadvantaged the Muslim-dominated Bosnian government and using Western air strikes to punish Serbian aggression. EU countries – particularly the UK and France – believed the US proposals would aggravate the war and feared Serb reprisals against their forces delivering humanitarian relief in Bosnia. They effectively vetoed the policy.

Further transatlantic tensions arose after a peace plan was developed by the UN and EU special envoys to ex-Yugoslavia, Cyrus Vance and David Owen, with provisions for Bosnia to be divided into ten ethnically-based cantons. Bosnian Serbs, who controlled over 70 per cent of Bosnia, rejected the plan. In any event, the Clinton administration's ill-concealed reluctance to commit US troops to a peacekeeping force mooted to enforce the plan made it a dead letter and encouraged Serb intransigence.

From the EU's perspective, the best hope for an early peace in Bosnia was thus jettisoned by US reluctance to participate as a full partner in a vital security operation in Europe. From the American side, Christopher charged that Western Europe was 'no longer the dominant area of the world'.[2] Clinton openly criticised France and the UK for obstructing US plans to use force against Serbian aggression. Congress pressed for a unilateral lifting of the arms embargo, a move widely viewed as 'a cheap vote, one that ran the risk of a bloodier war in Bosnia and a wider war in the region' (Drew 1994: 429).

Eventually, a myopic proposal to create 'safe havens' in Muslim-held areas of Bosnia was initiated by the US together with France, the UK and Spain – not with the EU as a whole. Frustration with the Union, and Russian refusal to support Western military action against the Serbs, led the Clinton administration to channel its diplomatic efforts through the *ad hoc* 'Contact Group', consisting of the US, France, Germany, the UK and Russia. As the war dragged on into 1995, the EU and NATO both appeared marginalized. The transatlantic alliance seemed to be in tatters.

Advocates of a European defence identity often made the prior assumption that the CFSP would lead to increased unity in EU foreign policy-making. Yet gradually it became clear that Maastricht had yielded no 'great leap forward' in the development of the EU's defence and security role. The foreign and security 'pillar' created by the Maastricht Treaty was a typical EU fudge between an Anglo-Italian proposal and a far more ambitious Franco-German plan. The 1991 Dutch presidency's insistence that qualified majority voting should apply to the CFSP was appeased by subjecting to majority vote the 'implementation' of broad policies agreed by consensus, but still allowing member states to opt out of such decisions 'in cases of imperative need'. The CFSP's decidely intergovernmental structure reflected agreement among member states that the 'Community method' of decision-making – majority voting on Commission proposals – was simply inappropriate for foreign or security policy.

The first 'joint actions' taken by the EU under the CFSP revealed a wide gap between vision and outcome (Ginsberg 1995). Most initiatives taken under it – such as sending monitors to South Africa for its first all-race elections and supporting the Middle Eastern peace process – begged the question of how the CFSP differed from the previous EPC arrangements. Petty squabbles about finance and the role of the Commission made the CFSP seem woefully inadequate to the Union's foreign policy aspirations.

On the other hand, one of the EU's first joint actions prompted a useful dialogue between East European states through the CFSP initiative on 'stability pacts', which sought to promote agreements on borders and to link commitments on the treatment of minorities to eventual EU membership. The OSCE was charged with the supervision of resulting accords, such as the agreement signed between Slovakia and Hungary in March 1995. Moreover, the war in ex-Yugoslavia led to the breaking of new ground in discussions about linking the WEU with the EU. The EU took on the task of administering the town of Mostar in Bosnia in collaboration with the WEU.

The Maastricht Treaty singled out the WEU as 'an integral part of the development of the Union' which could 'elaborate and implement decisions and actions of the Union which have defence implications'. It affirmed that the WEU would be autonomous but linked to both NATO and the European Union. The potentially divisive question of whether the WEU would eventually be incorporated within the Union itself was left open for future discussion, ostensibly at the 1996 IGC.

The waters were muddied further when Mitterrand and Kohl announced plans in May 1992 for expanding the existing Franco-German joint brigade from 4,000 to create a 'Eurocorps' of up to 40,000 troops. The plans explicitly referred to the eventual goal of incorporating forces of other EU member states into the Eurocorps. The French expended substantial diplomatic energy trying to convince other EU states to contribute forces to the new formation even before the announcement of the plan. But the Eurocorps's very hazy links to the WEU – let alone NATO – were viewed by potential partners such as Belgium and Spain as violating the spirit of what was agreed at Maastricht. 'Atlanticist' states such as the Netherlands and the UK shunned the Franco-German plan as creating new security structures with the potential to undermine NATO. In the words of a US Assistant Secretary of Defense, 'we were not consulted in the least about the creation of Eurocorps. It came when we were redoing NATO strategy and caused a lot of consternation on our side about the whole notion of a European security identity.'[3]

In short, after the Soviet threat disappeared, new fissures opened up between the US and EU member states. These divisions were reflected in controversy about how existing institutions should be altered and how the different memberships of the EU, the WEU and NATO could be reconciled in a new European security architecture. The UK and the Netherlands began to talk openly about linking membership of the EU to NATO. The French feared that to do so would be to sanctify NATO's primacy in European security, thus undermining efforts to create a common European defence. The German position remained equivocal. Italy and other EU states often urged the need not only for American involvement in European security but also for a stronger European defence pillar, so that Germany was both counterbalanced by the US and bound within Europe (Lesser 1992: 183). The challenge for US–EU relations became the search for compromise within a myriad of national agendas.

3 NEW DOCTRINES AND INSTITUTIONAL CHANGE

The early 1990s brought substantial reformulation of NATO's political and strategic mission. The London Declaration in 1990 confirmed a shift from traditional strategic deterrence to 'stabilization' and 'reassurance'

(NATO 1990). Supporters of a continuing central role for NATO in European security were strengthened by the accelerating break-up of the Soviet Union in late 1991. As NATO's Secretary-General, Manfred Wörner, put it:

> The classical threat has disappeared. The risk is uncertainty – about the future political structure of the Soviet Union, the bad economic situation and all its consequences in a country which still has more than 3 million people under arms and tens of thousands of nuclear weapons. . . . The Soviet Union, or even Russia, is such an enormous land mass that it needs a geopolitical counterweight. I don't think Europe alone can provide it.[4]

The declaration of the Rome NATO summit in November 1991 urged that, 'in an environment of uncertainty and unpredictable challenges, our Alliance, which provides the essential transatlantic link as demonstrated by the significant presence of North American troops in Europe, retains its enduring value' (NATO 1991a). Changes in NATO's military strategy and force and command structures were agreed. A new 'strategic concept' committed the allies to smaller, more mobile and flexible conventional forces which could intervene quickly in localized regional conflicts.

The Atlanticist plan for preserving the leading role of NATO became reform of the Alliance's strategic doctrine combined with calls for a new European security architecture based on 'interlocking institutions', including the EU, the OSCE and the WEU, along with NATO itself. A statement on the new strategic concept urged that 'the strengthening of the security dimension in the process of European integration, and the enhancement of the role and responsibilities of the European members of the Alliance are positive and mutually reinforcing' (NATO 1991b). Pointedly, it insisted that NATO would remain the 'essential forum' for consultation between alliance members. The declaration also contained a reaffirmation of the central strategic principle which had underpinned NATO since its origins:

> [The Sovet Union's] conventional forces are significantly larger than those of any other European State and its large nuclear arsenal comparable only with that of the United States. These capabilities have to be taken into account if stability and security in Europe are to be preserved. . . . Nuclear forces based in Europe and committed to NATO provide an essential political and military link between the European and North American members of the Alliance. The Alliance will therefore maintain adequate nuclear forces in Europe.
>
> (NATO 1991b)

The Rome summit also exposed tensions which no amount of consensus on the Soviet situation could obscure. In his opening address Bush departed from a prepared text to tell his European counterparts, 'If you want to go your own way, if you don't need us any longer, say so.'[5] The comment was clearly intended for domestic US consumption: Bush risked stoking pressures in Congress for outright US withdrawal from Europe if he appeared too enthusiastic about an independent European defence identity. It was also a rare case of the US speaking its mind in the debate about the future of European security and seeking to strengthen the arguments of Atlanticist states such as the UK and the Netherlands.

On the Europeanist side, France approved the summit declaration and supported the new strategic concept. But Mitterrand railed against the idea that NATO should have a 'new political mission'.[6] In early 1992, the French poured scorn on a US-backed plan to create a NATO 'humanitarian aid unit' to deliver Western aid to the Soviet republics. The proposed unit clearly duplicated EU aid mechanisms and seemed a bald attempt to conjure up new chores for NATO. It was quietly abandoned within months.

Later in 1992, NATO finally appeared to bridge differences between its Atlanticist and Europeanist members and settle on a clear statement of its new role and purpose. At a meeting of foreign ministers in Oslo, a new 'reinforcement concept' was unveiled under which NATO would act in the service of conflict prevention operations taken by other institutions. The idea of 'interlocking institutions' was being fleshed out as never before as NATO 'eschew[ed] leadership in favour of sharing roles, risks, and responsibilities' (Kegley and Raymond 1994: 227; see also Ferguson 1992).

France's position on NATO's role continued to soften considerably. The 1994 Brussels NATO summit saw the French embrace US proposals for Combined Joint Task Forces (CJTF), which offered France the possibility of participation in specific peacekeeping missions without having to accept the diplomatic bloody nose of rejoining NATO's integrated command. CJTF meant that 'coalitions of the willing' could be constructed when conflict erupted in Europe. In principle, such coalitions could draw upon NATO resources, even if they were based on the WEU and did not include the US.

The French also found themselves in the unfamiliar position of supporting the US line that only NATO possessed the resources needed to pose a credible threat to the Serbs in Bosnia. NATO's new reinforcement role was put to the test for the first time as it agreed to protect and serve the UN's humanitarian mission. The two institutions were truly interlocked by a 'dual key' system, which required that both sanction NATO air strikes before they could take place.

NATO launched several 'pin-prick' attacks on Bosnian Serb positions in 1994–5 in response to UN requests. However, the dual key system provoked severe tensions between the United States and Europe. The US argued for robust, punitive attacks on the Bosnian Serbs. The UN and West European states feared that such an approach would jeopardize the humanitarian relief mission and efforts to seek a peaceful solution to the conflict. Much of the Western media, as well as the Muslim-led Bosnian government, pilloried the Clinton administration and the EU for their divisiveness and inability to stop the war.

The UN humanitarian mission became increasingly untenable in 1995. Latent tensions between Croatia and Croatian Serbs again reached a boiling point. Meanwhile, the Bosnian government launched a large-scale offensive, leading the Serbs to respond with further strangulation of Sarajevo and other Muslim 'safe areas'. At the UN's request in May 1995, NATO initiated new 'pin-prick' attacks in order to try to bomb the Bosnian Serbs into line. The Serb response was to seize several hundred UN personnel as hostages. The effect was to illustrate, more clearly than ever, the paralysis of the West and the international community in the Balkans.

Western diplomacy at least succeeded in convincing Slobodan Milošević, the leader of Serbia proper, to stop supporting Serbian war efforts elsewhere in ex-Yugoslavia, in exchange for a partial lifting of economic sanctions on Serbia. Milošević leaned on the Bosnian Serbs sufficiently hard to persuade them to free their UN hostages. He also refused to come to the aid of Croatian Serbs when they were routed by Croatian government forces in summer 1995.

However, Bosnian Serbs overran the Muslim 'safe areas' of Srebrenica and Zepa with apparent impunity, amidst new reports of mass executions of Muslims. The recently elected French President Jacques Chirac urged a muscular Western military response to retake the safe havens. Without the participation of the US, and specifically the use of its transport helicopters, Chirac's pleas were hollow, exposing Europe's continued military dependence on the US. In Washington, Congress gave notice of its strong opposition to further US involvement in the war but voted overwhelmingly to lift the arms embargo unilaterally, in defiance of a Clinton veto. In effect, Clinton's policy on Bosnia was 'rebuked for moral blindness and diplomatic incompetence by both political parties' (Safire 1995).

Under fierce public pressure to do *something* about Bosnia, the major European contributors to the UN force in the Balkans formed the 10,000-strong Rapid Reaction Force (RRF) in June 1995 to protect the UN's larger contingent on the ground. The RRF consisted of French, British and Dutch troops. However, its purpose remained unclear. The UK continued to claim that the consent of all parties (including Bosnian Serbs) was needed for the RRF to be deployed in any serious way. For their part, the Bosnian Serbs seized forty more Dutch blue-helmets as hostages, several weeks before the RRF was operational, to gain leverage if the new force did in fact intervene. A clear illustration of the impotence of the West in the face of human tragedy was the much-touted vote in Germany to deploy German Tornado fighters as part of the RRF, even though it stood idly by as Bosnian Serbs continued ethnic cleansing in Eastern Bosnia.

Finally, after a Serbian mortar attack on a Sarajevo market killed thirty-seven people in September 1995, the West put aside its differences and launched the largest NATO operation in history. Repeated airstrikes on Bosnian Serb positions were reinforced by artillery attacks by the RRF. A US-led peace initiative finally appeared to put a negotiated settlement to the crisis within reach, especially when the Bosnian Serbs agreed to allow Milošević to represent them in peace talks.

The Bosnian conflict illustrated three wider points about the nature of European security in the post-Cold War era. First, unless the West wished its forces to intervene as combatants themselves, it had to wait until the balance tilted in a desired direction, as in 1995 when the Serbs suffered setbacks in both Bosnia and Croatia. At that point, NATO military intervention hastened the shift and thus persuaded the Serbs to discuss a negotiated solution to the conflict.

Second, it remained difficult to 'interlock' institutions without creating gridlock. Seeking to solve or avert conflict using more than one institution usually makes intellectual sense. A logical division of labour exists between the UN, NATO, the WEU and the OSCE, and all should have a role in achieving a secure Europe. But different institutions will often have different agendas and priorities, as the UN and NATO did in Bosnia.

Third, Western Europe still remained deeply dependent on the US, not only for its security, but also to resolve conflicts on its borders. A good illustration was the dispute between Greece and Macedonia, to which a tentative settlement was brokered not by the EU itself, but only after a determined US diplomatic effort in 1995. Regardless of what its Treaties said, the EU still only had three weapons at its disposal in times of crisis: public opinion, the threat of withdrawing diplomatic recognition, and economic sanctions. To be able to shoulder its security responsibilities, the EU/WEU clearly needed an integrated system for decision-making, a command and control system, and a rapid transport capability, or at least clear provisions for the use of US assets. It also needed full German participation.

In debates about giving the EU a military capability to back up its foreign policy, it was perhaps revealing that the term 'security identity' was used far more often than 'security institutions' (see Waever 1996). Arguably, the EU's problem was its lack of an actual 'security identity'. Most European citizens still felt more loyalty to their nation-state than to the EU as a whole.

The campaign to bomb the Bosnian Serbs to the negotiating table illustrated that, at least for the forseeable future, NATO remained the only security institution which had the structures and technology to wield the collective military power of the West. By contrast, in the words of a Pentagon official, 'it was a mistake by the US to let the WEU "handle" ex-Yugoslavia. The WEU, especially its command structures, turned out to be Hollywood storefront.'[7]

Meanwhile, the vexing issue of Russia's role in European security remained unresolved. A tacit 'Slavic alliance' between Russia and Serbia led Yeltsin to condemn the NATO bombardment of the Bosnian Serbs in 1995. If only to appease his nationalist critics in advance of a domestic Russian election, Yeltsin described the NATO action as 'a first sign' of how an expanded and US-dominated NATO would behave. He further warned that rapid NATO enlargement would provoke a 'conflagration of war throughout Europe'.[8]

Yeltsin's statements highlighted how difficult it would be to reconcile the demands of East European countries for Western security guarantees and the need to avoid isolating Russia. Following the demise of the Warsaw Pact, the Western allies sought a way out of the dilemma by creating new mechanisms for involving East European states in NATO's activities without offering them actual NATO membership. For example, at the 1991 Rome summit, NATO governments announced the creation of the North Atlantic Cooperation Council (NACC), which promised all former Warsaw Pact members annual meetings with NATO foreign ministers and regular consultations with military authorities and experts. NACC exchanges covered a range of issues including force planning, the conversion of military industries to civilian production and the political control of armed forces in a democratic society.

NACC was accepted grudgingly by East European states which continued to assert that NATO membership was a primary goal of their foreign policies. The new forum proved useful in that it helped to build confidence between former enemies. NACC also gave the West an institution in which to push the former Soviet republics with nuclear weapons to guarantee that the process of consolidating weapons in Russia and gradually reducing their numbers would continue. Eventually, however, NACC became little more than a discussion group. Eastern countries sought to ensure that NACC membership did not become a poor man's substitute for full NATO membership. The question about enlargement became 'not whether but when', according to official NATO policy. The cause of Eastern states was taken up by the new Republican majorities in the US Congress after 1994. Their advocacy goaded Clinton to embrace a more rapid timetable for NATO enlargement than his administration would have preferred out of deference to Russia.

Groping for at least a short-term solution to the dilemma of NATO enlargement, the Clinton administration backed 'Partnerships for Peace', an initiative to engage Eastern (and 'neutral') countries in NATO activities through joint training exercises, officer exchanges, etc. Perhaps the only Clinton foreign policy to attract the support of most Republicans, the programme made it more likely that the accession of Eastern states might be a major political step, though a small one in military or logistical terms. The Clinton administration repeatedly hinted that NATO expansion could occur in the first part of its second term.

The American position on NATO was driven by domestic political considerations more than any sober analysis of European security needs. The debate about NATO enlargment became a typically American debate about power, principles and morality. It lacked much appreciation of the dangers of creating new political divisions or exacerbating latent ethnic tensions in the region by isolating Ukraine or offering membership to Hungary but not Romania. It also took little account of the fact that most East European armies were poorly trained and equipped. Defence spending in the Visegrad countries in 1995 was less than half what it had been in 1989, and the departure of the USSR left them with no air defence system or viable command structure. In short, in the absence of considerable Western investments, Eastern states were destined to remain 'consumers', as opposed to 'suppliers', of security in Europe.

Many US Republicans found it impossible to conceive that Russia could ever be anything but an enemy of the US, particularly when bloody attacks were launched on the breakaway Russian republic of Chechnya in late 1994. Bringing the new Eastern democracies into Western institutions quickly, before Russia had a chance to threaten them again, became a logical policy option. Above all, US Republicans sought to use the NATO enlargement issue to cast Clinton as weak and an appeaser of Russia. For his part, Clinton had to be mindful of large ethnic Polish populations in Pennsylvania and Illinois, two US states that he *had* to hold to be re-elected in 1996.

The link between NATO and EU/WEU membership remained a delicate issue in transatlantic relations and a worrying one for Eastern states. For example, Kohl provoked considerable angst in Poland when he declared, in a speech to its Parliament in July 1995, that there was an 'internal connection' between Polish membership of the EU and of NATO.[9] Poles naturally became concerned that any such link might become an excuse to delay the integration of Poland into Western institutions.

By this point, the EU had signed 'Europe agreements' with the Visegrad states, the three Baltic republics, Romania, Bulgaria and Slovenia. Clearly, however, all could not join at once, leading to considerable concern in Eastern capitals about the prospect of being left for long periods on the wrong side of the EU's redrawn borders. In geopolitical terms, it made no sense to have Poland and Hungary in either the EU or NATO with a dissatisfied Slovakia between them. But concerns persisted about Slovakia's democratic credentials and record on human rights. Thus, the idea of 'Poland first' began to circulate, causing despondency in Budapest. For their part, the Poles and Czechs began to place more hope in NATO than in EU membership, since the former included the US – the only Western country clearly committed to Eastern Europe and able to show leadership – while the EU remained consumed with archaic debates about its internal structures and captured by special interests.

Arguably, EU membership remained a more urgent need for East European states seeking, above all, to modernize their economies. The link drawn at Maastricht between EU and WEU membership meant that the latter was likely to undergo considerable change in the near future with critical consequences for the development of a new European security architecture. A crucial point in debates about developing the WEU's role was the strength of the mutual defence commitment contained in its Brussels Treaty. The treaty stipulates that WEU member states must respond with all resources possible to an attack on any other member state. It allows for decisions to be taken within the WEU by two-thirds majority or simple majority vote in certain specific cases. By contrast, the NATO treaty commits each member state only to 'such action as it deems necessary' in the event of an attack on another NATO state. The difference is crucial, given new political and fiscal constraints on US internationalism, which could come into play if a crisis arose.

The WEU's treaty expires in 1998 and thus its future is an open book. It is difficult to imagine that its links to the CFSP will not be strengthened in some respect at the EU's 1996 IGC, despite enlargement to include non-WEU members Finland, Austria and Sweden, a year earlier. The insistence of the UK and France on maintaining their nuclear arsenals despite deep cuts agreed between the US and the USSR (and later Russia) in 1991–2 reflected the perceived need to keep options open and to preserve resources which conceivably could be used as the foundation for an exclusively European security structure. French nuclear tests in 1995 were justified by Chirac partly on the grounds that France did not want to be dependent on US computer simulation techniques to ensure the safety and reliability of its nuclear weapons. Regardless of his motives following global outcry against French nuclear tests, Chirac's declaration in 1995 that France might be willing to consider 'Europeanizing' its nuclear deterrent was a potentially important development.

Even if it remains a poor stepsister to NATO, the WEU has undergone considerable institutional development since the early 1990s. At French insistence, it created its own version of the NACC, including all East European states and the Baltic republics, but not CIS states. The move signalled closer relations between the WEU and those Eastern states

closest to future membership of the EU. The compatibility of a strengthened WEU with NATO was highlighted by the admission of Turkey,
Iceland and Norway as 'associate' WEU members. The Maastricht Treaty
made it possible for non-WEU members such as Denmark, Ireland or
Finland to play a political role in the CFSP without contributing forces
to the WEU.

The position of Germany remained a critical determinant of debates
about European security. The early 1990s saw the emergence of a new,
younger generation of German politicians. Klaus Kinkel, who replaced
Genscher as German Foreign Minister, and Volker Rühe, who became
Defence Minister, were notably less encumbered than their predecessors
by notions that German assertiveness would always be associated with the
experience of war in the minds of Western partners. Rühe led calls to
amend the German Basic Law to allow the participation of German troops
in peacekeeping outside the NATO area.

Still, the German foreign policy community remained steeped in the
art of consensus-building in the pursuit of multilateral actions and positions. The Kohl government's foreign policy record after unification
revealed a clear acceptance of the principle that Germany's primary role
was to provide leadership of collective institutions. Despite its unilateralism on Yugoslavia, it often overrode domestic political pressures when
Germany's broader national goals and image abroad were at stake. Friendship treaties were signed with Hungary and Czechoslovakia in 1992
despite resistance from ethnic Germans who refused to forsake longstanding property claims in both states. Anderson and Goodman (1993: 60)
argued that:

> Over the course of forty years, West Germany's reliance on a web of
> international institutions to achieve its foreign policy goals, born of an
> instrumental chioce among painfully few alternatives, became so com-
> plete as to cause these institutions to become embedded in the very
> definition of state interests and strategies ... Germany's institutional
> commitments in the post-1989 period [were] reflexive; they ha[d]
> become ingrained, even assumed.

As such, Germany became a crucial 'swing vote' in debates about
developing new European security structures. While supporting the
creation of the Eurocorps with France in 1992, Rühe stressed that it had
to remain compatible with NATO's command structure to avoid weakening the Atlantic Alliance. Eventually, Rühe's stance helped Spain, Belgium
and Luxembourg to join Eurocorps without fears of upsetting transatlantic relations. The Germans emerged as the key actors in bridging
the gap between Atlanticists and Europeanists.

By the mid-1990s the EU had prepared the ground for an independent
European security capability. It still had not gone far beyond developing

a fallback position in case of major changes in the US commitment in Europe. A true European 'defence union' was years away and the American commitment to NATO remained a generally non-partisan and robust one. In purely practical terms, the cost of keeping American troops in Europe was only about 15 per cent higher than the cost of keeping them in US. Meanwhile, opinion polls showed that nearly three-quarters of Americans thought that the US should stay in NATO. However, the same polls indicated that about two-thirds thought that the American 'should reduce its involvement in world affairs' (Sloan 1995b: 4–5). Eventual outcomes to the debate about European security structures will be determined primarily by the way in which US policy responds to American opinion, as well as the evolution of the CFSP and events in Eastern Europe. The debates will continue as a major focus of US–EU relations into the 21st century.

4 EUROPEAN SECURITY IN THEORY AND PRACTICE

For all its apparent shortcomings in a post-Cold War world, *neorealism* continues to offer clear explanations and predictions for international politics. Its proponents attribute the EU's impotence as an international actor, first, to the impossibility of a 'common' foreign policy, and second, to its lack of military power. Neorealists note that the US spends more than twice as much on its military than do the EU countries combined, and about ten times more than Germany. For them, the EU's continued weakness underscores the point that sovereign nation-states remain the only credible actors in international relations. Military power provides the only credible deterrent to aggression.

Neorealists doubt that the West can avoid conflict with Russia. Russian foreign policy has shifted primarily because most of its political class now shares neorealist assumptions. Shearman (1993: 158) argues that 'as an independent Russia, shorn of its empire, began to search for a new role in global politics, realists came to dominate both the academic research institutes and the Russian foreign policy establishment'.

If the US acts on neorealist assumptions, one must wonder how much longer NATO can survive in its present form. With the Soviet empire dismantled and Germany bound within the EU, it is hard to see why the US as a 'unitary-rational actor' should remain committed to European defence. Waltz (1993: 75–6) insists that 'we know from balance-of-power theory as well as from history that war-winning coalitions collapse on the morrow of victory, the more surely if it is a decisive one . . . NATO's days are not numbered, but its years are.'

For his part, Krasner (1993: 23) argues that:

The rhetorical vision now articulated by most major Western leaders –

the continuation of a strong NATO led by the United States and the development of a stronger European Community capable of formulating integrated security and foreign policies – is untenable.

Neorealists thus predict that the process of European integration will stagnate now that the Soviet threat is gone. In debates about European security, Atlanticists tend to share the neorealist view that European unity is fickle:

NATO enabled the process of European unification to go ahead at that speed. There is a substantial risk that if you took the US away and broke our alliance, that nations of Western Europe could fall back into competing alliances and counteralliances.[10]

Neorealist logic suggests that the break-up of the Warsaw Pact will ultimately lead the major European powers to compete to bring newly unattached states under their influence (see Thatcher 1992). Germany and Russia particularly will be tempted to develop client-states in Eastern Europe; with the possibility that blocs of states will emerge between which conflict is inevitable. Neorealists assume that any violent conflict in Europe will be 'indivisible' in political terms, and thus invoke the interests of the major European powers.

Ullman (1991: 144) offers the counter-argument that Germany, Russia and the US all lack vital interests in Eastern Europe, 'besides the negative one of seeking assurance that the region will not become a place where threats aimed at them originate'. Any purely national interest – such as Germany's interest in maintaining its economic influence in Eastern Europe – is likely to be outweighed by a common interest in maintaining the peaceful preconditions for economic reconstruction in the East, or at least ensuring that violent conflicts remain localized and do not make claims on national resources. For Hoffmann (1992: 218), the central threat to European security 'is not the neorealist nightmare of collisions among ambitious major actors, but economic chaos, political regression away from democracy, ethnic violence, and a void in cooperation'.

In contrast to neorealists, *institutionalists* argue that NATO, the EU and other existing institutions can be revamped to suit new realities and perform new tasks. Institutionalist logic suggests that the US and EU should 'seek to maintain the valuable international institutions that continue to exist, since the effort required to maintain them is less than would be needed to construct new ones' (Keohane 1984: 247). Thus, NATO should be preserved and reformed to accommodate a strengthened European pillar.

Many institutionalists insist that the OSCE remains useful in spite of its unwieldy membership and awkward decision-making arrangements. Despite its lack of a strict legal framework, the OSCE is applauded for having institutionalized 'peace-promoting' behaviour among its signatories, something which all members now take for granted and expect all other members to uphold (Hyde-Price and Roper 1991: 256–7; Efinger and Rittberger 1992). However, Keohane (1994: 236) disagrees: the OSCE 'has, it seems to me, been a failure, and is likely to continue to be ineffective'. Its structure may have been appropriate to using human rights issues against the Soviets, but it cannot be readily adapted for traditional security, democratic infrastructure or economic aid purposes. The lesson is that structures matter and there are limits to the malleability of Cold War institutions.

Still, nearly all institutionalists prescribe 'interlocking institutions' as the only solution to the new European security dilemma. NATO can act as a military insurance policy, but the WEU should be developed into a security organization with teeth. The European Union can link the economic power of Western Europe with the military capability of the WEU. Institutionalists remind us, in the words of a former Clinton administration official, that 'there is no tidy, institutional solution to the change in America's European role' (Walker 1991: 129).

Liberalism appears to have few prescriptions to offer in the debate on European security. Yet its central assumption – that free trade benefits all – points to the benefits of open defence procurement regimes and free trade in armaments. Creating a single EU market in armaments could lower the cost of European defence substantially and thus ease the transition towards reduced US contributions to NATO. Liberalism highlights the objective economic reasons for applying the EU's rules on open trade to the arms trade.

More broadly, recalling Kant's dictum that liberal states do not go to war with one another, empirical research suggests that liberal democracy *per se* is not a force for peace in any 'straightforward, uniform, or consistent fashion' (Morgan and Campbell 1991: 210). Yet the same research suggests that the domestic structures of states are crucial in determining their proclivity for aggression. Especially among the major liberal powers, relatively strong constraints on the autonomy of political elites lower the possibility that conflicts involving these states will escalate into war.

Liberals thus argue that the entrenchment of democracy in Eastern Europe is likely to make armed conflict less likely because domestic constraints on warlike behaviour will be strengthened. Liberal logic suggests that European security will be ensured first and foremost through the consolidation of liberal democracy in the former Warsaw Pact states. Incorporating them into Western security structures should be an urgent priority because this would pose additional constraints on decision-making by East European elites. Liberals add that expanding trade links between the former Warsaw Pact states and the West would provide further disincentives to violent conflict because war disrupts trade and stymies the economic growth which it engenders.

Reformists continue to deplore the US military presence in Europe. They believe that popular opinion can be mobilized to reject NATO and the continued existence of nuclear weapons, as it was in the early 1980s. Even analysts who spurned reformist assumptions conceded that the massive anti-nuclear street protests of that time were 'the most impressive display of populist muscle in the postwar era' (Joffe 1987: 3).

In 1995, France's nuclear tests were met with boycotts of French products throughout the industrialized world. Reformists relished polls which suggested that nearly 60 per cent of France's own citizens were opposed to the tests.[11] They also poured scorn on Chirac's offer to 'Europeanize' the French nuclear deterrent:

> Even if Germans' deeply ingrained inhibitions about any revival of a military stance could be overcome, the impossibility of a genuine sharing of ownership and control would rule it out. . . . Rather than stubbornly persevering with a morally and logically flawed project, he could, by revoking his 'irrevocable' decision [to commence French nuclear tests], take the lead in the movement for nuclear weapons' total removal.
>
> (Bonnart 1995)

More generally, the development of an EU role in defence is viewed with alarm by reformists. They stress that the creation of another superpower – defined in traditional military terms – is the last thing that Europe needs. Many argue that 'military concepts of defense should be replaced by civilian concepts, such as social defense', or non-violent resistance to external aggression (Spretnak and Capra 1986: 187).

Reformists insist that reforming political structures to ensure environmental protection and the observance of individual rights is the true solution to the new European security dilemma. The Western aid effort to Eastern Europe is derided by reformists as far too small and concerned with promoting capitalism, as opposed to democracy, human rights or ecology. Western aid programmes do not sufficiently link economic aid to democratic practices and protection of the rights of minorities.

Reformists noted with alarm that no Eastern army – except that of the Czech Republic – was firmly controlled by civilian authorities by the mid-1990s. The legitimation of East European military structures within the NACC and Partnership for Peace meant that the West was missing an opportunity to seize on a decline in public support in Eastern countries for the military and military values. Instead of enlarging or tinkering with NATO or the WEU, reformists favoured developing the OSCE process and particularly the Council of Europe, which puts the European Court of Human Rights at the service of citizens of new democracies whose human rights are violated.

Reformist arguments reflect the assumption that citizen-publics can become enlightened about their shared interest in peace and cooperation. They observe that the transmission of reformist values throughout Eastern Europe was critical to the revolutions of 1989. Reformists believe that 'increasing respect for both the ethics and effectiveness of non-violent approaches to achieving political change may be of enduring significance for European security' (Greene 1992: 142).

If nothing else, reformism at least highlights how the debate on European security often lapses into symbolic politics. On one side there is much French posturing about European unity. On the other, one finds alarmism among Atlanticists about the need to prepare for barely imaginable contingencies. The debate is far from settled, and it points to expanded scope for choice in US–EU security relations. But a political rebalancing of the Atlantic Alliance is a necessity and a prerequisite of US–EU partnership across a full range of security issues.

Part III

The case for the New Transatlanticism

Chapter 7

The changing essence of security

The expansion of Western foreign policy agendas to encompass a more eclectic set of issues mirrors an expansion in the very meaning of the term 'security'. Traditionally, political scientists working in the sub-discipline of 'strategic studies' assumed that international security was a product of the balance of nuclear terror between East and West. The potential horrors of nuclear war were precisely what preserved the 'long peace' of the Cold War period (Gaddis 1987). National security was viewed narrowly as military security.

The oil crises of the 1970s altered these perceptions. Economic well-being and access to natural resources became more important components of national security (Hager 1976; von Geusau and Pelkmans 1982). Then, the so-called Second Cold War of the early 1980s acted to reinvigorate strategic studies. The study of international relations became dominated by specialists concerned with nuclear weapons and the exotica used to measure their potency: megatonnage, throw-weight, first-strike capability, etc. MccGwire (1986: 56) summed up the frustration of many who believed that Western deterrence of the Soviets had become a 'dogma' propagated by 'a new breed of "tough-minded" strategic analysts, who liked to think through problems abstractly and in a political vacuum'.

The disintegration of the Warsaw Pact, increased awareness of environmental degradation and heightened concern about human rights point to the need for more holistic definitions of 'security'. This chapter links US–EU relations and recent debates about European security to new thinking about national and international security. It poses fundamental questions about whether and how stronger US–EU relations can promote a more secure international order.

Section 1 seeks to explain why the essence of security changed in the early 1990s. Section 2 offers an interpretative look at the implications of these changes for US and EU foreign policies and bilateral relations. The quest for new Western foreign policy doctrines is the focus for section 3. Section 4 assesses the extent to which changing notions of security are compatible with the assumptions of the four major theories of international relations.

1 REDEFINING SECURITY AFTER THE COLD WAR

The Second Cold War was not only a golden age for strategic studies. It also inspired the rise of eclectic and loosely organized peace movements on both sides of the Atlantic. Ranging from scruffy European Greens to commissions of the international great and good, members shared the conviction that the arms race and its massive financial costs heightened insecurity in the global system and drained resources away from basic human welfare needs (see Brandt Commission 1983; Palme Commission 1984; Spretnak and Capra 1986).

By the late 1980s many of the arguments of the peace movement had begun to creep into scholarly analysis of the Cold War system. Mueller (1989: 227) argued that a common set of values had emerged which made major war between developed states – even those on opposite sides of the East–West divide – obsolete:

> There has been a shift in values: prosperity has become something of an overriding goal, and war – even inexpensive war – is almost universally seen as an especially counterproductive method for advancing this goal ... prosperity and economic growth have been enshrined as major status, and even power symbols in the international arena, occupying much of the turf previously claimed by military prowess and by success in war.

By the mid-1990s, four norms, or established principles of behaviour, were widely accepted. First, wars were no longer viewed as a rational method of solving disputes between major powers. The three classical functions of military power were to seize territory, hold it or defend it against invasion. The most important change in international politics after the Cold War was a perceptible decline in the utility of military power for all but the third function (Ullman 1991: 23–7; Luard 1988).

The global order remained anarchic in that it lacked a global hegemon or authority higher than the nation-state. But the belief that major powers had nothing to gain from making war on each other became pervasive. Powerful states began to seek new methods for solving the problem which was often assumed to be insoluble in the strategic studies literature: the 'security dilemma'.

> Even if no state has any desire to attack others, none can be sure that others' intentions are peaceful, or will remain so; hence each must accumulate power for defense. Since no state can know that the power accumulation of others is defensively motivated only, each must assume

that it might be intended for attack. Consequently, each party's power increments are matched by the others, and all wind up with no more security than when the vicious cycle began, along with the cost incurred in having acquired and having to maintain their power.

(Snyder 1984: 461)

The break-up of the Soviet Union proved that nuclear weapons did not guarantee the national security of states. The main lesson of 1989 was that 'great shifts in power in the international system ... derived from relative economic performance, and the dynamism of economic institutions, and not the possession of weapons of mass destruction' (Walker 1992: 277). The economic, diplomatic and moral costs of using military power as a tool of foreign policy increased. Meanwhile, especially with an increasingly globalized economy, the benefits of territorial control or geopolitical influence diminished.

A second and related norm was that market economies became viewed as prerequisites for secure states with stable relations among themselves. The end of the Cold War made military competition between major states seem a waste of precious national resources. These same resources could be deployed to enhance national advantage in global economic competition, a game at which states needed to succeed to guarantee national economic security (see Moran 1990/1). Autarky was no longer a viable path to national economic security, if it ever had been. Economic growth and rising standards of living were available only to states which traded and competed in an open global economic order, which itself could be sustained only through international cooperation.

One effect of rising economic interdependence was to recast the nature of competition between major states. As Lister (1990: 103) argues, 'unlike ideological and territorial disputes ... [economic] issues are susceptible to non-zero-sum solutions which should make them more negotiable'. Another effect – particularly but not exclusively in the EU – was to alter the way that governments viewed their national sovereignty. National sovereignty increasingly became seen for what it is: 'the recognition by internal and external actors that the state has the exclusive authority to intervene coercively in activities within its territory' (Thomson 1995: 219). In other words, sovereignty came to be viewed more as a right than as a power, one which certainly did not bestow economic autonomy or control. Most governments began to realize that they could often better (indeed sometimes *only*) achieve their national economic goals through cooperation. For example, enhanced European competitiveness was possible only through pooling sovereignty to create the internal market.

A third norm was that Western states – at least under certain circumstances – were willing to take steps to prevent localized conflicts from becoming humanitarian tragedies (Harriss 1995). US and European governments often found it difficult to justify putting their own military forces at risk in countries which posed no direct threat to their own national security. On the other hand, increasingly globalized media made Western citizens less tolerant of genocide or starvation. As Robert Jackson (1995: 123) noted:

> It is becoming a world in which statesmen have international and humanitarian as well as national responsibilities. . . . If national responsibility was all that mattered in international relations the Somalia and Bosnia problems would be left to the people who live in those countries to sort out themselves.

A fourth norm was embraced by rich states and their scientific communities, if not globally: actions had to be taken to protect the planet from environmental degradation. Since pollution did not respect national boundaries, environmental degradation was a problem which threatened the security of all nations and peoples. Public support for increased EU powers in environmental protection was stronger than for any other area of policy (see Commission 1995c).

After the Warsaw Pact collapsed, these norms began to be reflected more clearly in Western security policies. In his 1989 Berlin speech, Baker (1991: 5) argued that, 'as we construct a new security architecture that maintains the common defense, the non-military component of European security will grow.' It remained difficult not to be vague about precisely what 'non-military security' meant. But its essence was a more 'stable peace' based not on fear but on positive relationships, and on an international system in which war was deterred by collective satisfaction with the status quo rather than by nuclear stand-off (Boulding 1987).

It primarily meant thinking about security *holistically* and embracing two key assumptions. The first was about the changed nature of international security. A balance of military power became just one basis of secure relations between states, which could only be achieved through mutual political accommodation. The second assumption concerned national security:

> A nation can no longer obtain security by unilateral means. It can enhance its own security only by enhancing the security of other countries. If it acts to increase the insecurity of other countries, it ends up increasing its own insecurity.
>
> (Miall 1991: 305)

These assumptions implied that the 'security dilemma' was far more likely to lead weak or insecure states – as opposed to strong or secure ones – to adopt violence as a response to real or imagined threats. Weak states were unable to ensure domestic economic security or command popular legitimacy, and thus remained dissatisfied with the status quo.

They existed as 'holes in the fabric of the international order' (Buzan 1991: 46). For example, weak states were unlikely to meet their obligations under international environmental agreements (Hurrell 1995). The contemporary international system included many more weak states than strong and stable ones. State-building thus became a logical goal for Western security policies, particularly in Eastern Europe and the CIS, but more broadly in the less developed world as a whole.

In the wake of the Cold War, security became mostly a product of domestic political economies. To some extent, the US and EU have tried to encourage economic stability and growth in the former Eastern bloc through the EBRD and G-24 aid effort. But the West failed to do what the US did in the immediate post-war period: create institutions such as the OEEC which offered aid in exchange for domestic economic reform. The lack of political will in the US and EU to give the Eastern countries clear policy advice was partly a consequence of divisions within the West itself. One particularly harsh assessment was that Eastern Europe witnessed the economic version of Western policy in Bosnia (see Gros and Steinherr 1995).

In fairness, the experience of building capitalist or democratic states in the West offered few guides for the East. The US or EU could hardly prescribe that the CIS and East European states modernize in the style of most West European states. If they did, they would encourage the construction of brutal and oppressive state structures in the hope that historical accidents (e.g. the rise of Hitler and Mussolini followed by a horrible war) might lead eventually to Western-style democracy (Tilly 1975).

Whatever their paths to modernization, the security problems of the former Eastern bloc and less developed countries had almost nothing to do with the problems associated with 'strategic studies'. Human rights violations increasingly took place against a backdrop of civil war or ethnic strife rather than through state oppression by authoritarian regimes, as illustrated by genocide in Rwanda and ethnic cleansing in Bosnia. The West could not remain aloof from human rights violations as these increasingly become the root cause of refugee problems (Amnesty International 1995). The wider point was that 'a secure international community will be one in which all or almost all the units are effective in meeting the basic needs of their citizens' (Booth 1991b: 349).

A holistic approach to security suggests that international cooperation on a scale previously unseen is needed to resolve the security problems of weak states, and thus create a more peaceful international order. Crushing debts keep LDCs poor. Poverty leads to ecologically unsound economic practices. Protection of Northern textile or agricultural industries leads LDCs such as India and China to develop export industries in armaments; the weapons produced are usually of such an inferior quality that other LDCs are the only viable markets for them. Aid agencies such as the IMF impose painful economic adjustment programmes; these erode the legitimacy of the governments that accept them and lead many to repress dissent (Thomas 1991: 286–7). Environmental protection is, by nature, a goal which can only be pursued by rethinking the present global allocation of finite resources. Results may have been disappointing, but the 1992 Rio summit and the 1995 Copenhagen UN Conference on Social Development at least prompted enhanced awareness of the environmental costs of Western consumption patterns and the urgent need for LDCs to have basic social programmes in primary education and health. They also yielded new ideas about lowering the debts of the poorest LDCs and about linking Western aid to LDC commitments to reduce pollution emissions.

A holistic approach also points to the importance of individual or 'citizen's security'. The people's revolutions in Eastern Europe and the former Soviet Union reaffirmed to many in the West that governments which deny their citizens' basic freedoms can and should be toppled by mass resistance. Western tolerance for governments which repress dissent and violate human rights has lessened since the Cold War ended. The heightened profile and influence of Amnesty International, and Western concern about repression in Burma, Mongolia and parts of Africa, are indicative.

Perhaps above all, a holistic approach lengthens the timeframe of security policies. Strategic studies offered no vision of the future besides one in which constant modernization of arsenals could prolong the balance of nuclear terror. It is now possible to imagine a more peaceful system of international relations, given creative, long-term thinking. In particular, coping with environmental degradation, the population explosion and nuclear proliferation will mean developing systems of incentives which could lead to adjustments in state behaviour. The alternative is future international insecurity. Security policies must become preventive, not just reactive.

New definitions of security imply 'more an attitude of mind than a set of concrete policies' (Booth 1991b: 336). A sea change in actual policies presupposes a fundamental change in attitudes. It will also require Western leadership of a sort rarely seen since 1989.

2 THE IMPLICATIONS OF THE NEW ASSUMPTIONS

The effects of redefined notions of security have become perceptible in Western foreign policies and US–EU relations. The Clinton administration refocused foreign policy on the goal of 'economic security', even if the US continued to spend almost as much on its military as the rest of the world combined (Borosage 1993/4). The EU's own self-image had long been informed by an expanded definition of international security, but it continued to lack the political unity to act as a 'civilian superpower'. In particular, the restructuring of European security arrangements was informed by new thinking about security and a general need to rebalance the Atlantic Alliance politically.

US foreign policy: old obstacles to new thinking

Formidable doctrinal and institutional obstacles must be surmounted before a more holistic view of security is embraced by the US foreign policy establishment. The record of the Bush administration from 1988 to 1992 suggested that the Cold War ethos of US foreign policy remained largely unchanged (see Mandelbaum 1991). The Gulf War was presented as a morally justified 'act of catharsis which should and would lead to higher standards of international behaviour in international affairs and particularly in the region' (Gittings 1991: 2). Yet, fearing that the territorial splintering of Iraq would upset geopolitical stability, the US gave little more than rhetorical support for the Kurdish and Shiite resistance to Saddam Hussein's regime after the war. Despite Bush's insistence that a new arms race in the Middle East would be 'tragic', his administration sought Congressional authorization to ship $18 billion in new US weapons to five states in the region soon after the war (Gittings 1991: 3).

Meanwhile, US policy towards the Soviet Union hinged on a stubborn, often blind faith in Gorbachev, despite his myopic plans to marry a free-market economy to the Soviet political system. Bush's December 1991 speech in Kiev, which warned of the dangers of the break-up of the USSR for regional stability, was remarkably ignorant of the groundswell of public support for Ukrainian independence. He repeatedly vetoed Congressional proposals to use economic sanctions to put pressure on China over human rights.

Pressures to shift US fiscal resources from defence to economic development or deficit reduction were counterbalanced in the 1990s by the political costs. Debate on the Bush administration's modest defence cuts did not occur along clear party lines because

> the military budget has been revealed as the world's largest jobs program. . . . The struggle is no longer just between the doves and hawks. It is now between the 'haves' (those with major weapons programmes in their districts and states) and the 'have-nots' (those who depend little on the military-industrial complex).
>
> (Isaacs 1992: 5)

The political economy of US military spending changed remarkably little after the end of the Cold War, despite the yawning federal budget deficit and the Republican agenda for reforming Congress. Clinton's lack of military experience and decision to tackle discrimination against gays in the armed forces immediately after his election combined to weaken his administration *vis-à-vis* the Pentagon and its supporters. Over time, his administration came to view sharp defence cuts as politically unthinkable, given the reliance on military spending of key states which he needed to win in order to be re-elected.

Meanwhile, a new debate about 'military readiness' bordered on the farcical. Pentagon complaints about the 'hollowing out' of US forces belied the fact that its budget was essentially unchanged from the late 1970s (Kaufmann 1994: 29). The new Republican majorities restructured and centralized the Congressional committee system, but left intact strong links between committees, constituent military industries and federal agencies (Hook and Cloud 1994).

The Clinton administration groped for new doctrines to guide its foreign policy. In May 1993, the State Department Under Secretary for Political Affairs Peter Tarnoff admitted that the US lacked the resources, inclination and will to lead on as many international issues as it had in the past. A year later, under the banners of 'enlarging democracy' and 'aggressive multilateralism', the administration pledged to seek democratic reforms in autocratic states, encourage 'state-building' in LDCs, and promote the development of more robust international institutions. However, the campaign had little resonance, particularly after the extension of trade privileges to China despite its human rights record, the UN débâcle in Somalia and the withdrawal of US forces from the policing of the arms embargo on Bosnia.

Meanwhile, the election of Republican majorities to Congress in 1994 reflected, perhaps above all, the rise of economic populism in the US. The declining fortunes of the US middle class were a powerful source of voter discontent. By some estimates, the economic situation of 80 per cent of US citizens did not substantially improve after the late 1980s. The first foreign policy experience of the large Congressional freshman class in early 1995 was the Mexican peso crisis, which prompted a huge, $40 billion 'rescue package' with a large US contribution. Although NAFTA provided safeguards against such crises, the immediate effect was to taint it and free trade generally in both popular and Congressional mind. Economic populists such as Ross Perot encouraged the widespread belief that NAFTA and cheap foreign imports were to blame for stagnant or falling real incomes in the US.

Many Republicans in Congress embraced 'aggressive unilateralism' as a foreign policy doctrine. In particular, a critical mass of newcomers expressed anxiety about the erosion of US sovereignty and its declining status as a trading power. On the Democrat side, many centrist moderates were defeated in the 1994 election. One effect was to empower left-wing, free trade sceptics in the Congressional party who tended to represent economically declining areas. Writing before the 1994 election, Nollen and Quinn (1994: 522) argued that 'few forces in support of free trade are left in US politics'.

Thus, an expanding foreign policy agenda was manifest above all in pressures for a tougher US trade policy. A National Security Directive in 1991 mandated a fundamental reshaping of the functions of US intelligence agencies such as the Central Intelligence Agency (CIA), which henceforth would gather data on natural resource shortages, global health problems and international R&D efforts. However, its bumbling attempts to gather 'economic intelligence' led to the so-called *affaire Pasqua* in 1995, when CIA agents were caught trying to bribe French authorities to obtain 'trade secrets' widely available already in the commercial press.

For his part, Kantor (1993) mused that:

> Past administrations have often neglected US economic and trading interests because of foreign or defence policy concerns. . . . [But] the days when we could afford to do so are long past. In the post-Cold War order, our national security depends on our economic strength.

American unilateralism in trade policy appeared to validate Krasner's (1982a: 33) maxim that declining powers naturally seek to realize short-term and politically motivated consumption goals; they rarely show leadership in developing international cooperation. Expanded notions of national security clearly create the potential for new tensions in US–EU relations. Strong transatlantic political links are vital if the pursuit of a new set of US national security objectives is not to result in a new round of bilateral trade wars.

EU foreign policy: a 'civilian superpower'?

The EU has long sought to translate its substantial non-military power into international influence. When the EPC mechanism was created in the early 1970s, Galtung (1973) was the first to suggest that the EU was a 'superpower in the making'. Common foreign policy actions gave the Union the potential to wield a type of political, economic and cultural power quite different from that of the US or USSR.

The EU cultivated the image of a 'civilian power' in its efforts to broker peaceful solutions to conflicts in the Middle East and Europe through the OSCE (Tsakaloyannis 1989: 243–5). But the civilian power concept was undermined by the EPC's institutional defects, the marginalization of the EU when armed conflict did arise, and the rise of Second Cold War in the 1980s. The EU was accused of wishful thinking by hard-headed sceptics who argued that it lacked the solidarity to wield its collective weight, while its individual member states could not remain aloof from superpower politics (see Bull 1983a, 1983b).

Changing notions of security rekindled interest in the 'civilian power' concept in the early 1990s. Its supporters claimed that the EU was developing into a credible political and diplomatic force which – compared to the US – was more sensitive to wider political realities and less eager to resort to military solutions (see Allen and Smith 1990; Hyde-Price 1992: 128–30). Perhaps ironically, the end of the Cold War helped to ease the EU into a role in the previously untouchable realm of defence and security (Buzan *et al.* 1990: 259). The development of the WEU as the defence arm of the Community became politically acceptable because it was clear that an EU defence identity would be purely defensive or preventive.

Yet both the Gulf War and the Yugoslav conflict highlighted the EU's impotence and utter dependence on American leadership when armed conflict erupted. The EU's 'civilian politics' approach to the Gulf War was possible only because US military power meant that there would be no dire consequences if it failed. Germany's contribution of funds instead of troops to the war effort seemed practical at the time, but sordid in retrospect. As Brenner (1991: 674–5) urged:

> The commercialization of mutual security commitments which are meant to be reciprocal encourages the United States to avoid facing up to the implications of its economic weakness, while permitting the Germans . . . to postpone indefinitely the moment of truth in confronting their obligations as world power.

Given the declining utility of military power, it seemed paradoxical to argue that the EU needed a military capability to meet its international obligations. However, in political terms, the pooling of military sovereignty came to be viewed as an acceptable method of inducing Germany to share fully in defence costs and burdens. It also promised to give the EU a more powerful voice in political decisions about how the West responded to international crises.

As interest in developing an ESDI increased, peacekeeping as a response to regional crises emerged as a growth industry. Between 1988 and 1992 the UN carried out fourteen peacekeeping operations, more than it had conducted in its entire previous history. Ullman (1991: 147) forecast 'plenty of opportunities for peacekeeping in the territory lying between Germany and the Urals'. The operation to protect Kurdish refugees after the Gulf War was the kind of crisis-management operation for which the EU remained unprepared (Galvin 1991: 7).

A defence capability would allow the EU to apply as much or as little pressure on those who threaten European security as is deemed politically necessary. If the same force were available for use beyond Europe, the EU could contribute on equal terms with the US and others to peacekeeping initiatives sanctioned by the UN. Above all, regardless of one's view of the viability of the notion of a 'civilian superpower', it is clear that the CFSP will always lack credibility without a defence force to act as a tool of last resort in the event of armed conflict.

European security and beyond

Future US support for an EU security and defence identity cannot be assumed. Despite its hesitations, the Bush administration encouraged the Union to develop common policies in the OSCE and the G-24 because it realized that the EU's non-military power could be harnessed to promote stability during a time of much uncertainty in the international system. But its insistence on preserving NATO's command, structures complicated internal EU debates concerning its security ambitions, and split EU members on the question of how important it was to keep the 'US in Europe'.

The Clinton administration welcomed the development of an ESDI in principle, but also faced pressures from Republicans in Congress to ensure that NATO was not undermined. Thus, it resisted any innovation in NATO command structures and expressed displeasure when EU states failed to consult the US in discussions about European security. For example, an informal meeting of EU foreign ministers in early 1995 linked the idea of a 'non-aggression pact' between Russia and NATO with a proposed EU trade agreement with Russia. A senior official in Clinton's National Security Council admitted that, 'for an EU meeting to discuss the future of NATO gave us considerable heartburn. . . . With more non-NATO members in the EU now, it's a question of propriety.'[1]

Nevertheless, attitudes about European security structures had converged considerably by the mid-1990s. The CJTF concept emerged as a way to reconcile an ESDI with a strong NATO. The WEU was still years away from developing the sort of operational capability which NATO already had. For practical reasons, virtually all EU governments wished to encourage the US to remain committed to European defence, even if some – in France and Greece – could not admit it publicly for political reasons.

In the run-up to the EU's 1996 intergovernmental conference, the Clinton administration let it be known that it favoured a UK proposal for a 'reinforced partnership' between the WEU and EU. An ESDI modelled on the proposal would not be impossible to 'sell' on Capitol Hill as an enhanced EU commitment to alliance burden-sharing and global peacekeeping. However, if the 1996 IGC resulted in a 'Fourth EU pillar' for defence – as outlined in a German counter-proposal – questions would clearly arise about the presence of four 'neutral' states in the EU, and whether they would have to join NATO to make WEU security guarantees credible. Such questions were unavoidable regardless of who or which party held the White House after 1996.

Transatlantic partnership required a *modus vivendi* on traditional security issues that had not emerged, but was not unimaginable, by the mid-1990s. More generally, Western solidarity on military issues loomed as a necessary but far from sufficient condition for global security. It was hard to argue with one Clinton administration official who claimed that investment in transportation, communications and environmental infrastructures in Eastern Europe would do far more to promote European security than reformulating NATO or empowering the WEU (Walker 1991: 136). A more general and vexing problem was that the US and EU still lacked clear foreign policy doctrines for a post-Cold War world.

3 TOWARDS A 'STABLE PEACE'

The debate about reformulating security structures in Europe is mostly about institutions, or different *means* to keep the peace. But the problem of adjusting US and EU foreign policies to expanded notions of security is more about *ends* than means. The US and EU need to develop a vision of a 'stable peace' before institutions can be designed or redesigned to promote its emergence. New policies must be informed by new doctrines.

An obvious starting point is the promotion of democracy. Western aid designed to facilitate free democratic competition made a difference in Hungary, Nicaragua, Cambodia, Namibia and South Africa as they took their first, tentative steps towards democratization in the 1990s. The presence of Western election monitors acted to focus world attention and helped to ensure that these countries' first elections were fair and relatively free of violence.

However, one free election does not mean that subsequent ones will be fair, or that governments will act democratically once elected. The governments which took power in the first elections in Poland, Hungary and Czechoslovakia were all complex coalitions of parties linked through 'umbrella groups'. Such groups were united in their opposition to previous communist regimes. But divisions between them naturally emerged when they took on the difficult task of actually governing (Greene 1992; Larrabee 1992). In Poland, fissures appeared immediately within Solidarity. The Hungarian democratic opposition eventually was toppled by its more conservative rivals. Czechoslovakia's legendary Civic Forum, with Vaclav Havel as its leader, could not prevent the country splitting in two by 1992. After Slovakia became independent, the Civic Forum became a rather unremarkable 'rightwing political party' in the Czech Republic (Kumar 1992: 340).

Expectations tended to run ahead of the harsh realities of the transition to market economies in Eastern Europe and the CIS. The effect was to put popular support for democracy itself into question. Moreover, Western actions to encourage rapid economic development often undermined the very principles of democracy and national sovereignty. For example, the IMF threatened to cut off aid to Poland in 1991 unless a Minister of Finance favoured by the West for his monetarist credentials was reinstated (Pugh 1992: 13). Ex-communist parties were elected in Poland, Hungary, Lithuania Slovakia and Bulgaria in 1994–5.

A wider problem is that the fall of the Soviet bloc unleashed a 'rediscovery of the past' in Eastern Europe (see Brzezinski 1989/90). Buzan *et al.* (1990: 255) saw Eastern Europe 'undergoing a kind of decolonization, and the outcome may have some Third World-type characteristics in the form of weak states, disputed boundaries, and ethnically dominated politics'. Only Poland, Hungary and Albania among East European countries had ethnically homogeneous populations. Even these countries were marked by territorial disputes rooted in ethnic divisions. Miall (1994: 8) observed that 'strong national identities and weak states combine with economic insecurity to make a dangerous cocktail'.

Western governments seemed slow to realize that 'macroeconomic change is one thing; changing attitudes, political language, and structures is another' (Syme and Payton 1992: 93). A long process of socialization was clearly needed before public institutions such as the civil service and police could become depoliticized and trusted (Greene 1992: 146). The upshot was that security in Eastern Europe could not be seen merely or even mostly as a question of developing the military means to intervene if ethnic conflicts threatened to spread across borders. It required preventive measures to ease the pain of the transition to capitalist economies and promote democratic institutions which could anticipate and contain political tensions. US and EU policies needed to embrace crisis prevention as opposed to crisis management. Yet the West – particularly the US – often seemed in danger of losing interest in the economic development of Eastern Europe unless one of the new democracies collapsed and suddenly turned into a traditional security concern.

The primary method the EU had at its disposal for promoting European security was to spell out clearly the terms of accession for East European countries. On the one hand, the 'Europe agreements' offered East European states a unique form of association with the EU. A timetable was set for the complete elimination of all quantitative restrictions on EU imports from states with these agreements. Considering the frequency of anti-dumping measures taken by the Union against East European imports, this was a significant step towards promoting export-led growth in the region.

On the other hand, provisions for opening up EU markets to Eastern exports of agriculture, textiles and clothing featured long transitional arrangements or failed to eliminate a range of formal or informal barriers (Hamilton and Winters 1992). Moreover, the Europe agreements remained bilateral agreements, or 'spokes', linking each East European country to the 'hub' of the EU. For Baldwin (1994), the effect was to marginalize the new democracies economically and politically. The 'herding' instinct of investors, the growth of inter-firm trade, and the lack of strong links between East European economies combined to favour investment in the EU itself. The EU offered no intermediate step between the Europe agreements and full membership, thus making continued progress towards the integration of East and West impossible before actual enlargement. From the East's perspective, the central problem was an under-articulation of the interests of EU consumers, who presumably would welcome cheaper East European products, and the over-articulation of sectoral interests – such as farmers – in EU policy-making. The consequence was that the EU could not fulfil its long-term political objectives because of entrenched short-term producer interests (Saryusz-Wolski 1994).

For their part, EU member states could point to the declaration of the 1993 Copenhagen summit, which firmly committed the Union to Eastern enlargement when (and if) East European economies were ready for the stiff competition they would face in the internal market. Meanwhile, the CFSP initiative to agree 'stability pacts' in Eastern Europe was a logical response to ambitions there to redraw national boundaries on the basis of ethnicity, even as national borders mattered less and less in the West (Waever 1996). By the mid-1990s, the EU and its member states were providing nearly two-thirds of all Western aid to the former USSR and 60 per cent of Western assistance to East European states. EU imports from Eastern Europe increased by 83 per cent in the five years after the Berlin Wall fell, while the North American imports from Eastern Europe actually fell by 9 per cent (Commission 1995d: 28–31).

Still, for many in the East, the selfish parochialism of the EU was illustrated by its plans to spend more than $35 billion on its internal regional development policy, but less than $8 billion on the rest of the world by 1997. The EU and its member states continued to promise more aid to Eastern Europe than they delivered: by the end of 1992, more than $75 billion had been pledged, but only about $17 billion had actually been dispensed (PMI 1994: 76). Unsurprisingly, popular support for the EU was in decline in most East European states by the mid-1990s.

The latter part of the decade promised to be a critical turning point for Eastern Europe. Many economists predicted that much of the region's advantage over the West in terms of labour costs and cheap energy would have disappeared by the time East European countries were due to join with the EU in a free trade zone. The economic consequences of failing to prepare the Eastern countries for further economic integration with the EU – let alone outright membership – could be devastating. The political consequences could be even more daunting.

The West has clear incentives for joint action in the region, given the potential repercussions of a failure of democracy there. East European security – defined in broad terms – is largely an EU responsibility, but the US can help by offering political support, as well as financial incentives, for rapid enlargement of the Union. A US–EU bilateral working group on Eastern Europe, created in 1994, succeeded in eliminating many petty rivalries and duplicated aid efforts. However, the EU had to prepare for the likelihood that the US aid contribution, already small, would decline even further.

Another candidate-issue for concerted US–EU action is environmental protection. The need for Western leadership in this arena is compelling. The horrors of environmental degradation in Eastern Europe and the former USSR became clear only after 1989. For example, the Severo nickel refinery in the Russian city of Monchegorsk by itself generated about as many sulphur dioxide emissions as all the Scandinavian countries combined. Western aid programmes to apply clean technologies and retool such 'dirty' industrial plants should be a matter of urgency for both the US and the EU.

The 1992 Rio UN summit on the environment was characterized by little meaningful Western leadership. Wary of being seen as concentrating on foreign policy during an election campaign and as imposing costs on US industry, Bush refused to accept a treaty on biodiversity, and only attended the summit to partake in the photo opportunities of its final few days. The US supported several new environmental initiatives with rhetoric but very little money, despite evidence that a majority of Americans supported a binding treaty on global warming (Usborne and Schoon 1992). The EU showed itself to be riddled with internal divisions – especially between the Commission under Ripa di Meana and poorer member states led by Spain – on new programmes to redistribute aid and 'clean' technologies from rich northern to poor southern countries.

The EU and US have provided global leadership on ozone depletion, but have mostly bickered over global warming and sustainable development. The West remains far from agreement on new programmes to encourage conservation, the efficient use of resources or pollution control in the West, let alone on programmes to transfer funds and clean technologies from rich to poorer states. New arguments have emerged to suggest that the EU and other industrialized countries (and key LDCs) should bypass the US on global warming in view of American resistance to multilateral agreements on the issue (Paterson and Grubb 1992). However, attempts to forge agreement on an EU-wide 'eco-tax' on CO_2 and carbon emissions foundered in 1994 when it was agreed that the tax could be implemented only if the US passed a similar measure. Recent evidence suggests that global carbon dioxide emissions will increase by more than 40 per cent by 2010 (IEA 1995). Clearly, multilateral environmental initiatives on reducing emissions or developing renewable fuels are unlikely without concerted US–EU commitments.

A third arena where the US and EU could accomplish far more together than separately is in controlling the proliferation of nuclear weapons. The behaviour of the West generally has set a bad example for states which aspire to join the 'nuclear club'. When Gorbachev unilaterally committed the Soviet Union to a ban on nuclear testing from 1985–7, the US, France and the UK refused to follow suit (Sharp 1991). Western insistence that non-nuclear states renew the Nuclear Non-Proliferation Treaty (NPT) – which committed them to abstain from developing nuclear weapons – thus rang hollow when it came up for renewal in 1995.

By this time, India, Pakistan and, most worryingly, North Korea and Iran were all close to developing nuclear weapons of their own (IISS 1995). More than twenty countries had the missile technology to deliver nuclear or chemical weapons over long distances. The Western response was the formation of the Missile Technology Control Regime (MTCR) to control the export of such technology. But the MTCR was viewed as yet another example of the 'nuclear club' which barred entry to new aspirants (Ullman 1991: 123).

The proliferation of nuclear weapons technology points to the need to convince near-nuclear powers that it is not in their interests to continue weapons development programmes. Severe tensions emerged in 1995 between the US and France when the latter refused to stop selling nuclear technology to Iran. Chirac's subsequent decision to initiate nuclear tests was met with derision both within the Clinton administration and in most of Europe.

The value of joint US–EU actions on non-proliferation was illustrated in Ukraine, which became the world's third largest nuclear power after the collapse of the USSR. The EU signed a cooperation treaty with Ukraine in 1994 and offered considerable aid for nuclear safety (Peterson and Ward 1995: 148–9). Meanwhile, the US offered $1 billion in nuclear fuel supplies and disarmament assistance. Ukraine eventually ratified the NPT and pledged to give up its nuclear weapons. It also enthusiastically embraced 'Partnership for Peace' and closer ties to NATO at a time when Russia's relations with the West were deteriorating.

Western solidarity is clearly needed if China and Russia are to agree to ban exports of militarily useful nuclear technologies. One potentially useful policy foil is a comprehensive test ban, which seemed within reach when Chirac responded to global outrage following French nuclear tests by endorsing the ban in principle, with the US and UK following suit. A more general pledge that the Western nuclear powers would never use nuclear weapons against states that did not possess them, in exchange for agreement by the latter not to seek them, is less unimaginable than it was during the Cold War (see Daalder 1995).

A fourth and related focus for possible joint US–EU actions is the poverty gap between North and South. Perhaps nowhere else is the holistic nature of security clearer than in LDCs, where lack of economic development threatens eventually to impose collective costs on the West in the form of humanitarian relief, as illustrated in Somalia. A failure to address Southern poverty promises to turn LDCs into increasingly important sources of environmental catastrophe, resource depletion and migration pressure.

The end of the Cold War, if anything, worsened the problem. Soviet aid to LDCs evaporated while aid from the richest countries began falling to reach a lower level in 1993 than at any time since the mid-1970s. More of it came in the form of 'tied aid', which required purchases of Western exports, or as IMF or World Bank packages, which primarily sought to lower inflation or meet balance-of-payments crises rather than to develop infrastructures needed for sustainable development. Much government-to-government aid from the West remained event- and media-driven and arrived only after droughts or natural disasters. Far too little was committed to promote clean water, better education systems or environmental protection.

Despite its central concern with aid to Eastern Europe, the EU continued to commit more resources to Southern aid than did the US. The third Lomé Convention signed by the EU and the African, Caribbean and Pacific (ACP) states in 1989 committed more EU money than ever before – $13.8 billion over five years – to aid and development. Although certainly not without its critics, the Lomé treaty was more comprehensive and programmatic than most other Western aid schemes.

Meanwhile, US foreign aid was targeted by Republican budget-cutters in Congress. The medium-term trend for the rest of the 1990s was certain to be large cuts in the American foreign aid budget. Declining aid budgets increased incentives for transatlantic burden-sharing on aid to LDCs, leading to increased coordination between the Commission and the US Agency for International Development in 1995.

By this time urgent reforms – which only the West could bring about – were clearly needed in the IMF and World Bank. The inadequacy of the IMF was highlighted by the Mexican peso crisis. The Fund's lack of preventive mechanisms and European discontent over its contribution to the Mexican rescue package prompted an overdue examination of the IMF's capital and liquidity. The US was in a strong position to take the lead on IMF reform, which could be sold as a way to promote market reforms in Russia (cheaply) and encourage open capital flows, from which the US benefited significantly.

IMF reform could be linked to an EU-led effort to reform the World

Bank, which is fast becoming an irrelevancy. The World Bank urgently needs to refocus its activities on aid to the poorest states in Africa, which are of special interest to the EU. An obvious way for the US and EU to start is by ending the informal system of 'fiefdom allocation', whereby the head of the World Bank is always an American and the managing director of the IMF is always a European.

Any discussion of new doctrines for US and EU foreign policies in an era of expanding notions of security must acknowledge both the desirability and difficulty of including Japan in new bilateral initiatives. As Ito (1990: 150) argues,

> Japan's foreign policy since the war has never clearly articulated the goals and values the country is willing to defend. Its seemingly value-neutral nature has invited considerable distrust from other countries, especially now that Japan has become rich and influential.

Japan needs to have its own debate about the future of its foreign policy. Thus far, the US and EU have worked together only on a narrow agenda – and only sporadically – to try to convince Japan to become a more responsible trading partner. The country's enormous wealth and influence in Asia suggest that the US and EU should embrace a wider agenda to urge the Japanese to take a more active role in the actual design of measures to promote democracy, environmental protection, nuclear non-proliferation and a narrowing of the North–South poverty gap.

4 CHANGING NOTIONS OF SECURITY: DOES THEORY HELP?

A key litmus test for any international relations theory has become its ability to incorporate changing notions of security. *Neorealism* seeks to explain structural change in the international system but tends to remain 'stuck' in its assumptions about the primacy of nation-states and military power. Some neorealists have begun to embrace expanded notions of security and the normative concerns of institutionalism and reformism (Windass 1985; Booth 1991b; Buzan *et al.* 1993). But even these theorists insist that anarchy will endure as an unalterable feature of the international system, which will remain state-centred. External threats will remain the major motivator of national security policies until there is a 'structural shift out of anarchy' (Buzan 1991: 34). These theorists argue that there are stark limits to the amount of 'order' which the US and EU, even acting together, can impose.

Other neorealists remain sceptical about whether the essence of security has changed much at all (see Mearsheimer 1990a, 1990b, 1994–5; Perle 1990, 1991). Some argue that states should develop 'non-offensive defence' structures, which do not reduce their military power but signal a shift in military strategy from offensive to purely defensive capabilities (see Møller 1992). But most neorealists assume that non-proliferation is doomed. They berate 'nuclear optimists' who wish to extend the NPT for making 'heroic assumptions about the rationality of states' (Sagan 1994: 102; see also Carpenter 1994).

Even 'unreformed' neorealists do not deny that economic power has become a more important determinant of international relations. However, even if economic issues are a more important feature of expanded foreign policy agendas, the outbreak of war in Eastern Europe or the Middle East would reassert military superiority as the primary source of international power. Waltz (1993: 68) argues that 'as military worries fall, economic worries rise. Competition continues, and conflict turns increasingly on technological and economic issues.'

Unsurprisingly, neorealism has come under increasing attack from theorists such as Kratochwil (1993: 66), who insists that 'the tolerance for cognitive dissonance in the profession is something bordering on the miraculous'. Several neorealist assumptions now appear outdated. First, the neorealist argument that power in international relations is fungible – that military power can compensate for economic weakness – seems untenable. The leverage which US military power provided in economic relations with the EU or Japan during the post-war period has clearly diminished.

Second, the internal characteristics of the US and the EU states have certainly not 'dropped out' or failed to affect their behaviour as actors in the international system. Domestic pressures in the US tightly constrain foreign policy on trade, environmental and foreign aid issues. The discussion about pooling military sovereignty in an ESDI flies in the face of many neorealist assumptions.

Above all, changing notions of security have led many theorists to ask what it means to be 'realistic' about modern international relations. The problem with neorealism is that it encourages acceptance of the grim interpretation of reality which naturally emerges from its assumptions:

> A profoundly insecure and unstable world, a world loaded down with expensive and lethal weapons; a world which flounders from crisis to crisis and from emergency to emergency; a world increasingly split between rich and poor; a world which daily compromises the future of its children and its ecological future; and a world which constantly lives beyond its income. Surely that is the ultimate lack of realism.
>
> (Urquhart 1992: 318–9)

By contrast *institutionalists* stress that economic, trade, environmental and traditional security issues have become more interconnected, with profound implications for international politics. For example, the globalization of national economies has weakened states and changed the nature of national security: 'interdependence increases vulnerabilities and threatens to weaken the state because military resources are increasingly found in global commercial markets over which states have little control' (Crawford 1994b: 25).

Hegemonic stability theory helps explain the rise of unilateralism in US trade policy and Congressional anxiety about American sovereignty and the WTO. Cafruny (1985: 83) argues that 'power resources not tapped by the hegemon-as-leader may be brought to bear by the hegemon-in-decline. . . . Many regimes therefore exhibit an inverse relationship between the decline of hegemony and the projection of power.' Most institutionalists admit that the weakness of regimes such as the UN or GATT is an essential problem of international relations in the absence of a hegemon to impose order.

Nonetheless, institutionalists insist that anarchy – as neorealists define it – is no longer a defining feature of the international system. Cerny (1996: 40) predicts that, in future, 'the "anarchy" of the international system will no longer be one of states competing for power, but one of neofeudal rivalries and asymmetric cooperation among a range of interests and collective agents' (see also Onuf 1989; Milner 1991). Many institutionalists believe that global competition will increasingly take place between regional economic blocs. Most assume that the process of European integration will continue, despite the problems of eastward enlargement. For example, many East European countries are preparing for membership by adopting EU environmental standards as fast as possible, with 'the de facto result [being] . . . considerable regional harmonization' (Levy 1993: 340).

Institutionalists develop novel prescriptions for national economic policies in response to changing notions of security. The keys to economic security in a world economy where private investment is increasingly mobile are public investment in education and economic infrastructures, not protectionism or barriers to FDI:

> Herein lies the new logic of economic nationalism. The skills of a nation's work force and the quality of its infrastructure are what makes it unique, and uniquely attractive, in the world economy. Investments in these relatively immobile factors of worldwide production are what chiefly distinguishes one nation from another; money, by contrast, moves easily around the world.
>
> (Reich 1991: 264)

In theoretical terms, institutionalists concede that

> Interdependence is unlikely to reduce conflict, and may increase it by giving states a broader agenda of issues over which their interests and

circumstances will differ. But where interdependence is strong, it should reduce incentives to resort to armed force.

(Buzan 1991: 43; see also Keohane and Nye 1987)

Institutionalism teaches that complex interdependence binds together industrialized economies, with the consequence that war has become an illegitimate policy instrument except to repel a military attack. The intermeshing of economies creates shared interests in stability and environmental protection. Global security has become a collective good. The problem is that international institutions lack legitimacy and the means to 'manage' interdependence. However, most institutionalists hold out hope that a 'stable peace' is possible through international cooperation, particularly if the US and EU can provide leadership in expanding the agendas of international regimes to embrace preventive action to forestall conflict.

Institutionalists are attacked by neorealists as naive. Mearsheimer (1994/5: 47–9) complains that 'although the world does not work the way institutionalist theories say it does or should, those theories remain highly influential in both the academic and policy worlds.' Policies based on institutionalist assumptions are 'bound to fail'.

Liberals offer a different perspective on changing notions of security. They caution that the pursuit of 'economic security' has the potential to destabilize the global free trade system. As security becomes identified with economic rather than military power, trade issues become more politicized, and protectionism more difficult to resist. The repercussions of this trend for US–Japanese relations are that ' "national security" is now such an elastic, convenient concept that protectionists in both countries have used it frequently without compunction' (Ito 1990: 144).

Yet, since liberal economies require liberal polities, advocates of liberalism claim that their paradigm of international relations is fully compatible with expanded notions of security. Open trade has encouraged the emergence of 'oases of stable peace' in the West (Booth 1991b: 337). Some liberals point to the possibility that these oases may be extended to include formerly non-liberal states through a more open system of global free trade.

Others argue that the sharing of liberal norms is not yet global, but rather confined to a 'core' of great powers. A close reading of Fukuyama's (1992) *The End of History* reveals this distinction: it argues that democratic capitalism is the only possible model of society for *advanced* countries. The upshot for the US and EU is that 'economic interdependence, political democracy, and nuclear weapons lessen the security dilemma; the major powers have no pressures for expansion. The result is a relationship consistent with a liberal model of international relations' (Goldgeier and McFaul 1992: 469).

By contrast, tribalism, fundamentalism or despotism may prevail in economically backward states. Pressures for territorial expansion still plague the less developed world because states which are internally unstable often seek wealth, population and protection. However, liberals argue that Western aid is a relatively ineffective tool for solving the problems of the South. Stronger international institutions cannot, by themselves, lead to a strengthening of liberal values. The key to a more stable peace is political leadership in the core to override the demands of powerful domestic interest groups for protectionism so that the benefits of open trade may be extended to the less developed world. Increased trade inevitably leads to increased cultural exchange, which can help to promote tolerance of ethnic and regional identities. In general, liberals insist that free economies promote peaceful, 'high-trust' societies (Fukuyama 1995). In particular, liberals castigate the EU for its stubborn refusal to open its markets to Eastern Europe.

For *reformists*, liberal economic prescriptions for Eastern Europe are naive and irresponsible:

> Those who speak, as many do so glibly, even mindlessly, of a return to the Smithian free market are wrong to the point of a mental vacuity of clinical proportions. It is something we in the West do not have, would not tolerate, could not survive. Ours is a mellow, government-protected life; for Eastern Europeans pure and rigorous capitalism would be no more welcome than it would be for us.
>
> (Galbraith 1990: 7)

Reformists condemn analysts who celebrate Western 'victory' in the Cold War (Hyland 1987; Fukuyama 1989) as arrogant and short-sighted. For reformists, Western self-congratulation obscured the urgent need for common US–EU initiatives to stop the descent of LDCs into economic misery and political instability. It also encouraged complacency about the nature of Western democratic institutions. Pressures to close the EU's democratic deficit and 'democratize' US foreign policy are viewed as part of a global movement which seeks to increase the participation of ordinary citizens in governance:

> Democratization in Eastern Europe could allow us to look critically at our own political and economic practices in the West. What we have experienced in the West is individual freedom. . . . [But] our ability to participate in decisions affecting our lives is much more limited. High levels of military spending and the way in which our identity as democratic nations has been defined by the Cold War are partly responsible for this lack of participation.
>
> (Kaldor 1991: 330)

On the environmental front, reformists urge that developing clean energy technologies, non-polluting transport systems and conservation programmes should be the primary issues on the US–EU bilateral agenda. They note that the US and EU together produce 36 per cent of all global carbon emissions, a primary source of acid rain and global warming. The CIS and Eastern Europe account for another 25 per cent (Commission 1991b: 4). Reformists warn that the single-minded focus of Western governments on promoting capitalist economies in East European states will lead them to develop Western production and consumption patterns which will worsen their environmental problems (Greene 1992: 160).

Reformist ideas on military security often seemed naive during the Cold War. However, the sea change of 1989 was reflected, and in some ways anticipated, by Mueller's (1989: 260) insistence that major war had become 'obsolete' and nuclear arms treaties were useless:

> There is an alternative: just *do* it. The arms buildup, after all, was not accomplished through written agreement; instead, there was a sort of free market in which each side, keeping a wary eye on the other, sought security by purchasing varying amounts of weapons and troops. As requirements and perspectives changed, so did the force structure of each side. If arms can be built up that way, they can be reduced in the same manner. It would be sort of a negative arms race.

By 1991 such a strategy was no longer a dreamy reformist vision: it had become official US policy. The Bush administration scrambled to put forth plans for unilateral reductions in the US nuclear arsenal in the hope that the USSR would reciprocate before centralized control of the Soviet nuclear arsenal collapsed. By 1992 sweeping reductions agreed by the US and Russia – which promised to reduce their strategic arsenal by two-thirds each – went far beyond cuts agreed in formal treaties.

On the EU side, no fewer than nine member states condemned the French nuclear tests of 1995. Eventually, Chirac responded by going much further in accepting limits on France's future nuclear activities than many in the French military thought wise. The point is that many reformist assumptions are now accepted in establishment thinking about international security.

Reformists share institutionalist assumptions about the need to nurture international cooperation, but specify that global institutions must embrace a global 'civic ethic' to guide action in the 'global neighbourhood'. In many respects, the reformist agenda was crystallized in the report of the Commission on Global Governance (1995), which included Delors and the Swedish Prime Minister, Ingvar Carlsson. It highlighted the unfulfilled potential of the UN Charter and the International Court of Justice in The Hague, which, it urged, should become the world's 'cathedral of law'. The Commission expressed the reformist hope that a new generation of young people was emerging with a greater sense of solidarity than any preceding generation. Reformists could cite the report as evidence that their assumptions had been embraced in the political mainstream.

The reformist commitment to 'think globally, act locally' is reflected in their assertion that security can no longer be defined in state-centred terms. Broader notions of security must 'encompass the individual human being at the lowest level and world society at the highest' (Booth 1991b: 341). International security is thus linked with the reformist critique of the state, which has become even more vehement since the end of the Cold War:

> With its removal, it is as if the ideological cement of Western civil societies has dissolved. Politicians lose their last semblance of ideological respectability and are exposed as self-seeking and ineffectual manipulators. . . . Liberal ideology quickly sheds its 1989–90 aura of triumphalism and appears incapable of managing the world crisis.
>
> (Shaw 1994: 176)

In short, reformists are the leading exponents of new holistic conceptions of security. For them, the 'New World Order' is characterized by four key crises – militarization, poverty, environmental destruction and human repression – which are interconnected in a single '*global problématique*' (Ekins 1992; Millar 1992; Peterson and Ward 1995).

Despite their disparate assumptions, nearly all international relations theorists could agree that three variables will be crucial in determining international relations in the twenty-first century. The first is whether there will be more occasions such as the Gulf War or Bosnia when the US asserts its military power, dictates the terms of Western policy and successfully obtains multinational 'cover' for its police actions. If so, then the argument of US conservatives such as Charles Krauthammer (1991: 23) that we are left with a 'unipolar world' is plausible.

A second critical variable is whether the EU can enlarge without further disharmony, and become a security and defence community as well as an economic community. To 'punch its weight' in global politics, the EU also must resist the temptation to 'define being "European" simply as being different from the United States – not necessarily contrary or opposed, but somehow visibly different' (Walker 1991: 130). Even as the EU develops its own identity in foreign and security policies, in most cases it will find that it wields far more influence and power if it acts in concert with the US.

A third factor will be the ability of the US to cope with rising aggressive unilateralism and economic populism. It is difficult to see how American power can be enhanced through withdrawal from international cooperation. Moreover, the spread of liberal values will not translate into a spread of US values unless the United States becomes able to provide for the basic human needs of a higher portion of its citizens. As Krasner (1989: 159) argues:

> Most of the world's peoples are not predisposed to accept the American version of individualism, democracy, and capitalism because their own national values are much more strongly oriented toward one kind of collectivity or another. . . . Most of the peoples of the world are, however, entranced by a high economic performance or quality of life. The future of American values, their external appeal and internal vigor, now depends more on the attainments of the American economy than on the power of the American military.

Arguably, US influence depends as never before on 'soft power', which springs from relatively intangible factors such as leadership and moral and cultural forces (Nye 1990: 32). American foreign policy-makers need to respond to the changing essence of national security and develop new doctrines which reflect this change. In broad terms, this means 'a new conception and style of leadership: it will have to be multilateral, institutionalized, and in partnership with others' (Hoffmann 1992: 212).

The central point of this chapter is that military power remains a potent source of influence in international relations, but it needs to be placed within a far more holistic conception of security. This point becomes clear not just from a look at the Brave New World of the 1990s, but also from common sense applied to the sources of violent conflict throughout history. Many armed states have been able to avoid competing with each other militarily because their relationships were secure in other dimensions. Secure relations between states in the political, economic, social and cultural arenas can solve the 'security dilemma'. A more stable peace requires secure relations between states across non-military dimensions. There is a strong argument to be made that the best place to begin is by developing a true partnership between the US and the EU.

Chapter 8

Conclusion

One of the central arguments of this study is that the behaviour of the US and EU as international actors has become subject to more diverse and powerful pressures. Western foreign policies have become more event-, media- and pressure group-driven, and thus more short term in focus. The attention of the West wavered in the absence of fresh reports of atrocities or ethnic cleansing in Bosnia. The Bush administration's political need to prise open markets quickly for US exporters led it to act impetuously during the Uruguay Round. Clinton reneged on his commitment to 'state-building' in Somalia almost immediately after grisly TV films were aired of dead US soldiers being dragged through the streets of Mogadishu.

The problem is that a more stable peace requires creative, long-term thinking. Even amidst new constraints, there remains more room for choice in US–EU relations than ever before. Some of the most important choices involve adapting political structures to accommodate rising economic interdependence. Production is increasingly globalized or regionalized while governance – collective problem-solving in the public realm – remains mostly nationalized (Caporaso 1996). The EU has become a more important level of governance as its member states have reacted to the interdependence which links their economies. On the US side, NAFTA, APEC and the Free Trade Area of the Americas initiatives reveal a similar dynamic of trying to make the political match up with the economic.

Meanwhile, most international institutions have undergone considerable transformation. Existing regimes have had to be adjusted or upgraded to accommodate changing notions of security and the need for preventive measures to preserve it. New links between NATO and Eastern Europe, the gradual empowerment of the WEU, and the increased prominence of the OSCE and UN reflect a new agenda to deepen and widen international cooperation. It is an agenda largely designed and promoted by the West, but the US and EU have clashed over its actual execution, as illustrated in Bosnia and on NATO enlargement.

This chapter focuses on some of the most critical choices which face the US and EU. It argues that the West can choose to develop a transatlantic relationship which is better able to regulate and manage the complex interdependence which links its economies. The US and EU have considerable scope to lead in translating expanded notions of security into actual policies.

Section 1 offers an interpretative assessment of the affinities and constraints which shape US–EU relations. Section 2 considers whether the pursuit of economic security must inevitably lead to regional 'trade blocs', which drive a wedge through global free trade as well as transatlantic cooperation. Section 3 surveys the landscape of existing international institutions and assesses the prospects for US–EU leadership within them. A final analysis of the four theories of international relations is offered in section 4.

1 AFFINITIES AND CONSTRAINTS IN US–EU RELATIONS

The New Transatlanticism of the early 1990s was a consequence of geopolitical change – the fall of communism and European integration – more than conscious political choices. Sceptics cautioned that the Transatlantic Declaration 'could turn out to be as meaningful as the declarations of undying friendship signed in former times between, say, East Germany and Algeria' (Wallace 1992: 21). However, the US–EU relationship is underpinned by affinities which are firmly ingrained. Their effects are difficult to pin down but they are critical in setting a context for political choices.

An important source of affinity is the evolution of the EU towards a political system which increasingly resembles that of the US. The European Union remains a rather loose confederation of mostly unitary and often fiercely independent states (Taylor 1991). Several of its members – particularly the UK and Denmark – remain allergic to the term 'federalism'. But the Union has gradually taken on many of the characteristics of a federal system, or one in which two or more levels of government have formal and defined powers over the same area and citizens. Elazar (1987: 11) argues that, 'the essence of federalism is not to be found in a particular set of institutions but in the institutionalization of particular relationships among participants in political life'. Since the mid-1980s, the EU has moved towards a unique 'segmented federalism' marked by 'treaty-based federal arrangements in certain policy areas, without having a formal, constitutionally based federalism' (Sbragia 1992: 260).

In key respects the EU will remain a more decentralized political system than the US. The primacy of national and subnational interests was reinforced by the Maastricht Treaty's commitment to 'subsidiarity'. The concept is a vague one, but the Treaty mandates that the EU should take action 'only if and in so far as the objectives of the proposed action cannot be sufficiently achieved by the member states' (see Peterson 1994b; Scott *et al.* 1994). In other words, the 'politics of scale' may justify common policies for external trade, the environment or the single market. Otherwise, powers should be devolved to the lowest level of government possible.

The EU is marked by substantial 'implementation gaps' due to the weakness of its common institutions and the political reluctance of its member states to force each other to comply with Community law. However, the EU arguably is a more integrated, authoritative level of government than the US federal government on many trade and economic issues. EU mechanisms for developing bargaining positions on trade (outside agriculture) are highly centralized. Multilateral trade agreements signed by the Union bind all levels of government in all member states. By contrast, the disparate rules and practices of individual US states – especially in financial services and public procurement – are persistent barriers to access to the American market.

Generally, however, the transatlantic relationship is one between partners whose political systems are becoming more similar. Particularly given its recent and future enlargement, the EU invites parallels with nineteenth-century America. These parallels promote mutual understanding and empathy, especially when domestic political forces pose constraints on each side's ability to bargain freely with the other. They reinforce a more general US–EU 'community in values' built on 'a common ground of democratic, capitalist and pluralistic values [which is] unequalled in relations between other corresponding units in the international system' (Heurlin 1992: 30).

Alongside such broad affinities must be set a number of important constraints. One is that the US often finds itself confronted with a Union crippled by internal squabbling, especially over EMU, its budget and enlargement. The EMS was nearly blown apart in a climate of severe recession and uncertainty about the viability of the EU's blueprint for a single currency in the early 1990s. An extraordinary book by a veteran Commission official with intimate knowledge of the EMS warned that tensions surrounding EMU could actually provoke war between Germany and France (Connolly 1995). However far-fetched the argument, tensions over EMU intensified. Polls suggested that as many as two-thirds of German citizens opposed it, as the Kohl government began calling for even stricter convergence criteria than were agreed at Maastricht.[1] Meanwhile, France accused Italy, Spain and the UK – whose currencies remained outside the exchange rate mechanism – of 'competitive devaluations'. EMU risked polarizing the EU and splitting the single market between those who were part of a single currency and those who were not. An EMU of all of the Union's member states was simply not on the cards.

Controversy surrounding the EU's budget often reflected conflict between 'convergence', or the need for EU states to achieve more uniform levels of economic performance in the run-up to EMU, and 'cohesion', or increased EU spending to reduce economic disparities between the rich North and poorer South. States such as Spain, Portugal and Ireland struggled to meet the strict EMU criteria by vastly reducing their public budgets and cutting public investment. In the short term, these measures promised to widen the gap in economic growth rates between richer and poorer EU states (Scott 1992).

The EU budget agreed for 1993–7 aimed to compensate poorer states by increasing regional aid to Greece, Ireland, Portugal and Spain. Still, the EU's budget equalled less than 1.3 per cent of its total GDP, a figure put into perspective by the fact that the US federal budget accounted for nearly 25 per cent of national GDP. The EU clearly lacked the funds to ensure greater 'cohesion' in the run-up to EMU. Further ahead, the budgetary implications of cohesion in a European Union including Poland, Hungary or the Czech Republic were mind-boggling.

Perhaps above all, the EU's unity was threatened by tensions over choices which needed to made about its institutional development in advance of enlargement. More flexible institutional arrangements were needed to accommodate an enlarged membership, particularly on issues which cut to the heart of national sovereignty such as foreign policy and defence. Enlargement threatened to increase disparities in economic development and geopolitical outlook within the Union. One particularly thoughtful analyst found it 'difficult to imagine how such a "post-sovereign, poly-centric, incongruent, neo-medieval" authority could possibly be stable in the longer run' (Schmitter 1992: 380). In short, the US may find itself having to interact with a far less politically coherent EU in the twenty-first century.

New constraints on a US–EU partnership may also arise from the evolution of politics in the United States. The rise of economic populism and 'aggressive unilateralism' was accompanied by unprecedented falls in the popularity of both major political parties, the polarization of right and left, and widespread voter disillusionment (Lowi 1995). Neither major party responded imaginatively to popular concerns about rising inequalities, the breakdown of the family, and the hard realities of global economic competition. The 'Contract with America' upon which Republican Congressional candidates ran – with considerable success – in 1994 contained a foreign policy section which pledged to curtail national participation in UN peacekeeping, increase defence spending, and reduce foreign aid. Yet, the overwhelming focus of the US political class on domestic, as opposed to foreign, problems, was reflected in the lack of a single word in the Contract about trade or foreign investment. An equivalent political platform in the 1950s would have contained no mention of the Cold War or communism (Judis and Lind 1995).

Competition between a Republican Congress and the Clinton White House boiled down mostly to a debate about how to cut public spending. Any spending on foreign policy or international cooperation became a soft target for cuts. More generally, the end of the Cold War lowered the electoral costs of opposing the President on foreign policy (Rhode 1994; Tierny 1994). Congress became more willing to substitute its collective judgement for the President's, as was illustrated on Bosnia, Somalia, Haiti, the WTO and NAFTA even *before* Clinton lost his 'friendly' majority in Congress. The EU faced the prospect of a more erratic and less coherent US foreign policy in the twenty-first century.

At the same time, the teething problems of NAFTA and APEC acted to weaken the assumption in Washington that the country's economic future lay in North America and Asia, not Europe. Even Newt Gingrich, the radically right-wing leader of the Republican House majority in Congress, insisted that he was, at heart, an internationalist and even pro-European. By 1995, proposals to slash spending on US farm programmes were being considered by a Congress determined to cut the national budget deficit, thus opening up the prospect of a transatlantic deal to free trade in agriculture.

On the EU's side, the run-up to the 1996 IGC produced growing evidence of political will to make the EU work more effectively. France brokered compromise on a financial assistance package for the Mediterranean region, where the Algerian civil war and rising Islamic fundamentalism raised new security concerns. The EU's 'Reflection Group', created to set an agenda for the IGC, urged member states to prepare for enlargement by agreeing provisions for suspending or even expelling members which violated fundamental human rights or democratic principles.

Despite its hard line on EMU, Germany showed signs of genuine leadership in proposing a four-year agenda to embrace sweeping reforms in areas not being considered within the IGC, particularly enlargement, farm policy, the launch of a single currency and future EU financing. The IGC seemed set to focus on the CFSP and its links to the WEU. Even Chirac acknowledged the need for more qualified majority voting (QMV) provided that member states could veto policies which threatened 'vital national interests'. Germany pushed for QMV on most foreign policy issues, except ones involving the deployment of troops, and supported a French proposal to appoint a single political Secretary-General of both the EU's Council of Ministers and the WEU to give the CFSP more coherence. EU foreign ministers backed the idea of a $4 billion 'Marshall Plan' for the former Yugoslavia, with a leading role for the Commission, after hopes of a political solution to the conflict in Bosnia rose in late 1995.

By this point, both the US and EU had acknowledged the need to re-examine transatlantic relations. In an obviously concerted initiative, the German, British and French governments all endorsed the idea of a new 'contract' or 'covenant' with the US (Sloan 1995a). Despite the daunting difficulties of a US–EU accord on agriculture or textiles, the main US trade agencies and the Commission (1995a) each launched studies on the idea of creating a 'transatlantic economic space' or even some type of US–EU free trade area. A 'transatlantic business dialogue' was created to feed the views of the private sector into discussions about how and which barriers to transatlantic trade could be eliminated. In 1995, the Clinton administration endorsed the creation of a bilateral group of senior-level representatives to develop 'a broad-ranging transatlantic agenda for the new century – an agenda for common economic and political action to expand democracy, prosperity and stability' (Christopher 1995: 15).

It is worth asking whether US and European citizens really support the notion of a US–EU partnership. On security issues, Levine (1992: 28) argues that '[while] a neutrally worded poll would be likely to show more Americans opposed to the US commitment to Europe than favouring it. . . . the question is of very little importance to most Americans'. However, after a decline in US support for NATO in the early 1990s, a solid majority (56 per cent) expressed support for keeping the US commitment to NATO intact (Rielly 1995: 35). The same poll found that far more citizens (49 per cent) considered Europe to be more important to US interests than Asia (21 per cent).

As for the EU, an extensive review of European public attitudes in the early 1990s led two US government analysts to argue that NATO 'is analogous to a comfortable and well-worn shoe; it has served its owner well over the years and continues to provide a comfortable fit' (Smith and Wertman 1992: 192). An apparent trend towards declining European public support for NATO – especially in Germany (Asmus 1992) – appeared to have been reversed after West European fears of growing political instability in Russia were fuelled by the strong electoral perform-ance of neo-fascists and the invasion of Chechnya. Polls suggested that nearly 80 per cent of Germans supported stronger US–European ties (Fitchett 1995).

Moreover, substantial latitude remained for political leadership to check any drift on either side towards inwardness or neo-isolationism. Less than half of the US public appeared to believe that the economic unification of Europe served their own national interests, compared to 85 per cent of US elites. A plurality (35 per cent) of the US public believed that the EU engaged in 'unfair trade'. Yet responses to both questions showed that a large percentage of US citizens – about one-third – simply did not know what they thought of European integration or EU trading practices (Rielly 1995: 24–30). Meanwhile, large numbers of Europeans acknowledged the existence of a transatlantic 'community in values' and took a positive view of the direction and substance of US foreign policy since the Reagan years. A sober cull of the evidence confirmed that 'as European policymakers begin the process of redefining US–West European relations they are not constrained by anti-American public sentiment' (Smith and Wertman 1992: 194).

Huntington's (1993: 71) masterful essay on the continued importance of 'primacy' in international relations argues that common values of the kind that unite the US and EU 'do not mean that these countries will have shared or even congruent interests'. However, his focus is almost exclusively on the Japanese threat to US primacy. The US and EU will always compete with one another, but there is a strong social consensus underpinning their relationship. Given that consensus, a true transatlantic partnership is not impossible in the twenty-first century, given sufficient political leadership on both sides of the Atlantic.

2 ARE TRADE BLOCS INEVITABLE?

As political structures are adjusted to reflect increasing economic interdependence, the emergence of protectionist or even mercantilist trade blocs could become a defining feature of the international order. Changing notions of security and stiffer competition have created new incentives for states which share the same agendas in global trade to form subgroups which allow them to pursue their collective interests. For example, the similarity of North American and EU economies has led Western figures, such as the Canadian Trade Minister, Roy McClaren, to argue that the continued existence of barriers to trade between them is anomalous and wasteful. The danger is that like-minded blocs of states will take actions which erode global free trade.

Critics of a US–EU 'economic space' or 'free trade area' warned that such notions risked undermining the development of the WTO when it was still in its infancy. The first Director-General of the WTO, Renato Ruggiero, condemned the proposals on the grounds that 'a free trade area of so many rich countries could give the feeling that we are again living in a divided world, with a rich area and a poor area'.[2] Others warned that a US–EU initiative 'might also drive Asian nations into their own trading bloc' (Duesterberg 1995: 78). In this context, a small but growing section of the Japanese political class began to urge that Japan should create its own sphere of economic influence in Asia in order to free itself from its dependence on Western markets and macroeconomic policies (see Ishihara 1989; Ito 1990; Drifte 1990). Waltz (1993) claimed that increased Japanese investment in Asia, due partly to an overstrong yen, was yielding a 'regional economic bastion'. One possible result was that incentives for Japan to liberalize its domestic market or take a more active global role more generally would be dampened.

Part of the problem is that the saliency of Cold War military alliances, which usually discouraged inward-looking or mercantilist trade policies, has declined. Defence commitments to Asia and Europe traditionally provided the US with substantial leverage in negotiations with the EU and Japan on trade and monetary issues. This leverage diminished as the Soviet threat receded. Meanwhile new tensions emerged on the industrial and economic side of military alliances. One of the forces fuelling the development of an independent European defence identity was the savings that could be had through the development of a single EU market in armaments, which would erode sales of US military technology to Europe. The controversy over the Japanese FSX fighter aircraft – which the Pentagon pressured the Japanese government to stop funding in 1990 – led US diplomats to bludgeon Japan into buying American F-16 technology.

The major US–Japanese trade disputes of the mid-1990s – particularly over cars and car parts – suggested that the leading US trade agencies wanted to treat Japan more like a 'normal' country, instead of one that had to be coddled for security reasons. For its part, Japan began acting like one, for example by continuing its trade with Iran despite the Clinton administration's insistence on an embargo. Worried that trade tensions would damage security relations, Clinton's Assistant Secretary for International Security, Joseph Nye, launched an intensified US–Japanese dialogue on security issues such as the risk of a nuclear North Korea and growing Chinese military power. Nye urged that 'ultimately, problems related to trade can undermine security, just as security problems can undermine trade and prosperity'.[3]

Thus, despite the lofty ambitions of APEC and political interest in a transatlantic economic space, the outcome of weaker security alliances and the pursuit of economic security could be the emergence of trade blocs in each corner of the 'triad' of Europe, America and Asia:

> A multipolar economic system with three separable but interconnected regions is emerging and could eventually produce a multipolar security system. Each region has the political capacity and technical-industrial foundations for independent action. The question is how the regions will relate to one another.
>
> (Borrus and Zysman 1992: 183)

For the US, NAFTA holds out the long-term promise of cheaper energy, and potentially rapidly growing markets for its high-tech products, particularly if plans to extend the agreement to more countries come to fruition.

The Clinton administration's initiative for a Free Trade Area of the Americas (FTAA) in 1994–5 sought to link NAFTA with Mercosur, a customs union agreed between Brazil, Argentina, Paraguay and Uruguay. However, the initiative was undercut by the peso crisis and trade liberalization fatigue on Capitol Hill. Little agreement was reached in a thirty-six-nation FTAA summit held in 1995 other than a deadline of 2005 for a negotiated agreement and consensus that all FTAA rules would be observed by all members. Still, the FTAA holds out the prospect of a future free trade area of 800 million consumers from Alaska to Cape Horn accounting for one-third of global GDP.

Of the three members of the triad, the EU probably is best equipped to assert its independence and to take on the characteristics of a more inward-looking trade bloc. Trade between EU states grew 75 per cent faster than the EU's external trade during the 1980s. Inter-European trade accounts for over half of the EU's total trade. Only about 10 per cent is with the US, and this share has fallen since 1990 (Commission 1995d: 22).

The enlargement of the EU and German tutelage in Eastern Europe will raise the stakes of political decisions still to be taken by the EU on foreign access to the internal market. Germany is politically and industrially committed to the economic reconstruction and eventual integration of Eastern Europe. It is not only the most economically and financially powerful of current EU member states, it also has – unlike the UK or even France – a set of policy preferences which provides it with many natural allies in debates about the EU's future (Keohane and Hoffmann 1993: 395–6). If and when EMU happens, a 'single currency area' stretching across Europe could ensue, of a sort unimaginable in North America or Asia. The emergence of a German-led, pan-European financial and trading bloc is not impossible in the twenty-first century.

For a time in the early 1990s, it became fashionable to argue that the logical US response to the economic and political development of the EU was to create a common market or free trade area with Japan (Ito 1990: 148; Attali 1990; Brzezinski 1991: 14). The Clinton administration's effort to breathe life into APEC acknowledged such arguments. Viewed in economic terms, the Pacific Rim offered the potential for a rational division of labour. The US bestowed its strengths in basic technological innovation and risk-taking. Japan possessed enormous capital investment resources and a penchant for developing and commercializing basic innovations. China and the Asian NICs offered abundant, educated and diligent work-forces (Kim 1988: 157–8).

However, Asia remained far more culturally heterogeneous than Europe, and the Pacific region far less politically, economically and socially unified than the North Atlantic area (De Santis 1993). US–Japanese relations remained strained as the American trade deficit with Japan

persisted. The Western perception that the Japanese state was less responsive to its electorate than the US or EU states, even after sweeping reforms
of the Japanese electoral system in 1993–4, was not entirely unjustified.
Japanese consumers, and thus Western exporters, remained disadvantaged by Japan's antiquated distribution system, its weak anti-trust legislation and myriad barriers to cheap imports.   A range of 'structural
impediments' to Japanese market access lingered due to 'an absence of
effective competition or transparency. . . . In most instances they exist
because of a *lack* of action by governments or the responsible authorities'
(Woolcock 1991: 2–3).

Joint action by two members of the triad to try to change the behaviour
of the third is most likely to be taken by the US together with the EU.
New evidence emerged in the 1990s to suggest that the mere threat of
joint action could produce results. For example, after Leon Brittan called
for US–EU cooperation in pushing Japan to apply stricter anti-trust rules,
prosecutions were launched in 1992 against several Japanese car companies for cartel-like behaviour.

Intensified US–EU political relations also have real potential to lead to
more intimate bilateral cooperation in sectors marked by domestic market
failures. Exchanges within the JCG could lead to a further pooling of
public funds for semiconductor research, which is massively expensive and
features daunting Japanese competition. Even as *l'affaire Pasqua* strained
Franco-US relations in 1995, the US and France, together with Germany
and the UK, signed an agreement to pool efforts on anti-missile research.
A useful transatlantic dialogue on 'information superhighways' promoted
interconnection and interoperability between networks despite differences of view on standards and government access to data.

Another sector where a bilateral political deal is needed is air transport.
The Clinton administration defied its own rhetorical support for European unity by signing 'open skies' agreements with individual EU states,
not the Union as a whole, despite the protests of Neil Kinnock, the
EU's Transport Commissioner. Kinnock argued that, in the absence of
European unity, the US would 'pick off' member states one by one and
thus dictate the terms of bilateral landing rights. Kinnock's warnings
seemed vindicated by subsequent US threats to seek new 'gateway' air-
ports in Germany rather than London if the UK did not offer better
terms.

A common US–EU market for air travel is difficult to imagine in the
near future, but many US Congressional Republicans favour increasing
the maximum stake that foreign airlines can hold in US carriers from 25
to 49 per cent (Skapinder 1995). Liberalization of air transport in Europe
has proceeded at a snail's pace, partly because of awareness that nearly
20 per cent of the US industry went bankrupt after the domestic market
was deregulated in the 1980s. Yet more transatlantic cross-investment

could result in wider choice for the more than 30 million passengers who travel annually between the US and EU, as well as in healthier airline industries.

In the airline sector, as in others, substantial divergences in the *type* of barriers which inhibit access to the US and EU markets will continue to strain transatlantic trade relations. By committing the EU states to the removal of internal barriers to trade, the 1992 project exposed many structural NTBs which limited foreign access to the EU's market. In contrast, most barriers to the US market remained 'statutory', or the result of legislative actions. Multilateral trade rules tend to eliminate statutory barriers but usually have little effect on 'structural impediments'. This point helps explain pressures in the US for legislative remedies to achieve 'fair trade' and general Congressional scepticism about the WTO (Woolcock 1991: 5). In short, despite the potential for intensified US–EU cooperation in sectors where market failures now exist or where access to the Japanese market is restricted, transatlantic tensions will persist on many broad questions of economic diplomacy.

Yet most discussions of trade blocs end up couched in generalities and ignore a major theme of this book: that is, rising and complex economic interdependence makes it difficult, and often impossible, for the US, the EU or Japan to target new policy measures on one member of the 'triad' without substantially affecting the other. The proposed EU banking directive of 1988 was primarily aimed at the powerful Japanese banking industry, but was altered after highly effective US lobbying (see Peterson *et al.* 1995). The high volume of cars manufactured in the US by Japanese 'transplants' means that the EU will come under severe political pressure from the US if it backslides on its promise not to treat US-produced Hondas or Toyotas as 'Japanese'. As O'Cleireacain (1991: 82) puts it:

> When 'Japan policy' becomes 'US policy', a different set of security and political considerations are brought to bear. Just like their European counterparts, US senators and congressmen and women respond to pressure from local constituents, whether they are the workers and managers of a US-controlled corporation or a Japanese-controlled corporation.

The degree to which public agencies or politicians share the concerns of a 'foreign' country depends largely on relative levels of economic interdependence. One reason why the USTR is more assertive in dealing with Japan than with Germany is that US multinationals invest far more heavily in Germany than in Japan. They often end up acting as advocates of German policies and interests in Washington (Graham 1991: 201).

Political rhetoric on one side of the triad often accuses governments on the other two sides of seeking to create protectionist trade blocs. This rhetoric is useful to domestic lobbies which seek protection. However, such pressures are counterbalanced by the increasing diversity of economic interests which must be accommodated in the trade policies of all industrialized countries. For example, if Hondas made in Ohio contain 75 per cent 'US content' (i.e. three-quarters of their parts are US-made), the EU has difficulty claiming that they are 'Japanese' cars. The USTR is obliged to defend Honda's access to the EU's market because Honda provides a substantial boost to Ohio's economy (O'Cleireacain 1991: 96).

The wider point is that investment, production and technology have become increasingly globalized. Reich (1991: 110) may exaggerate, but he makes the point effectively: 'there is coming to be no such organization as an "American" (or British or French or Japanese or West German) corporation, nor any finished good called an "American" (or British, French, Japanese, or West German) product'. This trend complicates trade policies but provides substantial disincentives to protectionism. Strengthened and sustained US–EU political relations can go far towards ensuring that fierce trade rivalries between firms can coexist with political cooperation between states, and that regionalism does not undermine multilateralism. As Smith and Woolcock (1993: 110) argue:

> Joint management of a new world order may be impractical and possibly undesirable, given the benefit of maintaining genuine multilateral structures. But unless the EU and US can agree on a common agenda and cooperate in supporting the international economic and political orders, a dangerous vacuum will develop.

More specifically, the political and economic fates of the US and EU are simply too intertwined for either side to choose to damage its links with the other by forming an exclusive or protectionist trade bloc.

3 NEW REALITIES, ALTERED INSTITUTIONS

The New Transatlanticism has already gone far beyond diplomatic niceties. Consultation and exchange between the US and EU at both the highest political levels and at 'micro' or 'expert' levels is more intensive now than at any time since the early post-war period. It might be argued that there is no transatlantic 'problem' that needs to be fixed. Agreement on a Transatlantic Economic Space, let alone a broader US–EU treaty, inevitably would involve long and difficult negotiations. With the EU's own IGC looming, the Commission (1995a: 20) argued that 'any overall formalization of the relationship cannot be envisaged in the near future'.

However, US–EU relations now involve higher stakes and wider opportunities. As a senior adviser to the Clinton administration argued, 'The US–European relationship is hardy but not indestructible, and it can be destroyed by neglect as well as by intent' (Steinberg 1993: 165). A genuine US–EU partnership in the twenty-first century offers clear benefits for both sides, but it will clearly require better-organized exchanges, joint efforts to provide leadership within multilateral institutions, and a large dose of creative imagination.

Perhaps the primary virtue of going beyond the Transatlantic Declaration to develop a formal US–EU treaty would be that it would bind the hand of the US Congress, since it would require ratification by the Senate. Awareness of the EU in Congress is alarmingly low. Given the blurring of domestic and foreign policies, linking domestic institutions becomes just as important as linking external agencies. Longstanding exchanges between the European Parliament and US House of Representatives have left the Senate as well as national EU parliaments out in the cold. In the mid-1990s, a continuing dialogue between US and EU governments facilitated hard-fought compromise on diabolical issues such as Bosnia. The lack of any such dialogue between parliaments invited irresponsible posturing by legislators (Rifkind 1995). The US and EU badly need a stronger parliamentary dialogue.

On a perhaps more mundane level, they also need a means for solving the problem of divergent technical standards, which is cited by business more frequently than any other barrier to transatlantic trade (Commission 1995a: 11). Progress has been made on regulatory cooperation, but there is far more to do to eliminate incompatible standards which distort trade. Both sides were committed to further movement on the issue by the mid-1990s.

A formal treaty could seek to impose more political direction on the transatlantic agenda by having bilateral summits set priorities for the myriad bilateral exchanges which take place between the US and EU (Commission 1995a: 7). It could also embrace more ambitious measures, such as agreed principles for a new security architecture. Over time, the New Transatlanticism has facilitated an emerging political consensus on two points: first, that the WEU has to be strengthened, with US encouragement and logistical support; but second, that NATO has to be retained as an insurance policy in the face of lingering uncertainties about the evolution of the geopolitical landscape in Europe (Heisbourg 1992; Asmus et al. 1993; Brzezinski 1995). A formal US–EU treaty could set the terms for a political rebalancing of NATO which accommodates a parallel European defence force based on the WEU and features active participation by France. It could also resurrect the goal of extending 'negative' security guarantees to East European and CIS states, which would prohibit any NACC member from stationing military forces on any other member's territory unless it was part of a multinational force (see Mueller 1989; Heisbourg 1992).

In a global context, the UN is the logical arena for joint US–EU initiatives on human rights, the environment and security issues outside Europe. EU states were often in the vanguard of a movement for reform of the UN's highly bureaucratic and state-centred structures in the early 1990s (see Hindell 1992; Spiers 1994). For example, the EU enlisted Japan's support to establish a UN register of all international transfers of conventional weapons in 1991. The action showed that the EU was capable of diplomatic initiatives which its member states – particularly active arms exporters such as France and the UK – could not countenance on their own.

However, going beyond such marginal changes would require, first, a re-drafting of the UN's Charter, and second, a much firmer US political commitment to the UN. Under the terms of the UN Charter, the sovereignty of its member states is absolute except in cases of threats to international peace and security. This caveat makes it impossible for the UN to intervene when citizens' human rights are abused by their own governments. The UN often appears ineffective as a peacekeeper at a time when 'world politics are increasingly characterized by levels of violence in micronationalist struggles that were not imagined by the framers of the Charter or by pundits even a few years ago' (Weiss et al. 1994: 84).

Moreover, the UN lacks any supranational authority to deal with issues such as the environment, AIDS, international crime or migration. Any change in the UN's Charter would require the unanimous agreement of the five permanent members of the Security Council, each of which holds effective veto power over any substantive UN action. The Security Council is a Cold War anachronism which ensures that the nuclear club of the US, Russia, France, China and the UK effectively dictates the UN's agenda (Haas 1993). Japan and Germany, the second and third largest contributors to the UN's budget, are excluded. So are potential representatives of the developing world such as India, Brazil or Nigeria.

Germany and Japan – with recent encouragement from the Clinton administration after 1992 – are likely to be admitted to the Security Council in the early twenty-first century. However, the EU as a whole could do much to enhance its credibility as an actor on the world stage by taking the lead in pushing for reform of the UN. Its authority within the UN would be enhanced enormously if a political settlement was reached which allowed the Union itself to take over one of the two European seats on the Security Council currently held by France and the UK, with Japan taking over the other.

The UK and France may be expected to resist such a step fiercely, but 'the question isn't what, exactly, will happen to the Security Council but when it will happen' (Newhouse 1991: 102). The Japanese pay more to the UN than the UK and France combined, and resent such 'taxation without representation' (Daley 1992: 41). The political capital the EU could accrue in its relations with Japan by lobbying for a Japanese seat on the Security Council is inestimable. Many reluctant LDCs might be drawn into a coalition for reform of the UN if proposals were pursued to give one or more of the large states among them a permanent Security Council seat without veto power (see Lister 1990).

Strengthening the UN would require a fundamental shift in US attitudes and a President willing to expose Congressional sceptics as myopic. The UN's total 1992 peacekeeping bill of $1.4 billion was dwarfed by an American military budget of over $300 billion. The US was spending $2,000 on its military for every dollar it was investing in UN peacekeeping (Coate 1994: 12). Washington's refusal to pay its fair share for the UN is widely viewed as proof of its hypocrisy as an international actor (see Nye 1992). Without US leadership, the UN will remain a good idea whose time never comes. The case of Bosnia was indicative: 'the UN's probability of firm reaction was in almost direct proportion to the interest that the United States took in the situation and Washington's willingness to act' (Weiss *et al.* 1994: 239).

The EU could help to provoke new American thinking about the UN's role. A useful project for bilateral relations would be to lead a diplomatic effort to revive the UN's Military Staff Committee and create a UN standing force which could form the core of 'peace enforcement units' to enforce ceasefires (Boutros-Ghali 1992). Despite its inadequacies, the UN remains better equipped for neutral intervention than regional organizations, such as the Organization for African Unity or OSCE. These organizations are often shunned by political leaders who fear a precedent for regional involvement which might justify future intervention in their own country. The point is that the UN is the only game in town for much of what it does (Rochester 1993; Weiss *et al.* 1994: 38–9).

The UN has significant potential to act as a forum in which the US and EU can 'multilateralize' bilateral initiatives on a range of non-military security issues. For example, the EU secured membership of the UN Food and Agriculture Organization (FAO) in 1991. The EU thus could join the US in pushing for a new fund to aid net food-importing states which faced increased food prices after the Uruguay Round. Both the US and EU supported refinements in the enforcement measures of the International Atomic Energy Agency, which enhanced its ability to monitor problem states, such as North Korea or Iraq, suspected of pursuing nuclear ambitions (Graham 1994).

The UN is also a sensible forum for global initiatives to protect the environment. The Rio summit of 1992 revealed that ambitious programmes to transfer Western funds and 'green technologies' to LDCs in exchange for environmental protection commitments are unimaginable in the foreseeable future. Eventually such arrangements could be hastened by developing the concept of 'responsibility-sharing' among the major industrialized countries. Responsibility-sharing could, for example, link US commitments to reduce its CO_2 emissions to increased Japanese aid to Eastern Europe or EU commitments to transfer environmental technologies to the Third World.

Responsibility-sharing came to be viewed within the Bush administration as a way to encourage Japan and Germany to take a more active role in international affairs. Cynics claimed that US enthusiasm for the idea was a reflection of its extraordinary success in convincing its allies to pay for the Gulf War: the US may even have made a 'profit' on the war (Niblock 1991). Critics of responsibility-sharing argued that it would lead the major powers to view their interests as more separable, less intertwined and less subject to compromise (Walker 1991; Asmus 1992).

Yet the G-24 initiative to aid Eastern Europe represented a first and largely successful attempt at responsibility-sharing. Despite the inadequate sums raised, it signalled a conscious US decision to give the EU primary responsibility for its own 'backyard', but to define and work towards common goals. Meanwhile, the US took the lead in efforts to reduce and dismantle nuclear weapons in the former Soviet Union, with the EU linking its own aid to continued progress in denuclearization.

Japan continued to shy away from assuming foreign policy responsibilities commensurate with its international economic power (Drifte 1990; Hellmann 1989). On the one hand, it became the world's largest aid donor in total monetary terms, and paid for nearly half of the massive UN operation to separate warring factions in Cambodia (Daley 1992). On the other, its longstanding dispute with Russia over the Kurile Islands was viewed by many in the West as a ruse to preclude any meaningful aid contribution to the CIS.

Proposals for developing responsibility-sharing often focused on the G-7 summits which brought together political executives from the US, Japan, Canada, the UK, Italy, France and Germany. Known as 'economic summits', the G-7 increasingly focused on wider political issues after separate meetings of finance ministers were launched in 1986. Many analysts began to urge that a 'core agenda' be developed for the G-7, which would consist of aid, environmental, defence, trade, investment and macroeconomic policy issues (Group of Thirty 1991; Ostry 1991; Bayne 1992). The G-7 came to be seen as a forum for agreements to determine which members were best placed to take the lead on which core issues. Summits could define clear objectives and tangible performance measures, with monitoring of progress to be undertaken by relevant institutions such as the IMF for economic policy, the UN for environmental policies, and the GATT/WTO for trade and investment.

The G-7 shares many of the same problems the UN Security Council. While G-7's members account for about two-thirds of global GNP, it provides inadequate representation for the EU as a whole. It is viewed by LDCs as a *directoire* of rich states. Yet new ideas for responsibility-sharing within the G-7 have innate appeal. Besides being far less bureaucratic and more adaptable than the UN, it is the only international forum which engages Japan as a full partner. It has the potential to link issues – such as aid and trade – which are normally dealt with in specialized international institutions.

Strengthening the G-7's role should not distract from efforts to reform the UN. Substituting the EU itself for its four member states on the G-7, to form a 'G-4', would make responsibility-sharing more credible, and set a useful precedent for the UN Security Council. It also would help to facilitate a genuinely shared US–EU agenda on foreign policy.

Such an agenda may be emerging already. The transatlantic summit of June 1995 identified an ambitious list of concrete issues upon which the US and EU would seek to develop joint actions. It included human rights, nuclear safety, assistance to Palestine, environmental protection in Eastern Europe, aid to Bosnia, international crime and state-building in Haiti (Commission 1995a). No precedent existed for truly common initiatives on such a wide variety of issues.

The strength of barriers to the ideas discussed in this section should not be underestimated. In particular, EU member states – notably France and the UK – continue to guard jealously their privileged positions in international institutions. The rise of aggressive unilateralism in the US hardly inspires optimism about the prospects for an American *volte-face* on questions such as strengthening the UN or embracing meaningful environmental protection agreements. Transatlantic relations are still marked by a 'pronounced focus on "deal-making" in order to cope with or manage interdependence, rather than the exercise of principled leadership or responsibility sharing' (Smith and Woolcock 1994: 464). The very term 'New World Order', which Bush claimed was a 'big idea', had come to be viewed as a 'grandiose facade' on both the left and right, and on both sides of the Atlantic, by the mid-1990s (Phillips 1992: 42).

However, a more 'stable peace' – perhaps a less loaded term – can be created only through 'big thinking' and political leadership, on a scale which was mostly absent in the mid-1990s. To Halliday (1994: 241), the culpability of the US and EU was clear:

It is a pity, indeed it is very dangerous, that just at the moment when a new international situation emerges, there should be a faltering of political nerve in the countries with the greatest international influence on what does, and does not, constitute a desirable political system.

The point is that a more desirable international system is unlikely unless the US and EU take the lead, and define a common agenda within multilateral institutions.

4 THE FOUR THEORIES – A FINAL ANALYSIS

Many of the criticisms of *neorealism* contained in this study would have seemed implausible or reckless in the 1980s. More recent international relations literature is full of scathing attacks on neorealism (see Booth 1991a; Urquhart 1992; Hoffmann 1992; Kratochwil 1993). The present study could be accused of flogging a dead horse.

Neorealist scepticism about schemes to bring about a 'stable peace' is often constructive. For example, strategies for peacekeeping must be rigorously thought through, as the war in Bosnia has shown. In the words of a Bush administration official, 'peacekeepers cannot begin as peacekeepers, become peace enforcers overnight and then switch back without any adverse consequences to themselves or the trouble spot in which they serve' (Bolton 1995).

Neorealism also performs the useful function of reminding us that international institutions should not be viewed as desirable for their own sake (Gallarotti 1991). There is no doubt that many parts of the UN (not to mention the EU) are a bureaucratic mess. Neorealists are on strong ground in arguing that the UN's FAO is so poorly run and addicted to outdated models of agricultural development that it actually perpetuates Third World poverty (Brooks 1986).

At the same time, the intellectual hegemony of neorealism is considerable, and is difficult to justify. James's (1989: 226) spirited defence of its principles is indicative:

> the study of inter-state relations is a conservative activity. In one very limited sense this is very obviously and necessarily true: the study of anything which exists is by definition the study of part of the status quo, and not of how it might be altered.

Many neorealists do little to advance theoretical debates. They are often dismissive of other approaches and focus on assserting 'the doomed utopianism of reformist projects' (Linklater 1995: 256). Perhaps the most glaring deficiency of neorealism is its inability to predict or even acknowledge change. The muscle-bound defence of neorealist assumptions often means that

> whole sectors of international reality become marginalized, such as the considerable amount of cooperation, the importance of common conventions for sustaining international systems, and the links between domestic order and efforts of institutionalizing international inter-actions.

> (Kratchowil 1993: 64)

The insistence of neorealists that many international organizations are poorly run often leads them to neglect the question of how pressing international problems can be resolved. The integration of the global economy and the political fragmentation of the East–West blocs mean that consolidating liberal democracy, stopping environmental degradation and checking nuclear proliferation will only be possible through collective, long-term international action. In this context, neorealism 'is often a euphemism for short-sightedness, self-interest, and policies which lack the necessary courage or vision' (Urquhart 1992: 311). The primary weakness of neorealism in explaining US–EU relations is that it cannot accommodate changing notions of security which give both sides stronger incentives to pool efforts and resources within international organizations.

Neorealists are right to insist that intense economic competition between sovereign nation-states will continue to be a central characteristic of the international system. Strengthened international institutions cannot eliminate the 'anarchy' of a system which lacks an overarching political authority. Theorists engaged in 'new thinking' about international security argue that these assumptions should not be abandoned in the quest for a new 'realist-idealism', which is both 'realistic and utopian' (Booth 1991a: 28). Others seek to develop neorealism, and claim that Waltz has been 'misunderstood' by his critics. They urge that theorists must focus more on international *relations*, as opposed to the international *system* (Buzan *et al.* 1993). Neorealism's systemic, or 'structural', obsession leads to prophecies which fly in the face of political reality. An example is Waltz's (1993: 20) insistence that Germany and Japan will inevitably become nuclear powers, because 'for a country to choose not to become a greater power is a structural anomaly. For that reason, the choice is a difficult one to sustain.'

If nothing else, neorealists must draw upon the insights of other schools of thought (Buzan *et al.* 1993: 20). In particular, the assumptions of *institutionalism* have been vindicated in the 1990s in so far as 'Institutionalists expect existing institutions to adapt and to persist more easily than new institutions, formed by states on the basis of changing interests, can be created. Realists make no such prediction' (Keohane 1993b: 297).

For example, the neorealist prediction of the collapse, or at least grave weakening, of the EU after the demise of bipolarity seems far-fetched, despite its continued problems of disunity. By contrast, institutionalists expect it to become larger and more significant, even if it is not often a 'single actor' in international politics. Institutionalists 'do not expect cooperation always to prevail, but they are aware of the malleability of interests and they argue that interdependence creates interests in cooperation' (Keohane 1984: 8).

Institutionalism sheds considerable light on the 'great dialectic between political fragmentation and economic integration' (Buzan *et al.* 1990: 11). The gap between economic realities and political structures threatens to widen because cooperation between private actors is *ad hoc*, driven by technological change, and runs ahead of formal political regimes to regulate it:

> Today's economic activities are being managed on a global basis already, while officials are still captives of the eighteenth and nine-teenth-century notions of 'national sovereignty' and 'national interest.' The high-tech economies of Japan and America are relentlessly advanc-ing toward a twenty-first-century unified global economy while their political systems remain stuck in the eighteenth-century model of the state.
>
> (Ito 1990: 146)

The globalization of production means that both the US and EU have incentives to 'deepen' cooperation on competition policy and standards (see Graham 1991). Once common rules are agreed, the logical step is 'multilateralize' them so that US and EU firms can avoid discrimination when they invest and produce beyond the transatlantic area.

More generally, institutionalists prescribe 'responsibility-sharing' through strengthened international institutions, especially because the US can no longer provide 'hegemonic stability'. Even those theorists who insist that 'in realist terms the United States will remain the world's largest power well into the next century' submit that Washington 'will have to combine traditional power and liberal institutionalist approaches if it is to effectively pursue its national interest' (Nye 1992: 95–6; see also Huntington 1992). Institutionalists cite the US near-invasion of Haiti in 1994 as an example. After a UN resolution authorizing a multinational force 'to use all necessary means' to remove Haiti's military junta – the first-ever UN authority for military action in the Western hemisphere – Haitian colonels gave way peacefully.

However, institutionalists caution that the UN and other widely inclusive regimes will always face severe collective action problems. Keohane (1994: 246) argues that institutions 'are often most useful when relatively few like-minded countries are responsible for both making the essential rules and maintaining them'. This axiom points to the importance of the US–EU 'community in values' as a basis for partnership. It also suggests that rapid incorporation of the CIS and East European states into new European security alliances, or the creation of a 'Pacific Economic Com-munity', is impossible.

Institutionalists remain vulnerable to the charge that competing insti-tutional agendas will undermine responsibility-sharing. Weiss *et al.* (1994: 39) clearly failed to foresee the problem in Bosnia: 'in Europe, UN diplomacy could well be combined with the use of NATO forces under a UN flag in regional disputes'. Moreover, many institutionalists forget that strong political leadership is needed for states to play 'two-level games' effectively so that international cooperation is not blocked by powerful domestic groups. The institutional development of the EU means that European leaders increasingly must play *three*-level games at the international, regional and domestic levels. Putnam (1993: 81) warns that:

> If the European Parliament were to gain increased powers of blockage without at the same time acquiring more coherent leadership, transatlantic tensions might well be exacerbated. Transatlantic cooperation in the years ahead is at serious risk unless Europe moves more quickly toward a genuine federal system with a chief executive who can resolve the conflicts among the three tables.

The problem of executives constrained by domestic imperatives has become a more explicit concern of *liberal* theories of international relations (Moravcsik 1992, 1995). In particular, the problem of 'system friction' between ostensibly domestic projects in the US and EU – such as EMU or cuts in the US budget deficit – could pose considerable obstacles to a new transatlantic bargain. Yet liberals tend to argue that the collectively declining power of the US and EU in global trade actually increases their incentives to seek collective action to ensure a liberal trading order, despite the emergence of new alternative economic partners (Kahler 1995). For example, a joint agenda for seeking changes in Japanese trade policy comes to seem logical:

> A liberal trading system may not endure if the second major single actor in the world plays by a different set of rules, even if these rules reflect the behavior of private companies and not necessarily an overt government policy. . . . A joint US–EU pressure on Japan may be called 'ganging up on the Japanese', but if exercised within the GATT framework it would become 'aggressive multilateralism' – a more palatable title. By whatever term, such pressures may produce results.
>
> (Kreinin 1991: 67)

At the same time, liberals point to the limited number of issues on which the US and EU can work in tandem to pressure Japan. The Bush administration needed alliances with Japan and the Cairns group in order to isolate the EU on the agricultural issue. The EU was forced to work with Japan and others to strike a deal on financial services after the conclusion of the Uruguay Round.

Recent evidence suggests that regional trade arrangements, such as the EU or NAFTA, have not impeded and may actually have promoted, global free trade (WTO 1995). Many liberals would concede that the elimination of lingering barriers to transatlantic trade is a useful project. The fact that the Clinton administration was seeking trade liberalization agreements with virtually every major economic area of the world – North

America, South America and Asia – except the EU as late as 1994 was difficult to fathom.

Still, liberals remain suspicious of initiatives such as APEC or FTAA on the grounds that they may add to trade discrimination instead of eliminating it, as another GATT round would do (Bhagwati 1995). They rightly view the WTO as a fragile institution which the US and EU must nurture. For liberals, the only way to justify a 'Transatlantic Economic Space' is as a means to kick-start another global trade round.

For *reformists*, the disparity between economic interdependence and political structures points to the more general inadequacy of the nation-state as an institution. Reformists wish to see the dissolution of states themselves in the long term. In the short term, international cooperation between major actors such as the US and EU is viewed by many reformists as the only solution to problems such as environmental degradation, the North–South divide and the proliferation of weapons of mass destruction. On these and other security issues:

> Some leading role for the great powers would seem to be inevitable and indeed desirable, just as the role of the major economic and financial powers is desirable and even necessary in the field of international economic management. The question is not whether they do or do not play a role, but rather whether this is unilateral, competitive and short-sighted, or whether it is a multilateral, more cooperative and long-term policy.
>
> (Halliday 1994: 239)

Perhaps ironically, reformists have much in common with neorealists in their criticisms of existing international organizations (see Gallarotti 1991). Aid schemes run by the World Bank, the IMF and even the EU are often grouped together in reformist critiques which insist that they perpetuate Southern poverty and Northern hegemony (Hayter 1974; Cox 1980; Cocks 1980). Reformist critiques of international organizations are sometimes as powerful as their critiques of the state:

> Our international institutions and procedures were designed for a set of conditions (the Cold War, simple technologies for transport and communication, relative immobility of capital, trade between national firms) and a set of objectives (defence through mutual deterrence, unlimited economic growth) that are no longer pertinent . . . the need for innovation comes at a time when funds to create new institutions are scarcer than they have been in decades, when there is dissatisfaction with the performance of most of the UN institutions, and when the United States continues to resort to unilateralism to implement its international agenda.
>
> (Glover 1994: 285)

However, reformists depart from neorealists in insisting that international organizations can be the only guarantors of global security. Reformists are hopeful that international institutions can embrace values such as concern for future generations in actual policy decisions. States cannot incorporate such concerns into their policies because they remain addicted to outdated notions of national sovereignty, which leads them to compete with each other for power and scarce resources. For reformists:

> The time of absolute and exclusive sovereignty has passed; its theory was never matched by reality. It is the task of leaders of states today to understand this and find a balance between the needs of good internal governance and the requirements of an ever more interdependent world
>
> (Boutros-Ghali 1992: 17)

Reformists must still contend with many of the criticisms faced by their intellectual predecessors, the idealists, about the role of military power in their theories. The reformist critique of the state is powerful, but it contains no solution to the problem of how to convince national leaders to accept supranational control of the means for defending their territories from aggressors. Reformists counter that international efforts must be made to enforce brokered agreements on ceasefires and arms embargoes when violent conflicts erupt between nation-states. The UN can play a leading role in sponsoring peacekeeping efforts. But reformists insist that the UN must become more than a great-power cabal and that the West must make firm commitments to its democratization (Falk *et al.* 1991).

Many reformists take an extremely pessimistic view of the chances for a 'stable peace' based on liberal values and Western leadership: 'We have now entered into the post-American era, but also the post-liberal era. This promises to be a time of great world disorder, greater probably than the world disorder between 1914 and 1945' (Wallerstein 1993: 4). Others castigate the US and EU for a failure of will and vision, but still contend that:

> These reservations do not invalidate the larger claim that on matters of primary normative and political concern there is a measure of international consensus around a set of values that, on grounds quite independent of their origin, can be based on reason and which bear, for reasons that social scientists can happily argue over, some relationship to economic prosperity and peace, both domestic and international.
>
> (Halliday 1994: 221)

A final assessment of the prospects for US–EU leadership towards economic prosperity and peace must assess three crucial variables. The first is the political evolution of the European Union. The end of the

Cold War gives the US the choice of relating to the EU as a more equal partner. But closer European unity is a prerequisite for US–EU partnership and it certainly cannot be taken for granted.

This study has stressed the crucial role of Germany in determining both the pace of European integration and the tone of US–EU relations. A rational American response to doubts about the sustainability of European integration might be to focus its diplomacy on Germany as much as on the EU, and far more on Germany than on other EU member states (Kegley and Raymond 1994: 198–9). The argument against such a strategy is that it would cause resentment among other EU states and undermine transatlantic relations. It would also be counterproductive to efforts to maintain a German domestic consensus on multilateralism in the conduct of its foreign policy. The US must nurture European integration if it wishes to sustain the New Transatlanticism. It must also be prepared for failures of German leadership: 'the notion of the new Germany embarking on a sinister power drive seems absurd, while that of a relaxed, united country able to juggle the many demands of its new political system seems unrealistic' (Kielinger and Otte 1993: 44).

A second key issue is public perceptions of US–EU relations. The trend towards the 'democratization' of US and EU foreign policy-making is visible in outcomes such as the Danish rejection of Maastricht and Clinton's trade policy. US public opinion in particular provides a daunting challenge to any further strengthening of bilateral relations. Looking at elite and mass attitudes over time, Wittkopf (1987) concludes that far more average Americans than elites have always favoured a 'hardline' or non-cooperative version of US internationalism, if they have favoured one at all.

Much of the blame for militant public attitudes, and the instability in US foreign policy which they encourage, rests with US political leaders and elites. Russett (1990: 117) argues that: 'if a finger of accusation for volatile policy is to be pointed, it should first be directed toward the elites ... they [have been] unable to produce a coherent and stable perspective on means and ends in American foreign policy'. The scope for political leadership to shape public attitudes is much wider than it was during the Cold War era. The goal for both the US and EU should be a more stable and less events-driven partnership, which facilitates long-term thinking and domestic consensus on means and ends for enhancing global security.

A third key issue is the extent to which the US and EU can multilateralize their bilateral commitments and build a global consensus to support their international policy agenda. New tensions are endemic in the process of adjusting political structures to accommodate rising economic interdependence or changing notions of security. Compared to military security, economic security can engender far more different types of state action, ranging from multilateral free trade agreements to outright economic nationalism. National environmental policies have become as politicized as military policies because they have begun to subsume the same set of ethical, welfare, employment and economic development issues. Because economic and environmental security are now 'core' issues for US and EU foreign policies, foreign policy-making has become subject to a far wider range of domestic political pressures than in the past.

One of the virtues of multilateral institutions is that they can often help to insulate political elites from erratic domestic pressures. The argument is not that foreign policy-making should remain the exclusive domain of elite political classes in the US and EU. It is that stronger bilateral and multilateral institutions can inspire thinking beyond short-term domestic political timeframes. The effect of taking actions multilaterally can be to legitimize those actions in the eyes of domestic interests which are asked to bear the short-term costs of measures to stem military aggression, open up trade, lessen Third World poverty or protect the environment. Pursuing 'holistic security' means trading short-term costs for long-term peace and stability. Domestic publics in the US and EU will not think in terms of this trade-off unless political leaders do so first.

A final thought: it is neither unreasonable nor ethnocentric to argue that the US and EU are better equipped than any other configuration of international actors to take on a role of collective global leadership in pursuit of a more stable peace and a more humane world able to meet the basic needs of far more of its citizens. One could equally argue, along with Newt Gingrich, that the transatlantic allies are not going stay together out of nostalgia (Brittan 1995: 14).

Appendix
The EU's institutions and member states

The EU is a complex political system. The reader who wishes to know more about its historical development and institutions is encouraged to consult George (1991), Nugent (1994), Dinan (1994) or Duff *et al.* (1994). Dinan (1994) offers a particularly thorough historical overview of the EU's historical development. Nugent (1994: 449–64) contains a chronology of major events in the EU's development as well as useful suggestions for further reading. What follows here is a brief overview of the EU's evolution and the role and functions of its institutions.

The Treaty of Paris of 1951 created the European Coal and Steel Community (ECSC) and a common market for coal and steel products. Its members were France, West Germany, Italy, Belgium, the Netherlands and Luxembourg. The six ECSC member states agreed to the Treaty of Rome in 1957 which created the European Economic Community (EEC) and European Atomic Energy Community (Euratom). The ECSC, EEC and Euratom were merged in 1965 to form the 'European Communities' (EC), which was most often referred to in the singular as the 'Community'.

The UK, Denmark and Ireland joined the EC in 1973 and were followed by Greece in 1981, and Spain and Portugal in 1986. In 1991, the Treaty on European Union – often called the Maastricht Treaty – was signed. When finally ratified in 1993, the European Union (EU) came into being. The EU groups together the pre-existing EC as well as two separate intergovernmental 'pillars' for the CFSP and internal security policy (see Duff *et al.* 1994). Austria, Finland and Sweden became EU members in 1995.

The Treaty of Rome created a unique quadripartite institutional structure for making EC policies (see Table A.1). The Council of Ministers is composed of national ministers and is the EU's main legislative organ. It is where national interests are expressed and pursued (Westlake 1995).

The European Commission is a hybrid executive and civil service which retains exclusive powers to propose EC legislation and represents the Union abroad in trade diplomacy. It exists to serve the 'general European interest' and is intended to be independent of the control of national governments (Peters 1992; Fitzmaurice 1994; Edwards and Spence 1994).

Table A.1 The institutions of the European Union*

Institution	Powers	Role
Council of Ministers	Legislative	Represents national interests
European Commission	Executive/civil service	Proposes EC legislation; represents EU in trade negotiations; serves 'general European interest'
European Parliament	Advisory amendment 'Co-decision'	Represents EU citizens; amends and alters legislation
European Court of Justice	Judicial	Interprets and applies EC treaties

Note: * The same institutions are concerned with the 'non-EC' policies of the European Union for foreign and internal security, but their powers and roles vary. The Council is by far the most powerful institution in the EU's two intergovernmental pillars and all policies require the unanimous endorsement of all member states.

The European Parliament (EP) played a largely consultative role prior to the coming into effect of the Maastricht Treaty, which gave the EP the power of veto through 'co-decision' with the Council in selected areas of policy. The Parliament is the only institution which represents EU citizens, and its powers have grown steadily over time (Corbett 1994; Westlake 1994; Corbett *et al.* 1995). The European Court of Justice (ECJ) interprets and applies what is formally called 'EC law', as there is no such thing as 'EU law'. Because the price of EU membership is the acceptance of EC law as superior to national law, the Court is viewed by many as a primary agent of European integration (Shapiro 1992; Bradley and Sutton 1994). Ultimately, however, the EU relies on national governments and authorities for the implementation of its policies.

The EU operates at multiple levels and resembles no other international organization (Peterson 1995). For example, the European Council, which is composed of national prime ministers and the French President, holds summits several times a year and acts as a sort of 'board of directors' for the EU. The summits have no firm legal basis in the Treaty of Rome, although their declarations have achieved 'quasi-legal status' as strategic guides for Union policy (Ludlow 1992). The Maastricht Treaty expanded the European Council's role by assigning it responsibility for linking the EC with the new intergovernmental 'pillars'.

The SEA committed member states to a system of weighted majority voting instead of unanimity on nearly all decisions taken by the Council of Ministers on the freeing of the internal market. This system assigns more 'votes' to large states (ten each for Germany, France, Italy and the UK) than to smaller states (Belgium has five votes and Luxembourg two). It is stipulated that more than 70 per cent of all votes must be affirmative for a Commission proposal to become law.

The primary effect of increased majority voting was to speed up considerably the EC decision-making process. However, unanimity prevails in some Community policy areas and – with few exceptions – within the two pillars for the CFSP and internal security. The EU's 1996 intergovernmental conference, which will consider further changes to the Treaty of Rome, will feature intense debates about extending QMV to all EU activities, as well as subjecting the CFSP and internal security policy to the 'Community method' of decision-making.

Notes

1 THE NEW TRANSATLANTICISM

1 Interview, DG I, April 1991.
2 Interview, DG I, April 1991.
3 Quoted in Peterson (1994a: 412).

2 THE HISTORICAL SETTING

1 Quoted in Grosser (1982: 201).
2 Quoted in Grosser (1982: 207).
3 Quoted in Smith (1992: 110).
4 Quoted in Larrabee (1991: 3).
5 Interview, March 1994.
6 Quoted in *Europe*, July 1989.
7 Interview, April 1991.
8 *Le Monde*, 16 December 1989.
9 Interview, April 1991.
10 Interview, November 1991.
11 *Agence Europe*, 12–13 November 1991.
12 Interview, DG I, November 1991.
13 Quoted in *The Economist*, 27 March 1993.
14 Quoted in Peterson (1994a: 420)
15 Interview, April 1991.
16 Quoted in Bennett (1991: 755).
17 Quoted in Kumar (1992: 339).
18 Quoted in *Agence Europe*, 12/13 November 1991.

3 THE NEW GEOPOLITICAL REALITY

1 Quoted in Bruce (1990: 76).
2 Quoted in *Independent*, 8 June 1992.
3 Quoted in Asmus (1992: 64).
4 Interview, Secretariat-General, September 1990.
5 *New York Times*, 22 December 1991.
6 Quoted in *The Economist*, 6 July 1991.
7 Quoted in *New York Times*, 24 December 1991.
8 Quoted in *Guardian*, 18 December 1991.

9 Interview, October 1994.
10 Quoted in *Boston Globe*, 28 July 1995.
11 Quoted in Kegley and Raymond (1994: 5).

4 THE DOMESTIC POLITICS OF US–EU RELATIONS

1 Interview, DG I, European Commission, September 1990.
2 Quoted in *International Herald Tribune*, 27–28 February 1993.
3 Interview, USTR, March 1995.
4 Washington Post/ABC News poll in *International Herald Tribune*, 19 September 1991.
5 New York Times/CBS poll in *New York Times*, 22 December 1991.
6 I am grateful to Mario Zuconni of the Centro Studidi Politica Internazionale in Rome for suggesting this point to me.
7 Interview, office of Congressman Richard Gephardt, November 1991.
8 Both quoted in Dunne (1995).
9 Quoted in *Independent*, 14 December 1991.
10 Quoted in *Agence Europe*, 8 July 1993.
11 Interview, December 1991.
12 Quoted in *The Economist*, 14 December 1991.
13 See Gallup poll results as reported in *Guardian*, 14 November 1991.
14 Gerster and Eichel quoted (respectively) in *Independent*, 12 June and 16 May 1992.
15 Quoted in Peterson (1994a: 411).
16 Interview, US State Department, March 1995.
17 Interview, November 1991.
18 US Under Secretary for Economic and Agricultural Affairs Joan Spero quoted in *Agence Europe*, 4 February 1994.
19 Interview, DG I, November 1991.
20 Interview, April 1991.
21 Interview, Irish EPC official, April 1991.
22 Interview, Congressman John Hostettler (Republican, Indiana), member of House National Security Committee, 31 March 1995.
23 Interview, November 1991.

5 TRADE AND MONETARY RELATIONS

1 Interview, March 1995.
2 Interview, September 1990.
3 Quoted in *Agence Europe*, 18/19 December 1989.
4 Quoted in *Financial Times*, 4 November 1991.
5 Interview, December 1991.
6 Interview, USTR, December 1991.
7 Interview, DG I, November 1991.
8 Interview, USTR, March 1995.
9 Quoted in *Financial Times*, 1–2 July 1995.
10 Quoted in *Agence Europe*, 12 October 1989.
11 Interview, April 1991.
12 Interview, April 1991.
13 Interview, March 1995.
14 Quoted in *Financial Times*, 26 April 1995.

15 Michael Fingers of the World Bank quoted in *Financial Times*, 13 October 1994.
16 The German Green MEP, F. W. Graefe zu Baringdorf, quoted in Green Group (1992: 10).
17 Quoted in Aaronson (1994: 54).

6 EUROPEAN SECURITY AFTER THE COLD WAR

1 Interview, March 1995.
2 Quoted in *The Economist*, 30 October 1993.
3 Interview, US Department of Defense, March 1995.
4 Quoted in *International Herald Tribune*, 26–27 October, 1991.
5 Quoted in *Independent*, 8 November 1991.
6 Quoted in *Agence Europe*, 9 November 1991.
7 Interview, March 1995.
8 Quoted in *International Herald Tribune*, 9–10 September 1995.
9 Quoted in *Financial Times*, 7 July 1995.
10 The former NATO Secretary-General, Manfred Wörner, quoted in *International Herald Tribune*, 26–27 October 1991.
11 *The Economist*, 9 September 1995.

7 THE CHANGING ESSENCE OF SECURITY

1 Interview, US National Security Council, March 1995. Austria, Finland and Sweden – none of which were members of NATO – joined the EU in January 1995.

8 CONCLUSION

1 See statements by the German Finance Minister, Theo Waigel, quoted in *Financial Times*, 12 September 1995.
2 Quoted in *Financial Times*, 24 April 1995.
3 Quoted in *The Economist*, 24 June 1995.

Bibliography

Aaronson, Susan (1994) 'The policy battle over freer world trade', *Challenge*, November/December: 48–54.

Adler, E. and Haas, P. M. (1992) 'Conclusion: epistemic communities, world order, and the creation of a reflective research program', *International Organization*, 46 (1): 367–90.

Albright, M. (1991) 'The role of the United States in Central Europe', in N. H. Wessell (ed.) *Proceedings of the Academy of Political Science*, 38 (1): 71–4.

Alger, C. F. and Mendlovitz, S. H. (1987) 'Grass-roots initiatives: the challenge of linkages', in S. H. Mendlovitz and R. B. J. Walker (eds) *Towards a Just World Peace: Perspectives from Social Movements*, London: Butterworths.

Allain, P. and Goldmann, K. (1995) *The End of the Cold War: Evaluating Theories of International Relations*, The Hague: Kluwer.

Allen, D. and Smith, M. (1990) 'Western Europe's presence in the contemporary international arena', *Review of International Studies*, 16 (1): 19–39.

Allen, J. (1995) 'Que peso? Why the key to Mexico's trade problems may be found in China', *Washington Post*, 26 February: C1.

Almond, M. (1994) *Europe's Backyard War: the War in the Balkans*, London: William Heinemann.

Amnesty International (1995) *Annual Report*, London.

Anderson, J. J. and Goodman, J. B. (1993) 'Mars or Minerva? A united Germany in post-Cold War Europe', in R. O. Keohane, J. S. Nye and S. Hoffmann (eds) *After the Cold War*, Cambridge: Harvard University Press.

Artis, M. and Ostry, S. (1986) *International Economic Policy Coordination*, London: Routledge & Kegan Paul.

Ashley, R. K. (1984) 'The poverty of neorealism', *International Organization*, 38 (2): 255–86.

Asmus, R. D. (1992) 'A unified Germany', in R. A. Levine (ed.) *Transition and Turmoil in the Atlantic Alliance*, London: Crane Rusack.

Asmus, R. D., Kugler, R. L. and Larrabee, F. S. (1993) 'Building a New NATO', *Foreign Affairs*, September/October: 28–40.

Attali, J. (1990) *Lignes d'horizon*, Paris: Foyard.

Avery, W. P. and Rapkin, D. P. (eds) (1982) *America in a Changing World Political Economy*, New York and London: Longman.

Baker, J. (1991) *Berlin Speeches*, addresses to Berlin Press Club, 12 December 1989 and The Aspen Institute, 18 June 1991, London: Embassy of the United States of America, July.

Baldwin, D. (ed.) (1993) *Neorealism and Neoliberalism: the Contemporary Debate*, New York: Columbia University Press.

Baldwin, R. E. (1988) 'An introduction to the issues and analyses', in R. E. Baldwin (ed.) *Issues in US–EC Trade Relations*, Chicago: University of Chicago Press.

—— (1994) *Towards an Integrated Europe*, London: Centre for Economic Policy Research.

Barber, L. (1990) 'Washington sees dual role for the EC in Latin America', *Financial Times*, 25 April: 8.

—— (1995) 'Brussels unveils blueprint for closer Chinese links', *Financial Times*, 6 July: 2.

Barnett, M. N. and Levy, J. S. (1991) 'Domestic sources of alliances and alignments: the case of Egypt, 1962–73', *International Organization*, 45 (3): 369–95.

Barrell, R., Morgan, P. and Pain, N. (1995) *The Employment Effects of the Maastricht Fiscal Criteria*, London: National Institute for Economic and Social Research, Discussion Paper 81.

Bayard, T. and Elliott, K. A. (1994) *Reciprocity and Retaliation in U.S. Trade Policy*, Washington: Institute for International Economics.

Bayne, N. (1992) 'The course of summitry', *The World Today*, 48 (2): 27–30.

Bennett, M. (1991) 'The superpowers and international institutions', *Western Political Quarterly*, 44 (3): 748–61.

Bergsten, C. F. (1990) 'The world economy after the cold war', *Foreign Affairs*, 69 (3): 96–112.

Betts, R. (1993/4) 'Wealth, power and instability: East Asia and United States after the Cold War', *International Security*, 18 (3): 34–77.

Bhagwati, J. (1995) 'The high cost of free trade areas', *Financial Times*, 31 May: 19.

Bolton, J. R. (1995) 'Dulles would disagree', *Washington Post*, 6 March: A17.

Bonnart, F. (1995) 'France's offer to share its arsenal is disingenuous', *International Herald Tribune*, 30 August: 8.

Booth, K. (1991a) 'Introduction – the interregnum: world politics in transition', in K. Booth (ed.) *New Thinking About Strategy and International Security*, London: Harper Collins.

—— (1991b) 'War, security and strategy: towards a doctrine for a stable peace', in K. Booth (ed.) *New Thinking About Strategy and International Security*, London: Harper Collins.

Booth, K. and Smith, S. (eds) (1995) *International Relations Theory Today*, Cambridge and New York: Polity.

Borosage, R. L. (1993/4) 'Inventing the threat: Clinton's defense budget', *World Policy Journal*, 10 (4): 7–16.

Borrus, M. and Zysman, J. (1992) 'Industrial strength and regional response: Japan's impact on European integration', in G. F. Treverton (ed.) *The Shape of the New Europe*, New York: Council on Foreign Relations Press.

Boulding, K. (1987) *Stable Peace*, Austin, TX: University of Texas Press.

Boutros-Ghali, B. (1992) *An Agenda for Peace: Preventive Diplomacy, Peacemaking and Peace-keeping*, New York: UN.

Bradley, K. and Sutton, Alastair (1994) 'European Union and the rule of law', in A. Duff, J. Pinder and R. Pryce (eds) *Maastricht and Beyond: Building the European Union*, London: Routledge.

Brandt Commission, The (1983) *Common Crisis*, Boston: MIT Press.

Brenner, M. J. (1990) 'Finding America's place', *Foreign Policy*, 79 (3): 25–43.

—— (1991) 'The alliance: a Gulf post-mortem', *International Affairs*, 67 (4): 665–78.

Brittan, L. (1995) 'The EU–US relationship: will it last?', speech to the American Club of Brussels, 27 April.

Brooks, R. (1986) 'Africa is starving and the United Nations shares the blame', *Backgrounder*, 480, Washington, DC: Heritage Foundation.

Brown, C. (1995) 'International political theory and the idea of world community' in K. Booth and S. Smith (eds) *International Relations Theory Today*, Cambridge: Polity.

Brown, J. F. (1991) *Surge to Freedom: The End of Communist Rule in Eastern Europe*, Twickenham: Adamantine.

Bruce, L. (1990) 'Europe's locomotive', *Foreign Policy*, 78 (2): 68–90.

Brzezinski, Z. (1989/90) 'Postcommunist nationalism', *Foreign Affairs*, 68 (5): 1–25.

—— (1991) 'Selective global commitment', *Foreign Affairs*, 69 (4): 1–20.

—— (1995) 'A plan for Europe', *Foreign Affairs*, January/February: 26–42.

Bull, H. (1977) *The Anarchical Society*, Oxford: Oxford University Press.

—— (1983a) 'Civilian power Europe: a contradiction in terms?', *Journal of Common Market Studies*, 21 (2–3): 149–70.

—— (1983b) 'European self-reliance and the reform of NATO', *Foreign Affairs*, 66 (4): 874–92.

Burley, A. M. S. (1993) 'Law among liberal states: liberal internationalism and the act of state doctrine', *Columbia Law Journal*, 92 (8): 1909–96.

Bush, G. (1989) 'Remarks at the Boston University commencement ceremony May 21 1989', in *Beyond Containment: Selected Speeches by President George Bush on Europe and East–West relations*, Washington, DC: United States Information Service.

Buzan, B. (1991) 'Is international security possible?' in K. Booth (ed.) *New Thinking About Strategy and International Security*, London: Harper Collins.

Buzan, B., Kelstrup, M., Lemaitre, P., Tromer, E. and Waever, O. (1990) *The European Security Order Recast: Scenarios for the Post-Cold War Era*, London: Pinter.

Buzan, B., Jones, C. and Little, R. (1993) *The Logic of Anarchy: Neorealism to Structural Realism*, New York: Columbia University Press.

Cafruny, A. (1985) 'The political economy of international shipping: Europe versus America', *International Organization*, 39 (1).

Calingaert, M. (1988) *The 1992 Challenge from Europe*, Washington: National Planning Association.

Caporaso, J. (1996) 'The European Union and forms of state: Westphalian, regulatory or post-modern?', *Journal of Common Market Studies*, 34(1):29–52.

Carnoy, M., Castells, M., Cohen, S. and Cardoso, F. H. (1993) *The New Global Economy in the Information Age*, University Park, PA: Pennsylvania University Press.

Carpenter, T. G. (1994) 'A new proliferation policy', *The National Interest*, Summer: 63–72.

Carr, E. H. (1940) *The Twenty Years Crisis: 1919–1939*, London: Macmillan.

Cecchini, P. with Catinat, M. and Jacquemin, A. (1988) *The European Challenge 1992: The Benefits of a Single European Market*, Aldershot: Wildwood House.

Cerny, P. G. (1996) 'Globalization and the changing logic of collective action', *International Organization*, 49 (4): 595–625.

Christensen, T. J. and Snyder, J. (1990) 'Chain gangs and passed bucks: predicting alliance patterns in multipolarity', *International Organization*, 44 (1): 137–68.

Christopher, W. (1995) 'Address on charting a Transatlantic Agenda', Madrid, 2 June, State Department, mimeo.

Coate, R. A. (1994) 'The future of the United Nations', in R.A. Coate (ed.) *U.S. Policy and the Future of the United Nations*, New York: Twentieth Century Fund Press.

Cocks, P. (1980) 'Toward a Marxist theory of European integration', *International Organization*, 34 (1): 1–40.

Cohen, B. J. (1987) 'An explosion in the kitchen? Economic relations with other advanced industrial states', in K. A. Oye, R. J. Lieber and D. Rothchild (eds)

Eagle Resurgent? The Reagan Era in American Foreign Policy, Boston: Little, Brown & Company.

Commission of the European Communities (1985) *White Paper on Completing the Internal Market*, COM 85, Brussels, 14 June. (Cited as Commission in text.)

—— (1988a) 'Proposal for a second Council directive on the coordination of laws, regulations and administrative provisions relating to the taking-up and pursuit of the business of credit institutions and amending directive', COM 87 (715), 77/789/EEC, Brussels, 16 February.

—— (1988b) 'Europe 1992: Europe world partner', Brussels, Office of Press and Public Affairs, 19 October.

—— (1989) 'Second Council directive on the coordination of laws, regulations and administrative provisions relating to the taking-up and pursuit of the business of credit institutions and amending directive', *Official Journal of the European Communities*, L386, Brussels, 30 December: 1–3.

—— (1990a) 'The Commission's programme for 1990: address by Jacques Delors, President of the European Commission, to the European Parliament and his reply to the debate', *Bulletin of the European Communities*, supp. 1/90, Brussels: 10.

—— (1991a) 'Fact sheet on contacts between the EC Commission and the US administration', Brussels: DG I, 8 August.

—— (1991b) 'A Community strategy to limit carbon dioxide emissions and to improve energy efficiency', communication from the Commission to the Council, Brussels, October.

—— (1991c) *Report on United States Trade Barriers and Unfair Trade Practices*, Brussels: DG I.

—— (1992) *Eurobarometer: Public Opinion in the European Community*, Brussels, 37, Spring.

—— (1993) *Opening Up of Public Procurement*, Luxembourg.

—— (1994) *EU–US: Progress Report on EU–US Relations*, Brussels: DG I, December.

—— (1995a) *L'Europe et les Etats-Unis d'Amérique: relations futures*, SEC (95) 1333/4, 25 July.

—— (1995b) *European Security Policy in the Run-Up to 2000: Ways and Means of Achieving Real Credibility*, Brussels: DG 1A, January.

—— (1995c) *Europinion Monitoring*, Brussels: DG X, April.

—— (1995d) *Partnership: the European Union and United States in the 1990s*, Washington, DC: European Commission Delegation.

—— (1995e) *Report on United States Trade Barriers and Unfair Trade Practices: Problems of Doing Business with the USA*, Brussels: DG I.

Commission on Global Governance (1995) *Our Global Neighborhood*, Oxford: Oxford University Press.

Connolly, B. (1995) *The Rotten Heart of Europe*, London: Faber & Faber.

Cooney, S. (1991) *Update on EC-92: A NAM report on Developments in the European Community's Internal Market Program and the Effects on U.S. Manufacturers*, Washington, DC: National Association of Manufacturers Publications.

Corbett, R. (1987) 'The 1985 intergovernmental conference and the Single European Act', in R. Pryce (ed.) *The Dynamics of European Union*, London: Croom Helm.

—— (1994) 'Representing the people', in A. Duff, J. Pinder and R. Pryce (eds) *Maastricht and Beyond: Building the European Union*, London: Routledge.

Corbett, R., Jacobs, F. and Shackleton, M. (1995), *The European Parliament* third edition, London: Cartermill.

Cox, R. (1980) 'The crisis in world order and the problem of international organization in the 1980s', *International Journal*, 31 (1): 370–95.

Crawford, B. (1994a) 'Germany's unilateral recognition of Croatia and Slovenia: a case of defection from international cooperation', *Center for German and European Studies Working Paper*, 2.21, Berkeley, CA: University of California, November.

—— (1994b) 'The new security dilemma under international economic interdependence', *Millennium*, 23 (1): 85–108.

Daalder, I. H. (1995) 'What vision for the nuclear future?', *Washington Quarterly*, 18 (2): 127–42.

Daley, T. (1992) 'Can the UN stretch to fit its future?', *Bulletin of Atomic Scientists*, 48 (3): 38–42.

De Clercq, W. (1988) '1992: the impact on the outside world', address to Europäisches Forum, Ansprach (mimeo).

DeConcini, D. and Hoyer, S. (1990) 'New organization for Europe', *CSCE Digest*, June: 2.

De Gucht, K. and Keukeleire, S. (1991) *Time and Tide Wait for No Man: The Changing European Geopolitical Landscape*, New York: Praeger.

de la Mothe, J. and Ducharne, M. (1990) 'Science, technology and free trade: towards an understanding of the new competitive agenda', in J. de la Mothe and M. Ducharne (eds) *Science, Technology and Free Trade*, London: Pinter.

Delors, J. (1989) 'Europe 1992 and its meaning for America', address at Harvard University, Boston, 22 September (mimeo).

—— (1990) 'Europe's ambitions', *Foreign Policy*, 80 (4): 14–27.

DePorte, A. W. (1986) *Europe Between the Superpowers: The Enduring Balance*, second edition, Council on Foreign Relations, New Haven and London: Yale University Press.

De Santis, Hugh (1993) 'Europe and Asia Without America', *World Policy Journal*, 10 (3): 33–43.

Destler, I. M. (1985) 'Executive–Congressional conflict in foreign policy: explaining it, coping with it', in L. C. Dodd and B. I. Oppenheimer (eds) *Congress Reconsidered*, third edition, Washington: Congressional Quarterly Press.

—— (1986) *American Trade Politics: System Under Stress*, Washington, DC: Institute for International Economics, Twentieth Century Fund.

Devuyst, Y. (1990) 'European Community integration and the United States: Toward a new Transatlantic partnership?', *Journal of European Integration*, 14 (1): 5–29.

—— (1995) *Transatlantic Trade Policy: US Market Opening Strategies*, Pittsburgh: University of Pittsburgh Center for West European Studies.

Dinan, D. (1994) *Ever Closer Union? An Introduction to the European Community*, London: Macmillan.

Dixit, A. K. (1986) 'Trade policy: an agenda for research', in P. Krugman (ed.) *Strategic Policy and the New International Economics*, Cambridge: MIT Press.

Dobbins, J. F. (1991) 'Toward a Euro-Atlantic community', keynote address to the Centre for European Policy Studies conference on Europe and North America, United States Mission to the EC, Brussels, 22 November.

Dole, R. (1995) 'Shaping America's global future', *Foreign Policy*, 84 (2): 29–42.

Doyle, M. W. (1986) 'Liberalism and world politics', *American Political Science Review*, 80 (4): 1151–63.

Drake, W. J. and Nicolaïdis, K. (1992) 'Ideas, interests, and institutionalization: "trade in services" and the Uruguay Round', *International Organization*, 46 (1): 37–100.

Drew, E. (1994) *On the Edge: The Clinton Presidency*, New York: Simon & Schuster.

Drifte, R. (1990) *Japan's Foreign Policy*, London: Routledge for Royal Institute of International Affairs.

Duesterberg, T. J. (1995) 'Prospects for a EU–NAFTA free trade agreement', *Washington Quarterly*, 18 (2): 71–82.

Duff, A., Pinder, J. and Pryce, R. (eds) (1994) *Maastricht and Beyond: Building the European Union*, London: Routledge.

Dumbrell, J. with Barret, D. (1990) *The Making of US Foreign Policy*, Manchester: Manchester University Press.

Dunne, N. (1995) 'Lake fires broadside at "new" isolationists', *Financial Times*, 28 March: 3.

Eatwell, R. (1994) 'The fascist and racist revival in Western Europe', *Political Quarterly*, 65 (3): 313–25.

Edwards, G. and Spence, D. (eds) (1994) *The European Commission*, Essex: Longman.

Efinger, M. and Rittberger, V. (1992) 'The CSBM regime in and for Europe: confidence building and peaceful conflict management', in M. C. Pugh (ed.) *European Security: Towards 2000*, Manchester: Manchester University Press.

Ehteshami, A. and Nonneman, G. with Tripp, C. (1991) *War and Peace in the Gulf*, Exeter Middle East monographs, Reading: Ithaca Press.

Eichenberg, R. C. (1989) *Public Opinion and National Security in Western Europe: Consensus Lost?*, London: Macmillan.

Eisner, R. (1986) *How Real is the Federal Deficit?*, New York: Basic Books.

Ekins, P. (1992) *A New World Order: Grassroots Movements for Global Change*, London: Routledge.

Elazar, D. J. (1987) *Exploring Federalism*, Tuscaloosa, AL: University of Alabama Press.

Emerson, M. (1991) 'Aspects of the economics of EMU', *European Economic Review*, 35 (2/3): 467–73.

EPC Secretariat (1990) 'Declaration on US–EC relations', 83/90, Brussels, 23 November.

Falk, R. (1991) 'How the West mobilised for war', in J. Gittings (ed.) *Beyond the Gulf War: The Middle East and the New World Order*, London: Catholic Institute for International Relations.

Falk, R. A., Kim, S. S. and Mendlovitz, S. H. (eds) (1991) *The United Nations and a Just World Order*, Boulder, CO: Westview Press.

Farer, T.J. (1977) 'The greening of the globe: a preliminary appraisal of the World Order Models Project', *International Organization*, 31 (1): 129–47.

Featherstone, K. and Ginsberg, R. (1993) *The United States and the European Community in the 1990s*, New York and London: St Martin's and Macmillan.

Ferguson, G. (1992) 'NATO's new concept of reinforcement', *NATO Review*, 7 (October): 31–4.

Fitchett, J. (1992) 'NATO as peacekeeping force: the momentum builds', *International Herald Tribune*, 24 April: 1,4.

—— (1995) 'Germans warming to use of soldiers on global missions', *International Herald Tribune*, 8 February: 2.

Fitzmaurice, J. (1994) 'The European Commission', in A. Duff, J. Pinder and R. Pryce (eds) *Maastricht and Beyond: Building the European Union*, London: Routledge.

Friedberg, A. L. (1992) 'Is the United States capable of acting strategically?', in C. W. Kegley, Jr, and E. R. Wittkopf (eds) *The Future of American Foreign Policy*, New York: St Martin's Press.

—— (1993/4) 'Ripe for rivalry: prospects for peace in a multipolar Asia', *International Security*, 18 (3): 5–33.

—— (1994) 'The future of American power', *Political Science Quarterly*, 109 (1): 1–20.

Fukuyama, F. (1989) 'The end of hysteria?', *Guardian*, 15 December.

—— (1992) *The End of History and the Last Man*, London: Hamish Hamilton.

—— (1995) *Trust: The Social Virtues and the Creation of Prosperity*, New York: Free Press.

Gaddis, J. L. (1987) *The Long Peace: Inquiries into the History of the Cold War*, Oxford: Oxford University Press.

—— (1990) 'Toward the post-cold war world', *Foreign Affairs*, 69 (2): 102–22.

Galbraith, J. K. (1990) 'Revolt in our time: the triumph of simplistic ideology', in G. Prins (ed.) *Spring in Winter: The 1989 Revolutions*, Manchester: Manchester University Press.

Gallarotti, G. (1991) 'The limits of international organization: systematic failures in the management of international relations', *International Organization*, 45 (2): 183–220.

Gallois, P. (1993) 'Vers une prédominance allemande', *Le Monde*, 16 July: 5.

Galtung, J. (1973) *The European Community: A Superpower in the Making*, London, George Allen & Unwin.

Galvin, J. R. (1991) 'Europe: Still vital to US security', *Defense '91*, July/August: 2–11.

Garten, J. E. (1992) *A Cold Peace: America, Japan, Germany, and the Struggle for Supremacy*, New York: Random House.

Gaster, R. and Bradshaw, R. (1993) *Leading the Learning Curve: The First 300 Days of the Clinton Technology Policy*, Washington, DC: North Atlantic Research.

Gazzo, E. (1991) 'Could the Union's "federal vocation" be simply a "trifle"?', *Agence Europe*, 5609, 15 November: 1.

George, S. (1991) *Politics and Policy in the European Community*, second edition, Oxford: Oxford University Press.

Geroski, P. and Jacquemin, A. (1985) 'Industrial change, barriers to mobility and European industrial policy', *Economic Policy*, 1 (1): 170–218.

Gill, S. (1990) *American Hegemony and the Trilateral Commission*, Cambridge: Cambridge University Press.

Gilpin, R. (1981) *War and Change in World Politics*, Cambridge, Cambridge University Press.

—— (1984) 'The richness of the tradition of political realism', *International Organization*, 38 (2): 287–304.

Ginsberg, R. H. (1989) *Foreign Policy Actions of the European Community: The Politics of Scale*, London: Adamantine Press.

—— (1991) 'EC–US political/institutional relations', in L. Hurwitz and C. Lequesne (eds) *The State of the European Community: Policies, Institutions and Debates in the Transition Years*, London and Boulder, CO: Lynne Rienner.

—— (1995) 'Principles and practices of the European Union's Common Foreign and Security Policy: retrospective on the first twenty months', prepared for presentation at the Second Pan-European Conference of the European Consortium for Political Research, Paris, 14–16 September, mimeo.

Gittings, J. (1991) 'Introduction', in J. Gittings, (ed.) *Beyond the Gulf War: The Middle East and the New World Order*, London: Catholic Institute for International Relations.

Glover, D. (1994) 'Global institutions, international agreements and environmental issues', in R. Stubbs and G. R. D. Underhill (eds) *Political Economy and the Changing Global Order*, Basingstoke: Macmillan.

Goldgeier, J. M. and McFaul, M. (1992) 'A tale of two worlds: core and periphery in the post-Cold War era', *International Organization*, 46: 467–91.

Goldstein, J. (1989) 'The role of ideas on trade policy', *International Organization*, 43 (1): 31–71.

Graham, E. M. (1991) 'Strategic responses of US multinational firms to the Europe-1992 initiative', in G. N. Yannopoulos (ed.) *Europe and America, 1992: US–EC Economic Relations and the Single European Market*, Manchester: Manchester University Press.

Graham, E. M. and Krugman, P. R. (1989) *Foreign Direct Investment in the United States*, Washington, DC: Institute for International Economics.

Graham, T. W. (1994) 'The International Atomic Energy Agency: can it effectively halve the proliferation of nuclear weapons', in R. A. Coate (ed.) *U.S. Policy and the Future of the United Nations*, New York: Twentieth Century Fund Press.

Green Group (1992) *Green Leaves: Bulletin of the Greens in the European Parliament*, 9, Brussels: European Parliament, April.

Greene, O. (1992) 'Transnational processes and European security', in M. C. Pugh (ed.) *European Security: Towards 2000*, Manchester: Manchester University Press.

Grieco, J. M. (1990) *Cooperation Among Nations: Europe, America, and Non-Tariff Barriers to Trade*, London and Ithaca, NY: Cornell University Press.

Gros, D. and Steinherr, A. (1995) *Winds of Change: Economic Transition in Eastern and Central Europe*, London and New York: Longman Higher Education.

Grosser, A. (1982) *The Western Alliance: European–American Relations since 1945*, New York: Random House Vintage.

Grotius, H. (1913) *De Jure Belli ac Pacis Libri Tres . . .* , Washington, DC: Carnegie Institute (first published 1646).

Group of Thirty (1991) *The Summit Process and Collective Security: Future Responsibility Sharing*, study group report, Washington, DC.

Haas, E. (1993) 'Collective conflict management: evidence for a New World Order?', in T. G. Weiss (ed.) *Collective Security in a Changing World*, Boulder, CO: Lynne Rienner.

Haas, P. M. (1990) *Saving the Mediterranean: The Politics of International Environmental Protection*, New York: Columbia University Press.

—— (1992a) 'Banning chlorofluorocarbons: epistemic community efforts to protect stratospheric ozone', *International Organization*, 46 (1): 187–224.

—— (1992b) 'Epistemic communities and international policy coordination', *International Organization*, 46 (1): 1–35.

Haas, P. M., Keohane, R. and Levy, M. (eds) (1993) *Institutions for the Earth*, Cambridge, MA: MIT Press.

Hager, W. (1976) *Europe's Economic Security: Non-Energy Issues in the International Political Economy*, Paris: Atlantic Institute for International Affairs.

Haggard, S. and Moravcsik, A. (1993) 'The political economy of financial assistance to Eastern Europe, 1989–1991', in R. O. Keohane, J. S. Nye and S. Hoffmann (eds) *After the Cold War*, Cambridge, MA: Harvard University Press.

Haggard, S. and Simmons, B. A. (1987) 'Theories of international regimes', *International Organization*, 41 (3): 491–517.

Hague, R. and Harrop, M. (1987) *Comparative Government and Politics: An Introduction*, second edition, London: Macmillan.

Halliday, F. (1994) *Rethinking International Relations*, London: Macmillan.

—— (1995) 'The end of the Cold War and international relations: some analytic and theoretical conclusions', in K. Booth and S. Smith (eds) *International Relations Theory Today*, Cambridge: Polity.

Hamilton, C. B. (1991) 'European Community external protection and 1992: VERs applied to pacific Asia', *European Economic Review*, 35 (2/3): 378–87.

Hamilton, C. B. and Winters, L. A. (1992) 'Opening up international trade with Eastern Europe', *Economic Policy*, 8 (April): 78–116.

Hanrieder, W. F. (1978) 'Dissolving international politics: reflections on the nation-state', *American Political Science Review*, 72 (4): 1276–87.

—— (1989) *Germany, America, Europe: Forty Years of German Foreign Policy*, New Haven and London: Yale University Press.

Harrison, G. (1994) 'US–European Union trade and investment', *CRS Report for Congress*, Washington, DC: Congressional Research Service, 95–34, 20 December.

—— (1995) 'European Union-U.S. trade relations', *CRS Report for Congress*, Washington, DC: Congressional Research Service, 95–342, 6 March.

Harriss, J. (ed.) (1995) *The Politics of Humanitarian Intervention*, London: Pinter.

Hart, J. A. (1992) *Rival Capitalists: International Competitiveness in the United States, Japan and Western Europe*, Ithaca, NY: Cornell University Press.

Hayter, F. (1974) *Aid as Imperialism*, New York: Penguin.

Heisbourg, F. (1992) 'From common European home to a European security system', in G. F. Treverton (ed.) *The Shape of the New Europe*, New York: Council on Foreign Relations Press.

Held, D. and McGrew, A. (1993) 'Globalization and the Liberal Democratic State', *Government and Opposition*, 28 (2): 261–85.

Hellmann, D. C. (1989) 'The imperatives for reciprocity and symmetry in US–Japanese economic and defence relations', in J. H. Makin and D. C. Hellmann (eds) *Sharing World Leadership: A New Era for America and Japan*, Washington, DC: American Enterprise Institute for Public Policy Research.

Herz, J. H. (1951) *Political Realism and Political Idealism*: Chicago: University of Chicago Press.

Heurlin, B. (1992) 'The roles of the United States and Soviet Union', in M. C. Pugh (ed.) *European Security: Towards 2000*, Manchester: Manchester University Press.

Hindell, K. (1992) 'Reform of the United Nations?', *The World Today*, 45 (2): 30–3.

Hinsley, S. H. (1989) 'The EC: body politic or an association of states', *The World Today*, 42 (1): 1–3.

Hoffmann, S. (1981) *Duties beyond Borders*, Syracuse: Syracuse University Press.

—— (1989) 'The European Community and 1992', *Foreign Affairs*, 68 (4): 27–47.

—— (1992) 'Balance, concert, anarchy, or none of the above', in G. F. Treverton (ed.) *The Shape of the New Europe*, New York: Council on Foreign Relations Press.

—— (1993) 'French strategies and dilemmas in the new Europe', in R. O. Keohane, J. S. Nye and S. Hoffmann (eds) *After the Cold War*, Cambridge: Harvard University Press.

Holmes, P. (1990) 'Telecommunications in the great game of integration', in G. Locksley (ed.) *The Single European Market and the Information and Communication Technologies*, London: Belhaven Press.

Hook, J. and Cloud, D. S. (1994) 'A Republican-designed House won't please all occupants', *Congressional Quarterly*, 3 December: 3430–5.

Hudec, R. E. (1988) 'Legal issues in US–EC trade policy: GATT litigation 1960–85', in R. E. Baldwin, C. B. Hamilton and A. Sapir (eds) *Issues in US–EC Trade Relations*, Chicago: University of Chicago Press.

Hufbauer, G. C. (1990) 'An overview', in G. C. Hufbauer (ed.) *Europe 1992: An American Perspective*, Washington, DC: Brookings Institution.

Humbert, M. (ed.) (1993) *The Impact of Globalisation on Europe's Firms and Industries*, London: Pinter.

Humphreys, P. J. (1990) 'The international political economy of the Communist revolutions: the case for a neo-pluralist approach', *Government and Opposition*, 25(4): 497–518.

Huntington, S. P. (1989–90) 'The U.S.: decline or renewal?', *Foreign Affairs*, 69 (1): 76–96.

—— (1992) 'The economic renewal of America', *The National Interest*, Spring: 4–18.

—— (1993) 'Why international primacy matters', *International Security*, 17 (4): 68–83.

Hurrell, A. (1995) 'International political theory and the global environment', in K. Booth and S. Smith (eds) *International Relations Theory Today*, Cambridge: Polity.

Hyde-Price, A. (1992) 'Alternative security systems for Europe', in M. C. Pugh (ed.) *European Security: Towards 2000*, Manchester: Manchester University Press.

Hyde-Price, A. and Roper, J. (1991) 'New directions in European security', in K. Booth (ed.) *New Thinking About Strategy and International Security*, London: Harper Collins.

Hyland, W. (1987) 'Reagan–Gorbachev III', *Foreign Affairs*, 67 (4): 7–21.

IEA (1995) *World Energy Outlook*, Paris: International Energy Agency.

IISS (1995) *Strategic Survey 1991–92*, London: International Institute for Strategic Studies.

Isaacs, J. (1992) 'Defence spending: workfare for the '90s?', *Bulletin of the Atomic Scientists*, 48 (3): 3–5.

Ishihara, S. (1989) *The Japan That Can Say No*, London: Simon & Schuster.

Ito, Kan (1990) 'Trans-pacific anger,' *Foreign Policy*, 80 (2): 131–52.

Jackson, J. H. (1995) 'US threat to new world trade order', *Financial Times*, 23 May: 17.

Jackson, R.H. (1995) 'The political theory of international society', in K. Booth and S. Smith (eds) *International Relations Theory Today*, Cambridge: Polity.

Jacquemin, A. and Sapir, A. (1988) 'International trade and integration of the European Community: an econometric analysis', *European Economic Review*, 32 (7): 1439–50.

James, A. (1989) 'The realism of realism: the state of the study of international relations', *Review of International Studies*, 15 (3): 215–29.

Joffe, J. (1987) 'Peace and populism: why the European anti-nuclear movement failed', *International Security*, 11 (4): 1–4.

—— (1992–3) 'The New Europe: yesterday's ghosts', *Foreign Affairs*, 72 (1): 29–43.

Jones, A. (1989) 'The realism of realism: the state of the study of international relations', *Review of International Studies*, 15 (3): 215–29.

Judis, J.B. and Lind, M. (1995) 'For a new nationalism', *New Republic*, 27 March: 19–27.

Kahler, M. (1987) 'The United States and Western Europe: the diplomatic consequences of Mr. Reagan', in K. A. Oye, R. J. Lieber and D. Rothchild (eds) *Eagle Resurgent? The Reagan Era in American Foreign Policy*, Boston: Little Brown and Company: 297–333.

—— (1995) *Regional Futures and Transatlantic Economic Relations*, New York: European Community Studies Association and Council on Foreign Relations Press.

Kaldor, M. (1990) *The Imaginary War*, Oxford: Blackwell.

—— (1991) 'Rethinking Cold War history', in K. Booth (ed.) *New Thinking About Strategy and International Security*, London: Harper Collins.

Kant, I. (1932) *Perpetual Peace*, Los Angeles: United States Library Association (first published 1796).

Kantor, M. (1993) 'Testimony before Senate Finance Committee', *USA Text*, Brussels: US Mission to the EC, 9 March.

Kaufmann, W. W. (1994) ' "Hollow" forces?', *The Brookings Review*, Fall: 24–9.

Kay, N. (1991) 'Industrial collaborative activity and the completion of the internal market', *Journal of Common Market Studies*, 29 (4): 347–62.

Kegley, C. W., Jr (ed.) (1994) *Controversies in International Relations Theory: Realism and the Neoliberal Challenge*, New York: St Martin's Press.

Kegley, C. W. and Raymond, G. (1994) *A Multipolar Peace? Great Power Politics in the Twenty-first Century*, New York: St Martin's Press.

Kegley, C. W. and Schwab, K. L. (eds) (1991) *After the Cold War: Questioning the Morality of Nuclear Deterrence*, Boulder, CO: Westview Press.

Kegley, C. W. and Wittkopf, E. R. (1993) *World Politics: Trend and Transformation*, fourth edition, New York: St Martin's Press.

Kennedy, P. (1989) *The Rise and Fall of Great Powers: Economic Change and Military Conflict from 1500–2000*, New York: Random House Vintage.

Keohane, R. O. (1980) 'The theory of hegemonic stability and changes in international economic regimes 1967–77', in O. R. Holsti, R. M. Siverson and A. L. George (eds) *The Global Agenda*, New York: Random House.

—— (1984) *After Hegemony: Cooperation and Discord in the World Political Economy*, Princeton: Princeton University Press.

—— (ed.) (1986) *Neorealism and its Critics*, New York: Columbia University Press.

—— (1989) 'Neoliberal institutionalism: a perspective on world politics', in R. O. Keohane (ed.) *International Institutions and State Power: Essays in International Relations Theory*, Boulder, CO: Westview Press.

—— (1993a) 'The diplomacy of structural change: multilateral institutions and state strategies', in H. Haftendoorn and C. Tuschhoff (eds) *America and Europe in an Era of Change*, Boulder, CO: Westview Press.

—— (1993b) 'Institutional theory and the realist challenge after the Cold War', in D. Baldwin (ed.) *Neorealism and Neoliberalism: The Contemporary Debate*, New York: Columbia University Press.

—— (1994) 'Redefining Europe: implications for international relations', in H. Miall (ed.) *Redefining Europe: New Patterns of Conflict and Cooperation*, London: Pinter: 229–40.

Keohane, R. O. and Hoffmann, S. (1990) 'Conclusions: politics and institutional change', in W. Wallace (ed.) *The Dynamics of European Integration*, London: Pinter for Royal Institute for International Affairs.

—— (1993) 'Conclusion: structure, strategy, and institutional roles', in R. O. Keohane, J. S. Nye and S. Hoffmann (eds) *After the Cold War*, Cambridge, MA: Harvard University Press.

Keohane, R. O. and Nye, J. S., Jr (1975) 'International interdependence and integration', in F. I. Greenstein and N. W. Polsby (eds) *International Politics: Handbook of Political Science*, Reading, MA: Addison-Wesley.

—— (1977) *Power and Interdependence*, Boston: Little Brown.

—— (1987) 'Power and interdependence revisited', *International Organization*, 41 (4): 725–53.

Kielinger, T. and Otte, M. (1993) 'Germany: the pressured power', *Foreign Policy*, 91, Summer: 44–62.

Kim, W. C. (1988) 'The era of Pacific co-prosperity', in M. Feldstein (ed.) *The United States in the World Economy*, Chicago: University of Chicago Press.

Kinkel, K. (1992) 'NATO's enduring role in European security', *NATO Review*, 7 (October): 3–7.

Kissinger, H. A. (1964) *A World Restored*, New York: Grosset & Dunlap.

—— (1973) 'The year of Europe', *Department of State Bulletin*, 14 May: 595.

—— (1982) *Years of Upheaval*, Boston: Little Brown.

Klingberg, F. L. (1983) *Cyclical Trends in American Foreign Policy Moods*, Lanham, MD: University Press of America.

Kohl, W. L. (1975) 'The Nixon-Kissinger foreign policy system and U.S.–European relations', *World Politics*, 28 (October): 1–43.

Krasner, S. D. (1982a) 'American policy and global economic stability', in W. P. Avery and D. P. Rapkin (eds) *America in a Changing World Political Economy*, New York and London: Longman.

—— (1982b) 'Structural causes and regime consequences', *International Organization*, 36 (2): 185–206.

—— (1983) *International Regimes*, Ithaca, NY: Cornell University Press.

—— (1989) 'Realist praxis: neo-isolationism and structural change', *Journal of International Affairs*, 43: 143–60.

—— (1993) 'Power, polarity, and the challenge of disintegration' in H. Haftendoorn and C. Tuschhoff (eds) *America and Europe in an Era of Change*, Boulder, CO: Westview Press.

Kratochwil, F. (1993) 'The embarrassment of changes: neo-realism as the science of Realpolitik without politics', *Review of International Studies*, 19 (1): 63–80.

Krauthammer, C. (1991) 'The lonely superpower', *New Republic*, 29 July: 23–7.

Kreinin, M. E. (1991) 'EC-1992 and world trade and the trading system', in G. N. Yannopoulos (ed.) *Europe and America, 1992: US–EC Economic Relations and the Single European Market*, Manchester: Manchester University Press.

Krieger, W. (1994) 'Toward a Gaullist Germany?', *World Policy Journal*, XI (1): 26–38.

Kristol, I. (1995) 'Who now cares about NATO?', *Wall Street Journal*, 6 February: 10.

Krugman, P. R. (1994) 'Europe jobless, America penniless?', *Foreign Policy*, 95, Summer: 19–34.

Kudrle, R. T. (1991) 'Good for the gander? Foreign direct investment in the United States', *International Organization*, 45 (3): 397–424.

Kumar, K. (1992) 'The revolutions of 1989: socialism, capitalism and democracy', *Theory and Society*, 21: 309–56.

Larrabee, F. S. (1991) 'The new Soviet approach to Europe', in N. H. Wessell (ed.) *Proceedings of the Academy of Political Science*, 38 (1): 1–5.

—— (1992) 'Democratization and change in Eastern Europe', in G. F. Treverton (ed.) *The Shape of the New Europe*, New York: Council on Foreign Relations Press: 130–71.

Latter, R. (1994) *The Continuing Need for Close US–European Ties*, London: Wilton Park Paper 87.

Lavin, F.L. (1993) 'Clinton and trade', *The National Interest*, 32, Summer: 29–39.

Lehman, J.-P. (1993) 'Japan and Europe in global perspective', in J. Story (ed.) *The New Europe*, Oxford and Cambridge, MA: Blackwell.

Lesser, I. (1992) 'Italy', in R. A. Levine (ed.) *Transition and Turmoil in the Atlantic Alliance*, London: Crane Rusack.

Levine, R. A. (1992) 'The United States', in R. A. Levine (ed.) *Transition and Turmoil in the Atlantic Alliance*, London: Crane Rusack.

Levy, M. (1993) 'East-West environmental politics after 1989: the case of air pollution', in R. O. Keohane, J. S. Nye and S. Hoffmann (eds) *After the Cold War*, Cambridge, MA: Harvard University Press.

Linklater, A. (1995) 'Neo-realism in theory and practice', in K. Booth and S. Smith (eds) *International Relations Theory Today*, Cambridge: Polity.

Lipson, C. (1984) 'International cooperation in economic and security affairs', *World Politics*, 37 (October): 1–23.

Lister, F. (1990) 'The role of international organizations in the 1990s and beyond', *International Relations*, 10 (2): 101–16.

Lodge, G. C. (1990) *Comparative Business–Government Relations*, Englewood Cliffs NJ: Prentice-Hall.

Lohmann, S. and O'Halloran, S. (1994) 'Divided government and U.S. trade policy: theory and evidence', *International Organization*, 48 (4): 595–632.

Lowi, T. (1995) 'America requires a third party, but don't hold your breath', *International Herald Tribune*, 25 August: 6.

Luard, E. (1988) *The Blunted Sword: the Erosion of Military Power in Modern World Politics*, London: I. B. Tauris.

—— (1990) *The Globalization of Politics*, London: Macmillan.

Ludlow, P. (1992) 'Europe's institutions: Europe's politics', in G. F. Treverton (ed.) *The Shape of the New Europe*, New York: Council on Foreign Relations Press.

Lunn, S. (1993) 'A reassessment of European security', in G. Merritt (ed.) *What is European Security After the Cold War,* Brussels: The Philip Morris Institute.

MccGwire, M. (1986) 'Deterrence: the problem – not the solution', *International Affairs*, 62 (1): 55–70.

McCulloch, R. (1988) 'Macroeconomic policy and trade performance: international implications of US budget deficits', in R. E. Baldwin, C. B. Hamilton and A. Sapir (eds) *Issues in US–EC Trade Relations*, Chicago: University of Chicago Press.

Mackinder, H. (1904) 'The geographical pivot of history', *Geographical Journal*, 23: 418–34.

—— (1943) 'The round world and the winning of peace', *Foreign Affairs*, 21 (July): 595–605.

McMath, J. (1995) 'The European Bank for Reconstruction and Development: an emerging determinant of EU policy?', paper presented to the fourth biennial conference of the European Communities Studies Association, Charleston, SC, 11–14 May.

Macrae, N. (1990) 'One Germany before one Europe', *Business Month*, February: 16–18.

Mahan, A. T. (1897) *The Influence of Seapower Upon History, 1660–1783*, Boston: Little Brown.

Major, J. (1993) 'Raise your eyes, there is a land beyond', *The Economist*, 25 September: 23–7.

Makin, J. (1989) 'International "imbalances": the role of exchange rates', *Amex Bank Review Paper* 17, New York.

Mandelbaum, M. (1991) 'The Bush foreign policy', *Foreign Affairs*, 70 (1): 5–22.

Mann, T. E. (1990) 'Making foreign policy: the President and Congress', in T. E. Mann (ed.) *A Question of Balance: The President, Congress, and Foreign Policy*, Washington, DC: Brookings Institution: 1–34.

Marquand, D. (1994) 'Reinventing federalism: Europe and the left', *New Left Review*, 203 (January/February): 17–26.

Mason, M. (1994) 'Elements of consensus: Europe's response to the Japanese automotive challenge', *Journal of Common Market Studies*, 32 (4): 433–53.

Maynes, C. W. (1990) 'America without the Cold War', *Foreign Policy*, 78 (2): 3–25.

Mearsheimer, J. J. (1990a) 'Back to the future: instability in Europe after the Cold War', *International Security*, 15 (1): 5–56.

—— (1990b) 'Why we will soon miss the Cold War', *Atlantic Monthly*, August: 35–50.

—— (1994/5) 'The false promise of international institutions', *International Security,* 19 (3): 5–49.

Miall, H. (1991) 'New visions, new voices, old power structures', in K. Booth (ed.) *New Thinking About Strategy and International Security,* London: Harper Collins: 293–312.

—— (1994) 'Wider Europe, fortress Europe, fragmented Europe?', in H. Miall (ed.) *Redefining Europe: New Patterns of Conflict and Cooperation,* London: Pinter: 1–15.

Millar, T. B. (1992) 'A new world order?', *The World Today,* February: 7–9.

Milner, H. (1991) 'The assumption of anarchy in international relations theory: a critique', *Review of International Studies,* 17 (1): 67–85.

Milward, A. (1992) *The European Rescue of the Nation-State,* London: Routledge.

Møller, B. (1992) *Common Security and Non-Offensive Defence: a Neorealist Perspective,* London: ICL Press.

Moran, T. (1990/1) 'International economics and national security', *Foreign Affairs,* 69 (5): 74–91.

—— (1993) 'An economics agenda for neorealists', *International Security,* 18 (2): 211–15.

Moravcsik, A. (1991) 'Negotiating the Single European Act', in R. O. Keohane and S. Hoffmann (eds) *The New European Community: Decisionmaking and Institutional Change,* Boulder, CO: Westview Press.

—— (1992) 'Liberalism and international relations theory', *CFIA Working Paper 92–6,* Center for International Affairs, Cambridge, MA: Harvard University.

—— (1993) 'Preferences and power in the European Community: a liberal intergovernmentalist approach', *Journal of Common Market Studies,* 31 (4): 473–524.

—— (1995) 'Explaining international human rights regimes: liberal theory and Western Europe', *European Journal of International Relations,* 1 (2): 157–89.

Morgan, C. T. and Campbell, S. H. (1991) 'Domestic structure, decisional constraints, and war: so why Kant democracies fight?', *Journal of Conflict Resolution,* 35 (2): 187–211.

Morgenthau, H. (1985) *Politics Among Nations,* fifth edition, New York: Knopf.

Mueller, J. (1989) *Retreat from Doomsday: The Obsolescence of Major War,* New York: Basic Books.

NAM (1986) 'US trade balance at a turning point', Washington, DC: National Association of Manufacturers.

NATO (1990) 'The London Declaration', reprinted in *Survival,* 32 (5): 469–72.

—— (1991a) 'The Alliance's new strategic concept agreed by the heads of state and government participating in the meeting of the North Atlantic Council', Brussels: North Atlantic Treaty Organization, 7–8 November.

—— (1991b) 'Rome declaration on peace and cooperation by the heads of state and government participating in the extraordinary meeting of the North Atlantic Council', Brussels: North Atlantic Treaty Organization, 7–8 November.

—— (1991c) 'Financial and economic data relating to NATO defence', press release, Brussels: NATO Press Service, 12 December.

—— (1992) 'Latest news', Brussels, NATO Press Service, 18 June.

Nau, H. (1990) *The Myth of America's Decline: Leading the World Economy into the 1990s,* New York and Oxford: Oxford University Press.

Nello, S. S. (1989) 'Recent developments in relations between the European Community and Eastern Europe', EUI working paper 89/381, Florence: European University Institute.

Neven, D. J. and Röller, L. H. (1991) 'European integration and trade flows', *European Economic Review,* 35 (6): 1295–309.

Newhouse, J. (1991) 'The diplomatic round: in a new era and groping', *The New Yorker*, 16 December: 90–104.

Niblock, T. (1991) 'Arab losses, First World gains', in J. Gittings (ed.) *Beyond the Gulf War: The Middle East and the New World Order*, London: Catholic Institute for International Relations.

Nicolaïdis, K. (1993) 'East European trade in the aftermath of 1989: did international institutions matter?', in R. O. Keohane, J. S. Nye and S. Hoffmann (eds) *After the Cold War*, Cambridge: Harvard University Press.

Niou, E.M.S. and Ordeshook, P.G. (1994) 'Less filling, tastes great: the realist-neoliberal debate', *World Politics*, 46 (2): 209–34.

Nivola, P. S. (1990) 'Trade policy: refereeing the playing field', in T. E. Mann (ed.) *A Question of Balance: The President, Congress, and Foreign Policy*, Washington, DC: Brookings Institution.

—— (1993) *Regulating Unfair Trade*, Washington, DC: Brookings Institution.

Nollen, S. D. and Quinn, D. P. (1994) 'Free trade, fair trade, strategic trade and protectionism in the US Congress', *International Organization*, 48 (3): 491–525.

Nugent, N. (1994) *The Government and Politics of the European Community*, third edition, London: Macmillan.

Nye, J. S. (1990) *Bound to Lead: the Changing Nature of American Power*, New York: Basic Books.

—— (1992) 'What New World Order?', *Foreign Affairs*, 71 (2): 83–6.

Nye, J. S. and Keohane, R. O. (1993) 'The United States and international institutions in Europe after the Cold War', in R. O. Keohane, J. S. Nye and S. Hoffmann (eds) *After the Cold War*, Cambridge, MA: Harvard University Press.

O'Cleireacain, S. (1991) 'EC policies toward Japan: implications for US–EC relations', in G. N. Yannopoulos (ed.) *Europe and America, 1992: US–EC Economic Relations and the Single European Market*, Manchester: Manchester University Press.

Olson, M. (1982) *The Rise and Decline of Nations: Economic Growth, Stagflation, and Social Rigidities*, New Haven and London: Yale University Press.

Oneal, J. R. and Elrod, M. A. (1989) 'NATO burden sharing and the forces of change', *International Studies Quarterly* 33 (3): 435–56.

Onuf, N. (1989) *World of Our Making: Rules and Rule in Social Theory and International Relations*, Columbia: University of South Carolina Press.

Ostry, S. (1991) 'The Group of 7 and responsibility-sharing', address at the Centre for European Policy Studies, Brussels, 22 November, mimeo.

Padoa-Schioppa, T. (ed.) (1987) *Efficiency, Stability, and Equity: A Strategy for the Evolution of the Economic System of the European Community*, Oxford: Oxford University Press.

Palme Commission, The (1984) *Common Security: A Program for Disarmament*, Boston: Pan Press.

Papp, D. S. (1991) *Contemporary International Relations: Frameworks for Understanding*, New York: Macmillan, third edition.

Paterson, M. and Grubb, M. (1992) 'The international politics of climate change', International Affairs, 68 (3): 293–309.

Pelkmans, J. (1995) 'How to explain EC-1992', paper presented to annual conference of the University Association for Contemporary European Studies, Cambridge, 6 January.

Pelkmans, J. and Murphy, A. (1991) 'Strategies for the Uruguay Round', Centre for European Policy Studies, Brussels, 22 November, mimeo.

Perle, R. (1990) 'The continuing threat', in G. F. Treverton (ed.) *Europe and America Beyond 2000*, New York: Council on Foreign Relations Press.

—— (1991) 'Military power and the passing Cold War', in C. W. Kegley and K. L.

Schwab (eds) *After the Cold War: Questioning the Morality of Nuclear Deterrence*, Boulder, CO: Westview Press.

Peters, B. G. (1992) 'Bureaucratic politics and the institutions of the European Community' in A. M. Sbragia (ed.) *Euro-Politics: Institutions and Policymaking in the 'New' European Community*, Washington, DC: Brookings Institution.

Peterson, J. (1989) 'Hormones, heifers and high politics: biotechnology and the Common Agricultural Policy', *Public Administration*, 67 (4): 455–71.

—— (1991) 'Technology policy in Europe: explaining the Framework programme and Eureka in theory and practice', *Journal of Common Market Studies*, 29 (3): 269–90.

—— (1993a) *Europe and America in the 1990s: the Prospects for Partnership*, Aldershot: Edward Elgar.

—— (1993b) *High Technology and the Competition State: an Analysis of the Eureka Initiative*, London: Routledge.

—— (1993c) 'Towards a European industrial policy: the case of high definition television', *Government and Opposition*, 28 (3): 496–511.

—— (1994a) 'Europe and America in the Clinton era', *Journal of Common Market Studies* 32 (3): 411–26.

—— (1994b) 'Subsidiarity: a definition to suit any vision?', *Parliamentary Affairs*, 46 (4): 116–32.

—— (1995) 'Understanding decision-making in the European Union: towards a framework for analysis', *Journal of European Public Policy*, 2 (1): 69–93.

Peterson, J. and Ward, H. (1995) 'Coalitional instability and the new multi-dimensional politics of security: a rational choice argument for US–EU cooperation', *European Journal of International Relations*, 1 (2): 131–56.

Peterson, J., Cowles, M. G. and Devuyst, Y. (1995) 'US lobbying and influence on the internal market', paper presented to the biannual conference of the European Community Studies Association, Charleston, SC, 11–14 May (mimeo).

Pfaff, W. (1994) 'Is liberal internationalism dead?', *World Policy Journal*, 10 (3): 5–15.

Phillips, K. (1992) 'American internationalism is no longer global', *New Perspectives Quarterly*, Summer: 42–4.

Pinder, J. (1991a) *The European Community and Eastern Europe*, London: Pinter for Royal Institute of International Affairs.

—— (1991b) 'The European Community, the rule of law and representative government: the significance of the intergovernmental conferences', *Government and Opposition*, 26 (1): 199–214.

PMI (1994) *Is the West Doing Enough for Eastern Europe?*, Brussels: Philip Morris Institute.

Ponnuru, R. (1995) *The Mystery of Japanese Growth*, Washington, DC: American Enterprise Institute.

Porter, M. E. (1990) *The Competitive Advantage of Nations*, London: Macmillan.

Powell, R. (1994) 'Anarchy in international relations theory: the neorealist-neoliberal debate', *International Organization*, 48 (2): 313–44.

Prestowitz, C. V. Jr (1988) *Trading Places: How We Allowed Japan to Take the Lead*, New York: Basic Books.

Prestowitz, C. V. Jr, Tonelson, A. and Jerome, R. W. (1991) 'The last gasp of GATTism', *Harvard Business Review*, March/April: 130–8.

Pugh, M. C. (1992) 'Introduction', in M. C. Pugh (ed.) *European Security: Towards 2000*, Manchester: Manchester University Press.

Putnam, R. D. (1988) 'Diplomacy and domestic politics: the logic of two-level games', *International Organization*, 42 (3): 427–60.

—— (1993) 'Two-level games: the impact of domestic politics on transatlantic bargaining', in H. Haftendoorn and C. Tuschhoff (eds) *America and Europe in an Era of Change*, Boulder, CO: Westview Press.

Ray, J. L. (1994) *Democracies and International Conflict*, Columbia, SC: University of South Carolina Press.

Reich, R. B. (1991) *The Work of Nations: Preparing Ourselves for 21st-Century Capitalism*, New York: Alfred Knopf.

Rhode, David W. (1994) 'Partisan leadership and congressional assertiveness in foreign and defense policy', in D. A. Deese (ed.) *The New Politics of American Foreign Policy*, New York: St Martin's Press.

Ricardo, D. (1911) *The Principles of Political Economy and Taxation*, London: J. M. Dent & Son (first published 1817).

Richardson, M. (1994) 'Issue of EC access complicates Asia's free-trade efforts', *International Herald Tribune*, 21 October: 11, 13.

Ridley, M. (1996) *The Origins of Virtue*, New York: Viking.

Rielly, J. E. (ed.) (1995) *American Public Opinion and U.S. Foreign Policy*, Chicago: Chicago Council on Foreign Relations.

Rifkind, M. (1995) 'Address to the Royal Institute of International Relations on Europe and America', London: Foreign and Commonwealth Office, 30 January, mimeo.

Risse-Kappen, T. (1991) 'Public opinion, domestic structure, and foreign policy in liberal democracies', *World Politics*, 43, July: 479–512.

Rittberger, V. (1993) *Regime Theory and International Relations*, Oxford: Clarendon Press.

Roberts, P. C. (1990) 'Europe 1992: free market or free lunch?', *Business Week*, 4 June: 26.

Rochester, M. J. (1993) *Waiting for the Millennium: The United Nations and the Future of the World Order*, Columbia, SC: University of South Carolina Press.

Rosecrance, R. (1986) *The Rise of the Trading State*, New York: Basic Books.

Rosenau, J. N. (1990) *Turbulence in World Politics*, Princeton: Princeton University Press.

Rousseau, J. J. (1975) *The Social Contract and Discourses*, London: J. M. Dent & Sons (first published 1762).

Runge, C. F. (1988) 'The assault on agricultural protectionism', *Foreign Affairs*, 67 (4): 133–50.

Russett, B. (1990) *Controlling the Sword: The Democratic Governance of National Security*, Cambridge, MA: Harvard University Press.

Safire, W. (1990) 'Bring on the CSCE', *New York Times*, 15 October: A15.

—— (1995) 'Clinton abdicates as leader', *New York Times*, 27 July 1995: A23.

Sagan, S. (1994) 'The perils of proliferation: organization theory, deterrence theory and the spread of nuclear weapons', *International Security*, 18 (4): 66–107.

Sandholtz, W. and Zysman, J. (1989) '1992: recasting the European bargain', *World Politics*, 62 (October): 95–128.

Sapir, A. (1988) 'International trade in telecommunications services', in R. E. Baldwin, C. B. Hamilton and A. Sapir (eds) *Issues in US–EC Trade Relations*, Chicago: University of Chicago Press.

Saryusz-Wolski, J. (1994) 'The reintegration of the "old continent": avoiding the costs of "half-Europe" ', in S. Bulmer and A. Scott (eds) *Economic and Political Integration in Europe*, Oxford and Cambridge, MA: Blackwell.

Sbragia, A. M. (1992) 'Thinking about the European future: the uses of comparison', in A. M. Sbragia (ed.) *Euro-Politics: Institutions and Policymaking in the 'New' European Community*, Washington, DC: Brookings Institution.

Schmitter, P. (1992) 'Representation and the future Euro-polity', *Staatswissenschaften und Staatspraxis*, 3 (3): 379–405.

Schott, J. and Buhrman, J. (1994) *The Uruguay Round: An Asssessment*, Washington, DC: Institute for International Economics.

Sciolino, E. (1991) 'U.S. reviews focus of security data', *New York Times*, 22 December: 9.

Scott, A. (1992) 'Making sense of Delors II', *Parliamentary Brief*, 1 (2): 54–6.

Scott, A., Peterson, J. and Millar, D. (1994) 'Subsidiarity: a "Europe of the Regions" vs. the British Constitution?', *Journal of Common Market Studies*, 32 (1): 47–67.

Sek, L. (1989) '1992, the GATT, and the Uruguay Round', in G. Harrison (ed.) *European Community: Issues raised by 1992 Integration*, Washington, DC: Congressional Research Service.

Shackleton, M. (1994) 'The internal legitimacy crisis of the European Union', *Europa Institute Occasional Paper 1*, Edinburgh: University of Edinburgh.

Shapiro, M. (1992) 'The European Court of Justice', in A. M. Sbragia (ed.) *EuroPolitics: Institutions and Policymaking in the 'New' European Community*, Washington, DC: Brookings Institution.

Sharp, J. M. O. (1991) 'Disarmament and arms control: a new beginning?', in K. Booth (ed.) *New Thinking About Strategy and International Security*, London: Harper Collins.

Sharp, M. (1995) 'Trade and technology policies: the influence of European programmes on the emergent industrial policy of Clinton's America', Brighton: University of Sussex (mimeo).

Sharp, M. and Peterson, J. (1996) *Technology Policy in the European Union*, Basingstoke: Macmillan.

Shaw, M. (1994) *Global Society and International Relations*, Cambridge: Polity.

Shearman, P. (1993) 'New political thinking reassessed', *Review of International Studies*, 19 (2): 139–58.

—— (1995) 'Russia and Europe after the Cold War', University of Melbourne, mimeo.

SIPRI (1995) *Yearbook 1995: Armaments, Disarmament and International Security*, New York and Oxford: Oxford University Press.

Sivard, R. (1995) *World Military and Social Expenditures*, Washington, DC: World Priorities.

Skapinder, M. (1995) 'Senator piles on Heathrow pressure', *Financial Times*, 6 July: 5.

Sloan, S. (1995a) 'European proposals for a New Atlantic Community', *CRS Report for Congress*, Washington, DC: Congressional Research Service, 95–374, 10 March.

—— (1995b) 'US perspectives on NATO's future', *International Affairs*, 71 (2): 1–15.

Smith, A. (1937) *The Wealth of Nations*, New York: Modern Library (first published 1776).

Smith, M. (1984) *Western Europe and the United States: The Uncertain Alliance*, London: George Allen & Unwin.

—— (1992) 'The "devil you know": the United States and a changing European Community', *International Affairs*, 68 (1): 103–20.

Smith, M. and Woolcock, S. (1993) *The United States and European Community in a Transformed World*, London: Royal Institute of International Affairs.

—— (1994) 'Learning to cooperate: the Clinton administration and the European Union', *International Affairs*, 70 (3): 459–76.

Smith, R. K. (1987) 'Explaining the non-proliferation regime: anomalies for contemporary international relations theory', *International Organization*, 41 (2): 251–81.

Smith, S. (1995) 'The self-images of a discipline', in K. Booth and S. Smith (eds) *International Relations Theory Today*, Cambridge: Polity.

Smith, S. K. and Wertman, D. A. (1992) 'Redefining US–West European relations in the 1990s: West European public opinion in the post-Cold War era', *PS: Political Science and Politics*, 25 (2): 188–95.

Smoke, R. (1987) *National Security and the Nuclear Dilemma: an Introduction to the American Experience*, New York: Random House.

Snidal, D. (1985) 'The limits of hegemonic stability theory', *International Organization*, 49 (3): 579–614.

Snyder, G. H. (1984) 'The security dilemma in Alliance politics', *World Politics*, 36 (July): 461–95.

Snyder, G. H. and Diesing, P. (1977) *Conflict Among Nations: Bargaining, Decision-making, and System Structure in International Crises*, Princeton: Princeton University Press.

Snyder, J. (1990) 'Averting anarchy in the new Europe', *International Security*, 14 (1): 5–41.

Spanier, J. (1987) *Games Nations Play*, Washington, DC: Congressional Quarterly Press.

Sperling, J. (1994) 'Germany foreign policy after unification: the end of cheque book diplomacy?', *West European Politics*, 17 (1): 73–97.

Spero, J. E. (1989) 'The mid-life crisis of American trade policy', *The World Today*, 45 (1): 10–14.

Spiers, R. I. (1994) 'Reforming the United Nations', in R. A. Coate (ed.) *U.S. Policy and the Future of the United Nations*, New York: Twentieth Century Fund Press.

Spretnak, C. and Capra, F. (1986) *Green Politics: The Global Promise*, Santa Fe: Bear & Company.

Stein, A. (1982) 'Coordination and collaboration: regimes in an anarchic world', *International Organization*, 36 (2): 299–324.

Steinberg, J. (1993) *An Ever Closer Union? European Integration and its Implications for the Future of US–European Relations*, Santa Monica, CA: Rand Corporation.

Stoeckel, A., Pearce, D. and Banks, G. (1990) *Western Trade Blocs*, Canberra: Centre for International Economics.

Strange, S. (1982) '*Cave! Hic dragones*: a critique of regime analysis', *International Organization*, 36 (3): 479–96.

—— (1988) *States and Markets: An Introduction to International Political Economy*, London: Pinter.

Syme, V. and Payton, P. (1992) 'Eastern Europe: economic transition and ethnic tension', in M. C. Pugh (ed.) *European Security: Towards 2000*, Manchester: Manchester University Press.

Taylor, M. (1987) *The Possibility of Cooperation*, Cambridge: Cambridge University Press.

Taylor, P. (1991) 'The European Community and the state: assumptions, theories and propositions', *Review of International Studies*, 17 (1): 109–25.

Thatcher, M. (1992) 'Europe's political architecture', speech to the Global Panel, The Hague, 15 May, mimeo.

Thomas, C. (1991) 'New directions in thinking about security in the Third World' in K. Booth (ed.) *New Thinking About Strategy and International Security*, London: Harper Collins.

Thompson, E. (1990) 'The ends of the Cold War', *New Left Review*, 182 (July/August): 139–50.

Thomson, J. E. (1995) 'State sovereignty in international relations: bridging the gap between theory and empirical research', *International Studies Quarterly*, 39 (2): 213–33.

Thucydides (1954) *The Peloponnesian War*, trans. R. Warner, New York: Penguin Books.

Thurow, L. (1992) *Head to Head: the Coming Economic Battle Among Japan, Europe, and America*, New York: William Morrow.

Tierney, J. T. (1994) 'Congressional activism in foreign policy: its varied forms and stimuli', in D. A. Deese (ed.) *The New Politics of American Foreign Policy*, New York: St Martin's Press.

Tilly, C. (ed.) (1975) *The Formation of National States in Western Europe*, Princeton: Princeton University Press.

Tonelson, A. (1991) 'What is the national interest?', *The Atlantic Monthly*, July: 35–42.

TPN (1994) *Towards Transatlantic Partnership: A European Strategy*, Brussels: Transatlantic Policy Network.

Tran, M. (1992) '$75 bn a year needed to restore environment', *Guardian*, 27 April: 10.

Treverton, G. F. (1990) 'Introduction: looking beyond 2000', in G. F. Treverton (ed.) *Europe and America Beyond 2000*, New York: Council on Foreign Relations Press.

—— (1991) 'Elements of a new European security order', *Journal of International Affairs*, 45, Summer: 91–112.

Tsakaloyannis, P. (1989) 'The EC: from civilian power to military integration', in J. Lodge (ed.) *The European Community and the Challenge of the Future*, London: Pinter.

Tyson, L. (1988) 'Making policy for national competitiveness in a changing world', in A. Furino (ed.) *Cooperation and Competition in a Global Economy*, Cambridge, MA: Ballinger.

UK Ministry of Defence (1995) *United Kingdom Statement on Defence Estimates*, London: HMSO.

Ullman, R. H. (1989) 'The covert French connection', *Foreign Policy*, 75 (3): 3–33.

—— (1991) *Securing Europe*, Twickenham: Adamantine Press.

Underhill, G. R. D. (1994) 'Conceptualizing the changing global order', in R. Stubbs and G. R. D. Underhill (eds) *Political Economy and the Changing Global Order*, Basingstoke: Macmillan.

United Nations (1994) *World Direct Investment Report*, New York, United Nations Centre on Transnational Corporations.

Urquhart, B. (1992) 'The United Nations in 1992: problems and opportunities', *International Affairs*, 68 (2): 311–19.

Usborne, D. and Schoon, N. (1992) 'Bush pledges aid to save rainforests', *Independent*, 2 June: 1.

US Mission to the European Community (1990) 'Bush–Haughey statement', *USA Text*, USAT PL 7, Brussels, Public Affairs Office, 27 February.

US State Department (1990) 'Toward a New World Order: address before a joint session of the Congress by President George Bush', *Current Policy*, 1298, Washington, DC: Bureau of Public Affairs: 1–4.

USTR (1991) *National Trade Estimate Report on Foreign Trade Barriers*, Washington, DC: Office of the United States Trade Representative.

—— (1995a) *1995 Trade Policy Agenda and 1994 Annual Report of the President of the*

United States on the Trade Agreements Program, Washington, DC: Office of the United States Trade Representative.

—— (1995b) 'The United States and Europe: new opportunities and strategies', *USIS Wireless File*, 26 April.

Vernon, R. (1989) 'European Community 1992: can the U.S. negotiate for trade equality?', in F. J. Macchiarde (ed.) *Proceedings of the Academy of Political Science*, 37 (4): 9–16.

Viner, J. (1950) *The Customs Union Issue*, New York: Carnegie Endowment for International Peace.

von Geusau, F. A. and Pelkmans, J. (eds) (1982) *National Economic Security: Perceptions, Threats and Policies*, Tilburg: John F. Kennedy Institute.

Waever, O. (1996) 'European security identities: a security reading of political identifications', *Journal of Common Market Studies*, 34 (1):103–32.

Wald, M. L. (1990) 'U.S. imports record 49.9% of oil', *New York Times*, 19 July: E4.

Walker, J. (1991) 'Keeping America in Europe', *Foreign Policy*, 83 (4): 128–42.

Walker, R. B. J. (1989) 'History and structure in the theory of international relations', *Millennium*, 18 (2): 163–83.

—— (1995) *Inside/Outside: International Relations as Political Theory*, Cambridge: Cambridge University Press.

Walker, R. B. J. and Mendlovitz, S. H. (1987) 'Peace, politics and contemporary social movements', in S. H. Mendlovitz and R. B. J. Walker (eds) *Towards a Just World Peace: Perspectives from Social Movements*, London: Butterworths.

Walker, W. (1992) 'Nuclear weapons and the former Soviet republics', *International Affairs*, 68 (2): 255–77.

Wallace, H. (1992) 'Which Europe for which Europeans?', in G. F. Treverton (ed.) *The Shape of the New Europe*, New York: Council on Foreign Relations Press.

Wallerstein, I. (1993) 'The world-system after the Cold War', *Journal of Peace Research*, 30 (February): 1–6.

Waltz, K. (1979) *Theory of International Politics*, Reading: Addison-Wesley.

—— (1986) 'Response to my critics', in R. O. Keohane (ed.) *Neorealism and its Critics*, New York: Columbia University Press.

—— (1993) 'The emerging structure of international politics', *International Security*, 18 (2): 44–79.

Weiss, T. G., Forsythe, D. P. and Coate, R. A. (1994) *The United Nations and Changing World Politics*, Boulder, CO and Oxford: Westview.

Westlake, M. (1994) *A Modern Guide to the European Parliament*, London: Pinter.

—— (1995) *The Council of the European Union*, London: Cantermills.

Williams, S. (1991) 'Sovereignty and accountability in the European Community', in R. O. Keohane and S. Hoffmann (eds) *The New European Community: Decision-making and Institutional Change*, Boulder, CO: Westview Press.

Windass, S. (ed.) (1985) *Avoiding Nuclear War: Common Security as a Strategy for Defence of the West*, London: Brassey.

Winters, L. A. (1991a) 'Comments on chapter 4', in G. N. Yannopoulos (ed.) *Europe and America, 1992: US–EC Economic Relations and the Single European Market*, Manchester: Manchester University Press.

—— (1991b) 'International trade and 1992: an overview', *European Economic Review*, 35 (2/3): 367–77.

Wittkopf, E. R. (1987) 'Elites and masses: another look at attitudes towards America's world role', *International Studies Quarterly*, 31 (2): 131–59.

Woolcock, S. (1990) *The Uruguay Round: Issues for the European Community and the United States*, Discussion Paper 31, London, Royal Institute of International Affairs.

—— (1991) *Market Access Issues in EC–US Relations: Trading Partners or Trading Blows?*, London: Pinter for Royal Institute for International Affairs.

WTO (1995) *Regionalism and World Trade*, Geneva: World Trade Organization.

Yannopoulos, G. N. (1988) *Customs Unions and Trade Conflicts*, London: Routledge.

—— (1990) 'Foreign direct investment and European integration: the evidence from the formative years of the European Community', *Journal of Common Market Studies*, 28 (3): 235–59.

—— (1991) 'Trade policy issues on the completion of the internal market', in G. N. Yannopoulos (ed.) *Europe and America, 1992: US–EC Economic Relations and the Single European Market*, Manchester: Manchester University Press.

Yoffie, D. B. (1989) 'American trade policy: obsolete bargain?', in J. E. Chubb and P. E. Peterson (eds) *Can the Government Govern?*, Washington DC: Congressional Quarterly Press.

Young, O. R. (1969) 'Interdependencies in world politics', *International Journal*, 24: 726–50.

—— (1980) 'International regimes: problems of concept formulation', *World Politics*, 32 (April): 331–56.

—— (1986) 'International regimes: toward a new theory of institutions', *World Politics*, 39 (October): 104–22.

—— (1991) 'Political leadership and regime formation: on the development of institutions in international society', *International Organization*, 45 (3): 281–308.

Yudken, J. S. and Black, M. (1990) 'Targeting national needs: a new direction for science and technology policy', *World Policy Journal*, 7 (2): 251–88.

Zoellick, R. B. (1990) 'Practical lessons for the post-Cold War age', *European Affairs*, 4: 79–84.

Zupnick, E. (1991) 'American responses to 1992', in G. N. Yannopoulos (ed.) *Europe and America, 1992: US–EC Economic Relations and the Single European Market*, Manchester: Manchester University Press.

Index